FROM THERE TO HERE

Irish Rugby in the Professional Era

FROM THERE TO HERE

Irish Rugby in the Professional Era

BRENDAN FANNING ∿

Gill & Macmillan

Gill & Macmillan Ltd
Hume Avenue, Park West, Dublin 12
with associated companies throughout the world
www.gillmacmillan.ie

Index compiled by Cover To Cover
Typography design by Make Communication
Print origination by Carole Lynch
Printed by ColourBooks Ltd, Dublin

This book is typeset in Linotype Minion and
Neue Helvetica.

The paper used in this book comes from the wood
pulp of managed forests. For every tree felled,
at least one tree is planted, thereby renewing
natural resources.

A CIP catalogue record for this book is available
from the British Library.

5 4 3 2 1

All interior photographs were supplied by Inpho,
unless otherwise noted.

CAPTIONS TO COVER IMAGES

Front top: October 1999: Ireland's Matt Mostyn (11) and Justin Bishop at the final
whistle after defeat by Argentina in the World Cup. (Brendan Moran/Sportsfile)
Front bottom: March 2006: Brian O'Driscoll with England's Julian White (*left*) and
Lee Mears in the background, RBS 6 Nations. (Brian Lawless/Sportsfile)
Back: Heineken Cup Final, May 2006: Munster's Marcus Horan, Federico
Pucciariello, Anthony Foley, Donncha O'Callaghan and Ian Dowling celebrate
with the Heineken Cup. (Inpho/Billy Stickland)

For Felicity, Anna and Liam

CONTENTS

ACKNOWLEDGMENTS   IX

INTRODUCTION   XI

1. Down Under: Australia, 1994   1

2. Last Drinks at the Free Bar: The Rugby World   25
Cup, South Africa, 1995

3. Exodus: The Departure of Ireland's   45
International Class, 1996

4. Trauma: Ireland's Development Tour to New   58
Zealand and Western Samoa, 1997

5. Divorce: The Separation of Pa Whelan and   84
Brian Ashton, 1998

6. Long Night in Lens: Ireland's Defeat by   100
Argentina, Rugby World Cup, 1999

7. Europe: Munster's March to Twickenham, 2000   120

8. Bloodletting: The Sacking of Warren Gatland, 2001 146

9. Waking the West: The Assault on Connacht, 2002 167

10. Coach and Captain: O'Sullivan and Wood, 2003 183

11. Clubs: The Never Ending Story, 2004   202

CONCLUSION   218

APPENDIXES

I   Development Squad, 1997   225

II   Charts and Statistics   233

    1.   Ireland Tour to Australia, May/June 1994   233

    2.   Ireland A/Development Tour to New Zealand
        and Western Samoa, May/June 1997   234

    3.   Munster's Heineken Cup Run, 1999/2000   236

    4.   Ireland in the 1995 Rugby World Cup   238

    5.   Ireland in the 1999 Rugby World Cup   240

    6.   Ireland in the 2003 Rugby World Cup   242

INDEX   244

ACKNOWLEDGMENTS

In writing a sample chapter for this book, for Fergal Tobin in Gill & Macmillan, I got stuck into Ireland's Development Tour to New Zealand and Samoa and feared I would never get any further. It's worth a book in itself. It was a harrowing trip for a group who thought touring was about something else altogether. Reliving those experiences was almost cathartic for some of those involved. Luckily for me, it was the beginning of a sequence where virtually everybody I approached for interview was happy to replay events that took us from where we were as a rugby nation to where we are now. I am indebted to them all for their help.

Along the way I was blessed to have the support of regular readers and prompters, principally my good friend Peter O'Reilly, who quit the teaching profession some time ago for life as a Sunday hack, but brought with him a selection of red pens. I'll fork out with thanks for the refills. He was abetted by Tom, Trent, and Sean at regular intervals. Thanks to Baz for early legwork in Pearse Street Library, and to Patricia Davis for transcription when that task became too much for me. A special thank you also to Yseult Thornley in RTÉ for putting up so cheerfully with the raft of requests for footage of times past.

Billy Stickland was a great help in choosing and supplying photographs to illustrate the story, and Des Daly's contribution both with facts and statistics was very useful. In Gill & Macmillan I was blessed to work with Deirdre Rennison Kunz, whose expertise in getting the project over the finishing line was always reassuring, and in the *Sunday Independent*, to sports editors past and present, Adhamhnan O'Sullivan and John Greene, for looking the other way when it suited me more than them.

Above all, thanks to my wife Felicity, for patience, love and support above and beyond the call of duty. Her ability to retrieve lost text, missing files and to remain calm in the regular crises, was special. And to our kids Anna and Liam, from whom "Are we there yet?" was a frequent question, well done for hanging in there. We are now.

INTRODUCTION

On the Tuesday night before Ireland played Australia in the quarter-final of the 1991 World Cup, Roly Meates had dinner guests. They were about to go to the table when the phone rang. It was Des Fitzgerald. Meates and Fitzgerald were props. One was in his 50s, the other half his age; one a coach and chairman of the Irish Rugby Football Union's amateur status sub-committee, the other a current player. But they were props, so they understood each other. And they were friends, so they could speak frankly. That was just as well because Fitzgerald spoke the way he scrummaged, and at that time he was one of the most effective tight heads in world rugby. He had learned much of his trade under Meates at Trinity. After minimal chitchat, Fitzgerald got to the point.

"You can tell your friends on the union there won't be any Ireland team running out on Sunday against Australia," he said.

It was a stunning threat to make. Four days before the biggest game of their lives, the Irish rugby team was threatening to go on strike. The only reason that Meates didn't keel over on the spot was because he understood better than any of his IRFU colleagues the depth of the players' frustration.

Rugby was going through a turbulent period in how it dealt with its international players. It had all started back in 1983, when Australian David Lord tried to set up a professional rugby circuit. That was what woke the International Rugby Board up to the pressure that would come on the game's amateur status. That was what prompted them to create a World Cup before someone else did it for them. By the time the second World Cup had rolled around, in autumn 1991, the momentum for change was gathering pace.

Ireland's players' representatives at this time were ideally suited to the task. Philip Matthews, Des Fitzgerald and Brendan Mullin were well educated, bright and articulate individuals. They made a formidable team. Behind them was a squad who now were prepared to take the ultimate sanction to stand up for what they believed in.

On the outside, Joe Public was reading reports that the Irish players needed clarification on some issues before they could get on with actually playing the World Cup. There was no sense of a dramatic stand-off, of relations between players and administrators deteriorating to a point unprecedented in the Irish game. Historically, the IRFU filled the role of landed gentry, and the players were its labourers. In the early days, you would be invited by letter to represent Ireland, and there in black and white would be the terms: the minimal kit that would be provided, and how you would have to fork out if it got damaged. Players would be told what they were entitled to in terms of refreshments, and trying to claim for something above and beyond that would invite a frosty response. It was Victorian stuff.

Of course the nuts and bolts had been updated over the years, but still there was a clear impression that those who ran the game considered themselves in a different class to those who played it. This was the attitude that was being challenged.

There were two battlegrounds during that World Cup. The first was the Participation Agreement, a 45-page document which everybody had to sign before they could take part in the tournament. The agreement gave Rugby World Cup a licence to do what they wanted with the images from the event. The Irish players had a big problem with this. Effectively they were being asked to sign away their rights for nothing. In fact they had no rights at all. They had another problem: the IRFU wanted to sign the documents on their behalf without the players getting sight of specifically what they were agreeing to. The union started coming up with excuses about why the agreements were not being produced. And the players became more militant with each side-step.

The other conflict was over the Commercial Scheme. The IRB had relaxed the laws on amateurism to a point where it was possible for players to benefit financially, albeit indirectly, from their involvement in the World Cup. There were all sorts of criteria that had to be satisfied in compiling this scheme. The Irish players believed they had complied. The union kept finding ways of telling them they had not. And with each delay the relations between players and administrators grew worse. There had never been anything like this before, and there has never been anything as rancorous since. This was four years before the start of the professional era.

The players had a plan to get around the image rights issue in the Participation Agreement: they would design a jersey logo, the rights to which would be shared between the union and the players. The union said no. Then they started digging their heels in over producing the agreement at all. So the squad went to London for the banquet to open the tournament with the document still unsigned. Manager Ken Reid addressed a squad meeting on the issue and urged them to get on with it. Matthews, Mullin and Fitzgerald sat up the front but said nothing, leaving it to the rest of the players to make the point because they believed Reid was trying to gauge the mood of the group.

"This was the 11th hour," Matthews says. "Guys could have been getting shaky, afraid they were going to miss this World Cup, that there was nothing to be gained here only principle. But to a man they were more militant than we were. It was unprompted and we didn't set them up. I had a wry smile on my face the whole time."

Two days later, back in the team's base in Finnstown House, a couple of IRFU officers arrived out to move things along. By the time they left to drive back into Dublin, the impasse had deepened. The message went back to the union that the players wouldn't take the field against Zimbabwe in the first game, five days later, until they had sight of the agreement. Eventually it was produced. The players signed it reluctantly and on the basis that the IRB were unlikely to abuse their images. They played, but the Commercial Agreement was still outstanding.

Ireland qualified from their pool, beating Zimbabwe and Japan, and losing to Scotland, and as the build-up began in earnest to the quarter-final with Australia, there was still no white smoke. That was when Des Fitzgerald called Roly Meates and spoiled his dinner. All Meates could do was to urge Fitzgerald not to jump off the cliff. In fact, the union blinked first. Two days after Des Fitzgerald's call, there was another meeting in Finnstown House. It was there the players and their representatives were told that the scheme would be OK. And two days after that they went out and played Australia.

The endgame in Lansdowne Road that day has become as big a part of Australian rugby history as Ireland's. What we didn't consider was how, if Michael Lynagh hadn't saved the day for the Wallabies, things would have turned out for Ireland in the years that followed. A few minutes before Lynagh's try in the corner, Gordon Hamilton had touched down almost directly opposite, 100 metres up the field. It was the perfect score. He received the ball far enough from the Australian line for it to develop into a storyline all on its own. Would he make it before the cover got to him? Surely not. Then you thought: well maybe. So by the time he crashed over to score, it was like the final episode of a gripping series. Suddenly you were looking at Ireland in a World Cup semi-final in Lansdowne Road. The euphoria was incredible, and even in the press box there was a whole lot of hugging and back-slapping going on—a reaction I hadn't seen before nor have I since.

The window on that view closed almost as quickly as it had opened.

In the years that followed, you wondered what would have happened to Irish rugby if they had held out that day, for it would have broken new ground in spectator interest in the country. You wondered if it would have given the players the affirmation they needed to kick on and force the radical change that was required in the IRFU, change that could have put them ahead of their peers in Europe when the race officially started with the game going professional in 1995. Instead, the team started to break up, and both Matthews and Fitzgerald had retired by the end of the season. A new manager came in as well, and if the old guard had been unhappy with Ken Reid they would have been even less enamoured of Noel Murphy, who soon set about getting the players back in line. By the summer of 1992, Meates had been dumped by his union colleagues. His demise removed the man best positioned to manage the stressful changes that were coming down the line.

The removal of Meates was the perfect illustration that the union weren't even close to moving forward. They had never quite understood what the class of '91 was about. And it certainly wasn't to cash in quick on the changes that were happening in rugby. "The critical thing from my point of view was that if we didn't make the changes ourselves, if we waited until they were forced upon us, the IRFU would lose control," says Des Fitzgerald. "The game would be driven by TV and the attendant media and speculators that go along with that, and that the influence on the game would be taken away and controlled by Sky or whoever it was at that time. And the team would just get slaughtered in all the matches, so that's where I was coming from. The guys in the IRFU—there's a massive amount of committed guys in there, whatever you say about them. They gave their life to rugby. There's no question about that and their intentions were always for the best. But my view was that they were trying to drive their car through the rear-view mirror. The game was always that way for them. It was very hard for them to accept changes because they didn't agree with them, and they could see all the danger and damage that would happen to the game as they knew it."

It was a matter of perspective. Some of us saw professionalism as Ireland's only chance of catching up with the leaders in the rugby world; others couldn't recognise that we needed it, and knew for sure that they didn't want it. In organisations such as the IRFU, change would not occur until a critical mass of people with power recognised that it had to happen. It would be a long time before that mass took shape. In the interim, we lurched from one crisis to the next.

There would be overseas tours and autumn internationals, Five Nations Championships and World Cups, all dealing in monumental hidings, a few good wins and too many moral victories. There would be sackings and resignations and moments when you thought it couldn't get any worse. In the media we were hard pressed trying to think of different ways to describe how bad it was. After Ireland were beaten 15-3 by Scotland in Murrayfield in 1993, I was instructed by an excitable newspaper editor to ring up each of the players and ask them "why they're such wankers". I rang them all, but may have changed the wording a little.

It wasn't until we came stumbling out of the 1990s that at last we got a bit of sun on our backs. And with that came the realisation in Lansdowne Road that the professional game didn't have to be the end of the world. In fact it could be a new beginning.

By the end of 2006 we'd seen how good that new life could be: Ireland had secured their second Triple Crown in three seasons, and beaten South Africa and Australia back to back to be ranked briefly among the top three nations in the world; Munster had become the second Irish province to win the European Cup, and Ulster had become the third Irish province to win the Celtic League. This kind of progress was unthinkable under the old regime. There is a generation of new rugby fans who have no idea where it all started, and where we have come from. Others have lost track of the journey. It started in the dark ages, and we pick up the story with what became known as the last of the great amateur tours.

Chapter 1

DOWN UNDER

Australia, 1994

When the coffee and chocolate biscuits had been demolished, we took our seats around the table. It was in the Donnelly suite in Dublin's Berkeley Court Hotel, the IRFU's favourite venue. This was a special occasion. Ireland were about to tour Australia and this was an official send-off of sorts. I was well up for it. Namibia in 1991 had been my first trip away with an Irish team, and while it was a strange and dull place, just being there had been enough. Now adventure number four was around the corner, and to a whole new destination.

The travelling media had been assembled so that the union could tell us what they were about. We were given personally inscribed hardback folders with facts and figures about who was going, where they were from, how we would get there and what would happen when we arrived.

It was choreographed but informal, a new approach to this sort of thing. Union president Mick Cuddy said a few words, as did tour manager Frank Sowman. The aim was to get everyone onside, to impart the message that this was a well-planned operation. But it wasn't clear how far forward the plan extended. The itinerary said that a couple of weeks later, on Wednesday 18 May 1994, Ireland would open their tour in Perth against Western Australia. There was no mention of the fact that almost a year later to the day, on Friday 17 May 1995, they would fly out to the World Cup in South Africa. You would have thought they would connect the two, and present them as a package: "Our World Cup preparation starts here." Maybe it didn't. Maybe the plan didn't go that far.

The Australian trip would be the first overseas venture for the senior squad since the calamitous tour to New Zealand in 1992. Some referred to that experience, with its three wins from eight games, as a wake-up call. If you consider being slapped in the head with a baseball bat to be a form of rise and shine, then it was an appropriate description. Even from the safety of the press box it had been a harrowing experience.

It had started with a selection process that saw 17 players, for one reason or another, dodging the draft. Their replacements were in no shape to cope with what followed. Neither were the old hands who showed up for duty. If it looked bad before the off, however, there was an even worse omen on arrival. There was nobody from the New Zealand Rugby Union in Auckland Airport to greet the tourists. After a short stopover we flew on to Christchurch where it was as cold inside the terminal as outside it. Again there was no reception committee to provide a bit of warmth.

Noel Murphy was the manager. He was fit to be tied. From a payphone in the arrivals hall he called Russ Thomas, one of New Zealand's representatives on the International Rugby Board, who lived locally.

"Russ, I'm at the airport," Murphy said, trying to regulate his breathing. "We're by ourselves. There's nobody in sight. Russ, I'm telling you, if you don't get down here with somebody, we're going home."

You wonder how history would have unfolded had Russ hung up and put another log on the fire. By the time the welcoming party had been mobilised, the press corps were settling in to the dark, dank and utterly bloody awful motel by Russley Park, the huge local amenity that serves the city so well. It didn't pick up much after that, and by the end of the four weeks Ireland were so battered and bruised that some of us took comfort from the experience: surely the IRFU would get motoring to try and make up the ground they had lost? They couldn't bring us down this road again, could they?

You didn't need extraordinary insight to see what route they had to take after that. Unless there was a radical change to the way the "elite" level were prepared—effectively giving them semi-professional status—then we would be going nowhere. And that was just the start. Suggesting this at the time was tantamount to pleading insanity.

Back then the World Cup didn't enthuse everybody around the committee table in Lansdowne Road. Rather, some of the blazers took their lead from the winter festival of the middle classes: the Five Nations Championship. It didn't have the commercial momentum that fed money into the minds of the players. It was easier to control. And if this was what defined your sporting life then what happened on a summer tour wasn't going to cost you too much sleep.

So the embarrassment of what happened in New Zealand faded quickly from the minds of those who were in a position to do something about it. It wasn't that they didn't do anything, but if somebody had one foot on the accelerator then somebody else had both feet on the brake.

Gerry Murphy had been assistant coach in New Zealand in 1992. It was arranged for him to stay on after that trip and gather what information he could. Then he was to do the same in Australia before coming back home. At the same time Willie Anderson, who was a technical officer with the IRFU, was building on his solid coaching contacts in Australia. He had been sent down to look at their systems, particularly how they had hooked up with the Australian Institute of Sport. Between them they had enough information to radicalise the game in Ireland.

"At the same time you had the tradition in the IRFU which, no matter what you said, wasn't buying into this because that wasn't the way they wanted to go," Murphy says. "Maybe I'm becoming very nice in my old age but that's the way it was. It was very, very frustrating, but there were elements within the organisation who were trying hard to do something about it."

The twin strategy would work like this. In the wake of Anderson's report the IRFU in June 1993 set up a Foundation to harness the best under 19s and mould them for future stardom. It made sense. It made even more sense to wade into it with financial and human resources and chase down the Australians. The Foundation needed to start with a turbo boost. That was where the other part of the strategy came in. Just because something was worth doing didn't mean everybody had to row in behind it.

Three years before Anderson put pen to paper, under 21s and future Wallabies Garrick Morgan and John Eales were well accustomed to the elite drill Down Under. "You'd go down to Canberra about four times a year, for about a week, and your work would let you go down," says Morgan, whose job conveniently was with a major rugby sponsor. "You'd be on base at the AIS and you'd get specialised coaching. Sports psychologists would talk to you about how to prepare for matches. So we were visualising our games the night before—stuff like that.

We had a dietician all the time. Another big thing was that we had specialised conditioners for weights and power."

This was how they produced the team that won the World Cup in
1991: they identified talent early and then invested in it like it was
the most valuable stock on the market. From the early 1980s they
had development programmes running across the country, under the
direction of Dave Clark, the widely respected coach. By 1987, rugby had
become part of the AIS programme, and Clark was its full-time director. From under 19s to the Wallabies, all the bases were covered. He
could see what was coming. "We went to the (1991) World Cup as the
best prepared team, mentally and physically, and that's why we won it,"
he says.

Ireland weren't in the business of winning World Cups. They were
in the business of bringing a fat bank balance to the agm every year and
purring over the figures. Well, there we were in the summer of 1994 and
the next chapter in our Overseas Experience was about to unfold.

————

The tour brass comprised Frank Sowman filling in as manager for Noel
Murphy who was unavailable; coach Gerry Murphy assisted by Willie
Anderson; and the late Locky Butler as liaison officer. The pairing of
Sowman with Murphy brought together two men who knew each other
well from the Wanderers club. Sowman, one of the Irish selectors, was
well liked and respected as a decent man.

His only experience of managing rugby trips was as chairman of
selectors with Leinster on short hops to England. This was a quantum
leap for him, one which he subsequently described as "somewhat daunt-
ing". Moreover his personality was far removed from the man he was
temporarily replacing. Not for nothing is Noel Murphy known as Noisy.
A domineering presence, he managed with both hands and many words.

Gerry Murphy had taken over from Ciaran Fitzgerald as Ireland
coach in the autumn of 1992. Traumatised by the summer tour to New
Zealand, Fitzgerald's next outing was in October when the Wallabies
stuffed Ireland 42-17 in Lansdowne Road. He did the sensible thing and
got out. Murphy did the irresistible thing and stepped in. When you
had watched him assisting Fitzgerald in New Zealand it was obvious

they were coming from different perspectives. Murphy had a lot more ideas and was unimpressed with some of Fitzgerald's coaching methods. Undermining him however would not have been on his agenda. Like Sowman he was liked as a decent man, and highly respected for his rugby knowledge. And anyway, the idea of confrontation left him cold.

I had seen this first hand when he coached in my local club, Clontarf. He was running the First xv and I was doing the Seconds when he heard Ireland's call. Mostly the sessions were combined and it was always instructive to work with him. He was generous and modest on the field, and always entertaining company over a pint after training on Thursday nights. Monday night selection was a different issue: if sometimes he skirted lashing players out of it in training, he frequently backed down on contentious selections.

Dealing with people who clearly didn't know as much as him, as soon as the argument would start Gerry would shrug his shoulders and concede. When he got the nod for Ireland I was happy for him, and enthused that Ireland were getting a more creative influence than Fitzgerald. But the fear was that his genial personality wasn't quite the cattle prod that the IRFU needed.

His record coming to the Australia tour was interesting. He had over-seen the first back to back wins over England since the five in a row era of 1972–76. And his third game in charge—against Wales in Cardiff in March 1993—ended a losing streak of 11 games. That second win over England was Ireland's only victory from the 1994 Five Nations. They kept up the losing streak at Parc des Princes, and also their end of the bargain in the curious relationship with Wales where we would win over there and they would win over here. Eric Elwood had the chance to clinch that game with what would have been his sixth penalty of the day, but hit the post with a handy kick. The last outing was against Scotland—a dull 6-6 draw where Ireland just didn't have enough to win.

So they could have been travelling to Australia with a Triple Crown under their belts. As it was, the spirit in the side was pretty good; there was continuity in selection with just 21 players being used over the five games (including Romania) that season; and there were a few decent prospects ready to get on board.

The most notable absentees were Nick Popplewell, who took a summer off, and Richie Wallace, who was recovering from a broken ankle. The bright young things were Keith Wood, who had been outstanding for Garryowen in the All Ireland League; Jonny Bell, David Corkery, Gabriel Fulcher and Niall Woods. For Jeremy Davidson it was validation of his promise and a chance to work with the big boys. Victor Costello had an even better opportunity to make a name for himself, having done well with St Mary's after packing in his shot-putting career the year before. Murphy had to make a case for him to the other selectors. Costello needed remedial work on his fitness ahead of departure. A few others should have joined him.

As for the how the press corps would prepare, I took my folder home from the Berkeley Court that day and read up on circadian rhythms. It was part of an entire section given over to jet lag and how to minimise its effects. There was a warning there for the players.

> "Some strategies have been discovered to speed up this recovery rate, and should be fully considered as part of the build-up for the first game . . . Large suppers, alcohol and caffeine are not recommended in the evening as they disturb sleep pattern—sorry!"

––––

Jeremy Davidson was all excited. He'd been to Canada with Methody and to New Zealand with the Irish Schools, but this was something else again. He had managed to squeak in for some action in one Ulster match that season but the province's under 20 team was his bread and butter. Ireland under 21s was as far as he'd gone. He had a strong work ethic, typical Ulster really. His parents were teetotalling Presbyterians and their outlook helped keep him on the straight and narrow now that he was in the University of Ulster at Coleraine. He liked a pint and a party, but the way he was stuck into rugby there wasn't much time for either. As a schoolboy in Methody his day would regularly start at 6 a.m., and a swim and weights session would be completed before breakfast. He knew what his priorities were.

Davidson slipped out of the Esplanade Hotel in Fremantle with David Corkery, not long after the squad arrived. Two young fellas, they felt like big men checking out the lie of the land.

"We thought we were the bees' knees, sneaking around, being bad," Davidson recalls. "And we passed this hotel bar. And inside there was nearly everybody who'd been on the plane that day! Knocking Australian beer into them like it was going out of fashion. It was as if it was Prohibition days. And we're there like: 'Jesus!' And they're going: 'Get this into you, compulsory drinking.' I thought it would have been frowned upon."

On the contrary. It seemed part of a plan. Victor Costello, who was delighted to be free of the isolation of athletics and back into the social bosom of rugby, explains the method to it.

"We were on the complete and utter piss but then we got up the next day at maybe 11 or 12 and we'd no jet lag. The jet lag was gone. We'd maybe one day of hardship but you slept that night."

The scientific angle lost its credibility when the tour developed into a pattern: drink hard, train hard, try and play hard. The problem was that the quality of the second two elements was compromised by the first. Drink was part of the fabric of team sport in Ireland, and because rugby teams got to tour more than any other code, they drank more as well. So when presented with the prospect of four weeks off work in a sunny climate, where most of your expenses were paid, it was easy to look on it as a holiday. If it quickly became apparent that you wouldn't be required for action in the test series then you would have been in a minority to look on it as anything else.

But the steep consumption wasn't confined to no-hopers, the dirt trackers as they were known in touring parlance. And the management weren't waving any big sticks at the culprits.

"You also have to take into consideration—and this is my opinion— that you're dealing with adults and it wasn't my position to be going around Sydney and Brisbane, walking around nightclubs looking for people who were on the fucking piss," Murphy says.

If he was dealing exclusively with adults then this would have been fine. But prominent in the group was a gaggle of wannabe teenagers: "The Under 14s". It was Willie Anderson who coined the phrase. He would have understood what they were about for he was only four years out of the team himself. And that in itself was a problem. Socially he was too close to the players than was healthy.

To be a member of the Under 14s you had to be from Munster, and the passion you brought to a game on a Saturday afternoon had to be matched by the same thirst for a bit of crack off the field. Its natural

leaders were Mick Galwey and Peter Clohessy. John "Paco" Fitzgerald
was a senior partner; Philip Danaher and Terry Kingston were board
members, and the 22 year old Keith Wood was an enthusiastic executive. They liked practical jokes, piss-ups and wading into the opposition. And nutrition wouldn't have governed their eating pattern. There
was no great pressure to rein them in, and the reasons for this were the
same as those which fed the IRFU's resistance to change. The odd big win
sustained those who wanted to trundle along in their comfort zone.

The Under 14s could point to some serious achievements on their
CV: the win over the Wallabies in Musgrave Park in 1992; the back to
back triumphs over England in 1993 and 1994. These had been secured
with the boys at the heart of the effort. If they could lead double lives
then let them at it. And in Australia they were at it.

"It was a piss-fest but at the same time it's what we knew about
touring," says Mick Galwey. "And we were probably trusting our
courage. Touring at that stage was like . . . touring was good fun. You
think of the end of season tour and you're thinking fun, you're thinking crack. You'd probably have to play Australia a couple of times in the
middle of it, but we weren't thinking that way. We weren't there to be
disruptive or be anything different but . . . in some ways people would
be trying to correct us and say stop messing and all that but messing to
us was trying to create a bit of crack and a bit of atmosphere. There was
a serious side; there was a fun side; and there was the match. We had the
fun side as well as the serious side whereas other people just had the
serious side."

Philip Danaher reckons that the drink was inseparable from the
sporting culture. "It was: 'Jaysus lads, let's have a few pints, we're all
in this together.' So we're all hemmed in, we'll do it out of pride and
we'll train hard in the morning and then drive on. It's where we were
coming from at the time."

Well, not quite everyone. The Ulster crew were not averse to the
pleasures of a few pints but they were temperate by comparison, and on
a different planet to their Munster cousins when it came to physical
preparation. And even Leinster's least enthusiastic trainer, Neil Francis,
had become a disciple of Matt Talbot.

There were cliques on that trip, one of which was the London Irish
set. Francis hung out with them. They were ahead of the Ulster boys
who were well ahead of the Munster boys on anything to do with

preparation. It was noticeable how often he would be having a quiet night with Jim Staples and Simon Geoghegan while the 14s were heading off for fun.

"It [that tour] was my first awareness of mortality in a sense that: 'Fucking hell, I have at most three years left. I've buggered my whole career away,'" says Francis. "What a waste of talent and whatever else and I haven't achieved anything. We'd beaten England that year but other than that we'd been losing and losing and I just decided to take it seriously. I didn't go out on the piss."

That didn't mean that he persuaded others to do likewise. He just accepted that that's the way it was. And the reaction to this Pauline conversion?

"They were quite surprised," he says. They weren't the only ones.

Francis's temperance was also influenced by the odds. It would be a hard enough slog without having to cope with hangovers. After the 1987 World Cup he spent a season playing in Sydney with Manly. Bob Dwyer, the Australia coach, remembered him as being talented but lazy. It was a fair description. Francis wanted to go back to Australia a better player. And given the progress Australian rugby had made in the meantime it was the least that would be required. Ireland were on the hard shoulder and in need of assistance. The Aussies were in the fast lane.

Soon after we arrived that gap became even clearer. There was an item on the news one night about the Australians' star centre partnership of Tim Horan and Jason Little. In a wretched twist of luck, both had suffered serious knee injuries playing for Queensland in the Super 10 final against Natal Sharks in Durban. The sight of the pair of them hobbling into arrivals in Brisbane was a sickener for the Australians. The World Cup was a year away. There was no time to be lost in repairing the ruptured ligaments and rehabbing the world's best midfield combination.

Horan's injury was by far the worse, so once the operation to reconstruct his knee was complete they would ship him down to Sydney to an apartment close to his physio. That way they could monitor his progress daily. Like Little, Horan was employed by Castlemaine Perkins, brewers of XXXX beer, who were a major sponsor of Australian rugby. Time off wasn't an issue. Back in Ireland, players struggled to get leave for a summer tour. Frank Sowman watched the report on TV in his hotel room. He wondered what the hell his lot were up against.

"If you'd taken out the IRB rulebook and looked at what Australia were doing it wouldn't have remotely resembled a comparison," he says. "I learned that we weren't going to be able to compete, yet we were dealing in theory with an amateur country."

Later in the trip he was lavishly entertained on a glorious afternoon cruising Sydney Harbour. There he met Ian Ferrier, chairman of New South Wales and a board member of the Australian Rugby Union. Ferrier filled him in on their equivalent of Richard Nixon's Committee to Re-Elect the President. It was called Mission Repeat. Sowman stepped ashore a wiser man that day. He understood that in Australia there was a powerful business lobby prepared to fund the Wallabies. This committee operated separate to the official ARU sponsorships, which put money into Wallaby Players Marketing Ltd—a fund for the players. Mission Repeat channelled more cash into the business of retaining players rather than see them go to rugby league, or to Italy where the rugby establishment made no bones about forking out loot. In 1993 the estimate was that a regular test player earned at least Aus$29,000.

For the men running Mission Repeat it wasn't the hardest sell. Even before the 1991 World Cup win there was a case of the suits fighting over access to a player's face on their brand. In May of that year Michael Lynagh became embroiled in a bitter dispute between Castlemaine Perkins, who at the time were pumping Aus$7m over 10 years into Queensland rugby, and their rivals, Powers. When Lynagh appeared in a television commercial plugging Powers Light Bitter, all hell broke loose. In Ireland the problem would have been over an amateur rugby player cashing in on his rugby fame. In Australia it was over a conflict of interest with a sponsor, one whose input to, and relationship with, the game made Irish rugby look like a cottage industry in the third world.

At provincial and national level in Australia there were promotions companies raising funds to subsidise the players' futures. If you lived down there it was easier to see where the game was going, and so it made sense to do these things, to prepare for the grand opening day. Paul McLean, who played opposite Ollie Campbell in Ireland's 2-0 series victory Down Under in 1979, was a national selector when we went there in 1994.

"We knew something had to be done or else these guys would just drop out of the main stream of rugby," he says. "That was our thinking at the time and we wanted to accelerate the payment of players rather than keep it in the cupboard. We wanted to be open about it because that was exactly the way the game was going to go."

It was small beer then that they should also bypass the IRB regulation, designed with amateurism in mind, which required teams to assemble no more than 72 hours before a test match. Back in 1991 Bob Dwyer started unravelling that red tape by getting his squad together earlier in the week. Typically this would be for a lunch gig on the Tuesday, whereupon they would train in the afternoon. And for their attendance for the week they would pick up $250. This innovation came three years ahead of the IRB sanctioning such payment.

———

None of this would have dimmed the enthusiasm of the big Irish contingent in the WACA in Perth for the opening game. They got more than they paid for: a record Irish tour win, with nine tries en route to a 64-8 score line. Western Australia had their usual quotient of Kiwis on board—11 in this case—and while they were physical they were also extremely limited. The only downside for the tourists was the 17 stitches which Keith Wood needed in a head wound. It would rule him out for at least the games against New South Wales and ACT.

The NSW game was on the Sunday, just four days later. We expected Gerry Murphy to throw in the test team against such strong opposition, and wait until ACT to fire in the rest of the party. We were wrong in the first instance, and in the second it was ignorant to assume that there was any safe haven in this itinerary for introducing virgin flesh. And it certainly wasn't in the Waratah Stadium, on a lovely Sydney afternoon. A very warm welcome, then, to the new boys, Roger Wilson and Philip Soden.

Wilson was a leggy and energetic number eight; a 22 year old medical student from Instonians. He had taken the traditional route through Schools, under 21s and Ireland A, and the previous summer had toured Africa with Ireland's first development side.

Against the Waratahs he pulled his hamstring chasing a kick-off in the first half. That would be the end of his tour.

Soden (25) had taken almost an identical route to Wilson, except that his starting point had been from CBC Cork. Despite the similar career path however the loose head prop had nothing like the same ambition. It was as if his representative honours were gifted to him. Shortly before he played for Irish Schools he didn't even know the team existed. When he arrived into Cork Con there was a heavyweight pack waiting to propel him up the ladder. Running his own business was something that excited him; and rugby was fantastic for the friends you could make.

"I was propping against Mark Hartill that day," he says. "And I always remember thinking: This fella's a fat lump. He always looked a bit heavy. But fuck me, the power of the man. It took every ounce of energy to scrummage that day. They might as well have given me a wheelchair to get around that pitch, he was so powerful. That was the main difference at that stage: their power, their fitness. They were so far ahead of us. We weren't conditioned really."

It's likely that had Noel Murphy been on hand, he would have pushed Gerry Murphy into playing the best possible selection against NSW. It would have made no difference. For the Waratahs it was their eighth game of the season. They were humming. And Ireland were all over the place. Eric Elwood started the day failing to make 10 metres with the kick-off and it was all downhill from there. If Elwood's boot wasn't working then neither was Ireland's game. He was awful. Meanwhile the Waratahs racked up phase after phase, as if playing by rote. Some time later Elwood got talking to a couple of NSW technical officers.

"They were able to tell us that they were playing to a five ruck pattern," he says. "And that after five rucks Joe Soap would get the score. I was there: 'What the hell are they talking about? That's way off.' We'd be getting the ball back off the second ruck and I'd kick it. But no, they had a five ruck pattern. And this was nineteen ninety fucking four? We were going: 'Well, fair play to ye.'"

The game threw up all sorts of questions. The most frequently asked was how Ireland could sleepwalk into such a fixture. Did they not howl in protest when presented with the itinerary? Well, no. Getting beaten up in your second outing wasn't a new experience. It had happened in New Zealand against Canterbury in 1992. A handy opener, followed by the serious stuff. That was the way it was for everybody.

For those of us who had witnessed this kind of thing in 1992 it was thoroughly depressing to see that it was all about to unfold again. There was a massive disparity in skill and physical conditioning, not the kind of stuff you could rectify over a few weeks. Wallaby hooker Phil Kearns though had an opinion on what might happen next.

Straight after the game I headed down with an Australian colleague, Greg Growden of the Sydney *Morning Herald*, to the NSW dressing-room area to get some quotes. Expecting to be waiting outside in the corridor for whoever we could nab coming out, I was amazed when he made to go in. This was standard stuff in GAA, where reporters would pick their way between gear bags and bodies to talk to whoever they wanted. In Irish rugby however there was a strict demarcation line: players inside, hacks outside.

So I tagged along. The Waratahs had just beaten an international side by 55-18 but they were more satisfied than elated with their achievement. Kearns was reclining on a bench, taking up the space of two men, stripping off tape and getting water on board. Growden asked him how he expected Ireland to react after such a shellacking.

"Aw mate, I wouldn't be surprised if they put a bit of a stink on in the test," he said.

It took us an age to get out of the dressing-room because David Campese was giving an interview in the corridor and TV crews had the place jammed. I tried to imagine a Leinster player being similarly in demand. At last I got to ask Greg what the hell a "stink" was.

"Some stoush," he said.

I tried again.

"He means there'll be a bit of slipper."

Ah, the old reliable shoe. Kearns's comments made good copy and the daily journalists got some mileage out of it. Sowman and Murphy responded as you would expect—in high dudgeon—but by then Kearns had got his message across to referee Joel Dumé who would be handling the first test in Brisbane in a fortnight. The implication was that the only way Ireland could win was by kicking the Wallabies to death. It was an instructive piece of media manipulation. That was another area Ireland hadn't explored. It dawned on me why in Australia they let the hacks inside the door.

Neil Francis was one of the few Irish players to emerge with any credit from the hammering. In the dressing-room beforehand he had warned his team-mates that something awful would unfold if they didn't play out of their skins. Even so, he hadn't foreseen the scale of the disaster.

"I was actually sort of shocked we were so far behind them. They really fucking destroyed us. You know the way you play against a really, really good side? It was like a poor Schools side against a really good Blackrock side. They blew us out of it. You couldn't get near the ball. It was a bit like the 'Boks: they cleaned the rucks so aggressively that if you were fringing or doing a bit of ruck inspecting you were in trouble because they'd take you out. They cut us to shreds. It was then I realised what had happened in New Zealand in '92."

He talked to Willie Anderson about whether rucking or mauling would be the best way to make some progress. Anderson was a devotee of rucking. "Right," said Anderson. "It's out with the nets." He used a low-slung net, suspended from poles, to drill the players in the right body position. "Get lower, get lower!" was soon ringing around the training ground as the Dungannon man went to work, whacking those who failed to assume the correct position. It was hard going, all the harder for those who had had a late night. Which never seemed to bother Willie. Such was his constitution that the more he drank, the more enthusiastic he seemed on the training ground the next morning.

————

Canberra seemed the ideal place to get the tour back on track. It was sleepy to the point of numbness, so there was nothing to focus on other than ACT and what history suggested would be a negotiable obstacle. There were warning signs, however: over the previous four seasons they had beaten Tonga and Samoa, and lost to Wales and France by only four points and one point respectively. The previous week they had run Queensland to 36-15. More immediately you only had to look at the curtain raiser to get a feel for the opening paragraph of the comment piece in the match programme: "In the 15 years since Ireland last visited the ACT, the National Capital Union scene has changed beyond recognition." Hmmm.

That curtain raiser at Manuka Oval, on another lovely sunny afternoon, featured the ACT Colts against their Sydney counterparts. That's when we first saw Joe Roff. He scored two tries—the first called back—in as many minutes from inside his own half.

He appeared to be gliding over the ground. Philip Danaher watched with the rest of us.

"When I saw him I just went: 'Oh mother of Divine Jesus.' He'd be on our team instead of me and all the other seasoned internationals. There was a realisation for some of us that while we could use our experience and enthusiasm and a bit of cheating and whatever to get by, if this kid was a part of the next batch coming through in Australia then, man, we've got a problem in our system."

The most pressing problem was that recurring theme: bigger, faster, stronger. And all of those attributes were being exhibited by the home team. Ireland had let loose the five tourists who hadn't been involved to that point: Brian Walsh on the wing; Alan McGowan and Alain Rolland at halfback; Shane Byrne at hooker and Paul Hogan at wing forward. Byrne had arrived out as cover for Keith Wood. Hogan was carted off injured before half time.

They were wiped, 22-9. ACT, with a promising young George Gregan at scrumhalf, scored three tries to nil and their centre Matt O'Connor pushed himself into pole position for a test spot. The most significant Irish selection featured Gary Halpin moving across the front row to loose head. He had been hoping to get in there for the test ahead of Paco Fitzgerald, but it didn't work out. Afterwards ACT coach Geoff Stokes was asked if there was anything about the Irish performance that impressed him. "Yes," he said. "Their goal kicking."

He couldn't understand why tackling was causing so many casualties among the Irish. "It wasn't that we were making really big hits," he said. Maybe fitness had something to do with it? Naturally, the injuries were beginning to mount: Peter Clohessy—who had a big game—Maurice Field and Mick Galwey were all hurt.

The next morning the roadshow moved up to Brisbane where the delightful warmth of a Queensland winter was balanced by a date in Ballymore with the Super 10 champions. This didn't look good. And then we got one of those performances that made the coaching staff believe they were on the right track.

Despite the poor conditioning base and the casual attitude to grog, the training sessions were well planned and well executed. Suddenly the rucking game started to work. Anderson reckoned it was the best rucking performance he had ever seen from an Irish side.

They led 19-13 at half time and despite being overhauled to 26-19 with time almost up, they had the legs to pull out a try from Keith

Wood, which Conor O'Shea converted for 26-26. Outstanding! Gradually, O'Shea's kicking duties were extending beyond the long-distance efforts given the diminishing confidence of Eric Elwood. The outhalf butchered a try for Jonny Bell midway through the second half and it cost Ireland the game, as well as increasing anguish for him personally.

"I remember talking numerous times to Willie Anderson and, being a young fella, getting into tears a few times because I wasn't able to cope," Elwood recalls. "The pressure was getting to me because I was performing badly. It was my first time away from home and I was playing shite. The rugby ruined the holiday."

Typically, Michael Lynagh rammed the point home when he stepped up and planted a winning penalty in the sixth minute of injury time.

The man of the match award went to John Eales but it could easily have been picked up by Neil Francis who was terrific out of touch. So the performance provided a selection dilemma for Murphy and Sowman and Anderson with the first test a week later. David Corkery had been so good that the incumbent open side, Denis McBride, injured since the NSW game, was now under serious pressure. Gabriel Fulcher's display had put Mick Galwey in the same boat. Luckily for Galwey, he wasn't fit for what happened next. Neither was McBride, but he would take two injections in his right shoulder to try and prove that he was. Mount Isa and an Australian XV was his shot at recovery.

"I was on the bench that night—it was three days before the first test—and you'd want to have seen their team: they had Willie O, a young Joe Roff picked from the ACT under 19s; Pat Howard in the centre. It was a great rugby side. We were warming up down one end of the pitch, and I was on the bench with Brads, and our guys were going through their thing and Brads turned to me and says: "You know what? I've a really, really bad feeling about this."— Conor O'Shea

The pilot of flight AN690 told us to fasten our seat belts and fold away our table tops; we would soon be landing in Mount Isa. As you do, you look out your side of the plane to see what you can see. Nothing. Not much action on the other side either. Just before we started the final descent somebody spotted what looked like a small settlement in the distance.

Frank Sowman thought he was in a unique position: the first man to manage an Irish side landing on the moon. Alain Rolland was still trying to cope with the fact that the Australian players were on the same flight when he looked out the window and felt even worse. Jeremy Davidson reckoned the ARU had come up with a master stroke to promote rugby in the desert. Nobody expected Las Vegas but this wasn't funny. There was a mixture of groans and whimpers among the tourists as the reality set in. The Aussies passed no comment. It got worse when you got up close.

"I remember arriving there," says Davidson. "The bus pulled up and we were sort of saying: 'Well, we're going to get there soon; shouldn't be too long.' There was nothing other than these wee rectangles of boxes that looked like fuck all else on earth. But there we were in this dodgy motel in Hicksville. And the sun was beating down for 22 hours a day. And you'd get up and say: 'I wonder what it's like today?' And your hand would get frazzled in the window. It was terrible. Fucking awful."

There was a lot wrong with this tour but Mount Isa was the nadir. It is a hot, dusty hell-hole with nothing to do and all day in which to do it. The players looked to Frank Sowman for an explanation as to why they had fetched up in the outback. But the manager had no input to the itinerary. He tried to put a brave face on it.

There were two things about Mount Isa that convinced the ARU that this remote armpit of the Queensland outback was a good place to bring the Irish. Firstly, it was the ideal mind bender in the week of a test match. Secondly, they were getting bunged by the local Irish club. And not just any old Irish club: the biggest Irish club in the southern hemisphere, no less. The jewel of this mining town was an aircraft hangar with more slot machines than you've ever seen in your life. This was the Irish club. They had a night there for the players: diddle-eye-do music and a bit of faith and begorrah. Oh, and there was a trip down the mine. This excited Denis McBride, who was an engineer, but it left the others cold, which in the circumstances was not a bad thing.

Then there was the game. One of the selling points of Munster's victory over the All Blacks in 1978 was the ropey footage which left so much to the imagination. Well in Rugby Park, Mount Isa, the lights weren't up to the standard required by TV. So the stories of what happened that night would go without challenge. I've heard a few accounts and never felt the need to question them. It was the worst experience. Ever. It even served to perfectly illustrate the state of Irish rugby: the previous Saturday the team had played above themselves and lost in heartbreaking circumstances; and then in the next game they were beaten out the gate. Yes, it was the second string, but that only emphasised the pitiful playing strength. All the problems which had been cast in a different light by the glow from the display against Queensland were back in full technicolour.

It was an ambush, but not on the scale people liked to think. The Irish never nailed down exactly what the Aussies meant by an "Australian xv". The tourists thought this would mean a development team. Afterwards they claimed they had been up against Australia A. Sadly that's not true. None of this opposition for example was in contention for the first test. Certainly there was a handful of big hitters—Alistair Murdoch, Dan Crowley, Brett Robinson and Willie Ofahengaue—but there were a few who wouldn't have been considered second-choice players and never made the step up.

All of them however had physical presence, and in a comparatively short preparation period their coach, Rod Macqueen, had them looking like a well-drilled provincial side. They started the game at a ferocious pace and by the time they stopped to admire their handiwork they were 30-3 up. They used the occasion to ease Willie O back from injury. He didn't last the game but the damage he did when he was there was irreparable. Afterwards Ken O'Connell slumped into his seat in the dressing-room and announced triumphantly to Willie Anderson that he had side-stepped the great Willie O. "The only problem was, he had the ball," added O'Connell.

The Sunday's Well flanker was a fine player. At the time though he was hopelessly unfit after a month on the lash following his club's triumph in the Munster Senior Cup. At his peak he wouldn't have been mapped in the Australian set-up. All over the field there were hopeless mismatches and there were more casualties. Four players had to leave the field, and for Alain Rolland, who tore knee ligaments, it would be an early flight home.

"What struck me at the time was that we were so far behind it was just unreal," he says. "And it was only highlighted for you when you were over there. We had streets to make up. The void between the two was so immense. It was frustrating. But when you got back here you got back into training in the sort of environment you were accustomed to. You weren't up against guys of that size any more; you were back in and around your own size. It wasn't so apparent when you got home because you were no longer around it. Out of sight out of mind."

His team-mates had another 10 days to endure before they could escape back to the land of the little people. They had just been beaten by 57-9, conceding nine tries, and the first test awaited them in Brisbane on Saturday.

The squad scrambled out of town like they were fleeing a car wreck that was about to explode. Back to the Travelodge, back to the city, back to normality. The team was announced the next day and the new caps were presented to the media. Jonathan Bell (20), Niall Woods (22), David Corkery (22) and Keith Wood (22). They had all shown up well and were expected to make the team. Bell in particular looked like he was on a similar conditioning level to his opponents. He was a tremendous prospect.

For those not in the match squad it was party time. Willie Anderson got the ball rolling for them soon after the test team was announced.

"I said: 'OK guys, we're gonna do this wee thing; we're gonna go to the team room, the door's going to be locked and you're going to be in there and say whatever you want. There's going to be a load of piss in there, and you can get as drunk as you want and stand up and say whatever you want.' And it was one of the best events I've ever been involved in because they got up and said: 'Well my opposite number is fuckin whatever,' and got it off their chests and had a bit of crack and whatever. They were able to get a vent."

It's hard to imagine how disappointed they could have been. The test team almost picked itself, and for some of the rest the prospect of being thrown into test rugby would have been alarming. That's exactly how it appeared to Philip Soden on the morning of the game.

He hadn't got that much sleep from the session the night before when he was rousted to fill in at lineout practice. Then it emerged that Gary Halpin had developed food poisoning and had to withdraw from the bench.

"Man, it was horrendous," remembers Soden. "I'll never forget, we were training on a pitch near the hotel and I saw Gerry Murphy coming down. I'm great at sensing things. I remember looking across and thinking: 'Oh fuck.' I remember Anderson shaking his head and then getting the: 'Come here.' And I was sent back to bed for two hours."

THE FIRST TEST

Lookadim go! The Human Skewer
Lookadim! Lookadim! Ilie Tabua
Lookadim running low to the ground
Lookadim hammer! Lookadim pound!
Lookadim poised like a heavyweight punch
*Lookadim launch! Lookadim crunch!**

Gerry Murphy had a plan for Ballymore. It involved winning the toss and getting into the game immediately via an Irish put-in to a scrum a good 10 metres inside the Australian half. It would happen like this: Eric Elwood would scud the kick-off along the ground straight to Wallaby flanker Ilie Tabua. As the poem suggests, the Fijian was a scary prospect in full flight, but he would have to gather the ball first. Murphy reckoned his hands weren't the best. And with it hurtling this way and that, and the Irish pack in hot pursuit, a knock-on and scrum seemed a reasonable outcome to hope for.

In training the coach outlined the plan to Elwood. "Murph, you're fucking having a laugh," the outhalf said.

"No," said Murphy. "Just hit the top of the ball and it will bounce and scutter."

Come the day the stage was set perfectly and Elwood got to start the game with a kick-off into the Australian forwards. He took one last look at where Tabua was standing and started his run-up. He hit the top of the ball perfectly. It bounced and scuttered, just like Murphy said it would. The direction too was spot on: straight at the target. Had Tabua fumbled it the story might have had a different ending. Instead he gathered it first time and went from 0 to 60 in record speed. This was especially bad news for Brian Robinson.

No matter how many times you watch it on replay it only seems to get worse. Tabua on the charge; Robinson in his way; top of Fijian head meets Ulster jaw-line in sickening collision. Robinson collapses in a heap but for Tabua it's no more than a speed bump. The game goes on with the Wallabies on the attack.

* Poem written by Rupert McCall, taken from *John Eales, The Biography* by Peter Fitzsimons (ABC Books)

Robinson is helped to the touchline and a couple of minutes later the Wallabies move the ball across the midfield where new cap Matthew O'Connor is tackled and sets the ball back. Enter stage left, Paco Fitzgerald, pausing only to stomp on O'Connor's chest before exiting the far side of the ruck. The touch-judge picks up the incident and flags it to referee Joel Dumé. Fitzgerald is spoken to. Robinson struggles back onto the field in time to see Michael Lynagh lining up the penalty against Fitzgerald on the half way line. Three nil to Australia and the game has barely started. This wasn't what Gerry Murphy had in mind.

It got better, but not much. The Irish forwards were aggressive and disruptive and it took Australia a long time to cope with it. Then they lost Mick Galwey and Paddy Johns had to shift into the second row. Phil Kearns's prediction of a "stink" didn't materialise but Peter Clohessy was blessed to avoid detection for walking on the head of Tim Gavin. As ever, the Claw was unfussy about where he put his feet, and it was noticeable that in the opening minute of the second half, when he took a ball on in midfield and was tackled to the ground, there was a mad scramble among the Australian forwards to give him some shoe. He was as accustomed to taking punishment as he was to doling it out. He saw both as different chores in the same job.

However it would take more than a foot-loose approach from the Irish forwards to swing the game their way. The difference between the teams when in possession was stark: Ireland either kicked it away—and mostly badly—or they ran it, looking like it was a task they knew would end in tears. And often it did. Dump tackles were the order of the day in Australia, and it was unsettling for the tourists to see the likes of Philip Danaher, who at home would have had some physical presence about him, being tossed about the place.

Tabua got Australia's first try just before the break for a 13-3 lead, and then in the second half they rattled up to 28-6 before Paddy Johns stretched and scored after good Irish pressure. That came almost on full time, but the Wallabies scored again through wing Damian Smith. At least it allowed for a bit of levity to end it all. Conor O'Shea was injured in trying to stop Smith, so just before Michael Lynagh could line up the game's final kick, Maurice Field raced on as a replacement. Eric Elwood still has a vision of it in his mind

"We're standing under the sticks waiting for the conversion going: 'Oh blow the fucking thing up will you?' And Maurice—track suit off—

came on and ran out to the corner. We're under the sticks and he's high kneeing it out to stop Lynagh's kick. Referee blew the whistle. Maurice hadn't touched the ball. And he goes to Lynagh: 'Swap shirts?'"

If the Aussies had drifted off to sleep in the week between Brisbane and Sydney you could have understood it. They didn't. Bob Dwyer prided himself on detailed analysis of the opposition, but he didn't have to extend himself to figure out the limited danger posed by the tourists. Neil Francis was the obvious threat. Conor O'Shea too looked like he enjoyed test football a bit too much. And there was always the possibility that Eric Elwood would find a kicking groove that would get his pack going forward. Outside of that, the Irish forwards had the capacity to cause intermittent harassment but it wouldn't be sustained. And with the other three channels blocked off, all they had to worry about was perhaps Simon Geoghegan getting the ball in space.

The only thing that had changed in the intervening week was that Ireland had secured their second tour win. The day after the first test they moved camp to Lismore, another sleepy retreat, this time a drive south from Brisbane. Waiting for them were New South Wales Country. It was supposed to be a gimme. No ambush, no heavyweight players sneaked into the home team, and still it was an uphill slog. Indeed if Alan McGowan hadn't succeeded with his fifth penalty— from inside his own half and with two minutes on the clock—it would have been another defeat. Somehow Country managed to miss eight from nine attempts on goal.

It was a win, but 20-18 was hardly a morale boost ahead of the second test. The build-up to that game was against the magnificent backdrop of the Pacific Ocean. If it wasn't for the fact that the Wallabies were waiting you could have forgotten about the rugby altogether, and simply enjoyed the setting of Manly Beach. Not quite finished yet.

THE SECOND TEST
Conditions in the Sydney Football Stadium were perfect, and this time Eric Elwood bypassed the Ilie Tabua option. It couldn't have gone better. The Irish pack swept over the Aussies leaving the ball on a plate for Michael Bradley. His up and under deep into the Wallaby 22 was perfect. Two rucks later and Conor O'Shea was dropping a goal for a three point lead. Thirty four seconds on the clock: what a start!

Then we looked across the field where Neil Francis was in a heap. Negating his influence had been the first part of the Australia game plan. "He was the lynchpin of your team in a funny way, the leader of your forwards," says Garrick Morgan. "I was still a bit pissed off from the Queensland match (he had his head opened by a boot) so I just wanted to get anyone I could. But I don't know who got Francis."

Whatever had happened Francis was out cold. Eventually he got up but thereafter it was new cap Gabriel Fulcher who delivered what there was of Ireland's lineout game.

And that wasn't much. By four minutes Australia had wiped out Ireland's lead with a try for debutant Daniel Herbert, but Ireland were going well enough.

Then they blew any chance of getting momentum. Having been awarded a penalty under their own posts, Peter Clohessy and David Corkery were done for shoe and the penalty was reversed. Three points to Lynagh and a big psychological swing with it. Australia were in danger of getting out of sight altogether by half time but for a tremendous try from Clohessy. It was by a distance Ireland's best sequence of the series, countering from their own 22 after Elwood had missed a penalty, and keeping control of the ball for the tight head to burst two tackles to score.

Starting the new half 21-13 down wasn't bad if it was followed by Ireland scoring first, but that didn't happen. Creditably, they managed to stay in touch, and overcame a howler from referee Dumé when he denied Simon Geoghegan a try. The referee was more relieved than anyone when Francis scored straight after. It was a reward for the huge effort they were making, but Gerry Murphy was deluding himself afterwards when he said he thought Ireland could have won a test. By the end of the trip, the daily training had given them enough lung capacity to get around the park, but the power deficit—not to mention skill—was still massive. In its own way, the plucky finish served only to distract from the scale of the problem.

Frank Sowman could have written his end of tour report long before the flight home. In fact it wouldn't have killed too much time on the first leg of the journey, from Sydney to Bangkok. He had seen enough for himself. Willie Anderson and Gerry Murphy had seen it all already. Years later, when asked about his frustration at the pace with which the

IRFU addressed change, Anderson simply passed himself off as a young man in a hurry. Gerry Murphy was more direct.

"Willie had been to Australia in '92, learning all these things. He saw what Australia were doing and he saw what we weren't doing. So it used to drive him round the fucking bend."

What Ireland weren't doing was investing in success. They weren't developing relationships with sponsors who could employ players and give them the latitude to develop their rugby. So obviously they weren't investing in full-time personnel to implement and monitor the programmes they didn't have. The notion of full-time coaches was one they found distasteful. In the IRFU Committee report at the end of that season, it was noted under the heading of "Amateurism":

> The Committee were disappointed that the (International) Board rejected recommendations by the IRFU to restrict coaching by paid officials to the under 21 age group.

So some more unpleasant statistics from the summer holidays were unlikely to move the earth in Lansdowne Road. Combined with the trip to Namibia in 1991, and New Zealand in 1992, Ireland had played 10 weekend matches—either tests or against frontline provinces—and lost them all. Moreover there was a string of midweek howlers to go with them. This was the backdrop to Sowman's report.

He pointed out what the Aussies were at; recommended that Ireland put more resources into the top end of their game, and left it at that. He was a solicitor, not a student of organisations and how they work, but he would have understood that change—the kind of radical change that had moved Australia so far down the track—would not come unless and until the power brokers reappraised their values. For the IRFU, the game was about preservation of the amateur principles. Frank Sowman wasn't about to suggest they abandon them.

Set against that scenario there was no reason to jump up and down with excitement that five new caps had come home from the tour. There had been a few good moments, and, by the end, the daily training meant players were far fitter than when they had gone out. But that wouldn't carry any benefits over to the next season. At the end of that one there would be a World Cup. Now how much time do you think the South Africans were devoting to the regulations on amateur status?

Chapter 2 ⌒

LAST DRINKS AT
THE FREE BAR

The Rugby World Cup, South Africa, 1995

*The IRFU will oppose the payment of players to play the
game and payment to others such as coaches, referees,
touch-judges and members of committees for taking part
in the game because the game is a leisure activity played
on a voluntary basis.*—IRFU *statement 16 May 1995*

T he Ireland squad flew out to South Africa the day after the IRFU
issued those words. As a statement of an ideal it was fine. As a
statement of fact—that rugby was a leisure activity played on a
voluntary basis—it was wide of the mark. At least for those countries
with serious designs on winning the Webb Ellis Trophy it was. Ireland
had no notions whatever about winning. How could they? Through
their own inertia they had fallen so far behind the world leaders they
were in danger of being lapped. Instead they were focused on qualifying from their pool. The game plan didn't go any farther than that. The
bigger plan was that they stand guard over the game itself.

It had been a busy year for the union's Amateur Status brigade. In
January, the chairman of that sub-committee, Billy Lavery, produced a
report on the trend towards professionalism. In February, the IRFU
looked at another report written by the IRB's Working Party on
Amateurism. Between the two documents they came up with their
policy statement that rugby was no more than a hobby.

Regardless of the reference material, the IRFU knew exactly its
position on this issue. It was idealistic; it was deep rooted. Rugby had
always known where it stood in Irish society. The game here began to
develop in the latter part of the 19th century, and its bedrock was the

professional classes for whom it was a leisure activity. It never moved out of that social stratum. The effect of this was to create a comfort zone: the games were highly competitive because of the rivalries which inevitably grew from such a narrow base; also there was an attraction to the social and business contacts that flowed from this regular interaction.

Its cosiness eventually would become a discomfort. There simply weren't enough people playing the game. There had always been a neat carve-up of turf for the field sports in Ireland. The GAA and FAI looked after the bread and butter; the IRFU cultivated the cream. And there wasn't enough of it.

So when people started talking about professional rugby the IRFU knew that it wasn't a runner for them. Leave aside for a moment whether or not they liked the idea of payment for a pastime; their protectionist policy meant that they hadn't the numbers to make professional rugby work. And if they hadn't the numbers they hadn't the money either. In any case, they hated the idea of pay for play. Historically, there was a social superiority enjoyed by the sportsman who competed for the love of the game. He looked down on the man who played for coin. This snobbery would define the IRFU through the generations.

For the moment, they were still fighting what they saw as the good fight. They called a press conference to reiterate this position, timed specifically so that the World Cup squad would fly out with a clear mission statement: there were matches, and then there was The Game.

Two key members of the team were living proof of the union's position. Peter Clohessy and Philip Danaher made themselves unavailable for the tournament for work reasons. Both had been ever present in the Five Nations. There was no persuading them to change their minds.

Danaher was tiring of combining representative rugby with life in the real world. The real world for Danaher was getting a career. For example, when he came home from the New Zealand tour in 1992, he was faced with ending his job with an insurance company who hadn't been wild about him taking a month off for rugby. Five months later the Australians were in Ireland for a short tour. Munster coach Garrett Fitzgerald asked Danaher if he would captain the side. Problem was that two days before they assembled in Cork for that game, Danaher had a job interview in Dublin. "That was the reality of it," he says. "So that coupled with: do I want to improve my speed?" He wanted to improve his career.

For Peter Clohessy, the Australian tour in 1994 ended with him in decent nick physically, and the scorer of one of the best tries Ireland had managed in years—far ahead of the set piece move that had everybody wildly excited when Simon Geoghegan crashed over in the corner in Twickenham four months earlier. By the time he arrived home from Australia, he had played in eight of Ireland's previous nine tests. He would play in the next five in a row before declaring his unavailability for the World Cup. He had just set up his own courier business. Just like that, Ireland had lost their tight head.

On the plus side, however, there was the return from retirement of Brendan Mullin. I was ambivalent about his comeback because of how it would be interpreted. On the one hand there was the attraction of him lining up in the centre with Jonathan Bell. On the other was the implication that the IRFU had taken significant strides in the two and half years he had been away from the international game, and that his return was an endorsement of this. They hadn't. Mullin had packed his bags in 1992 citing pressure of work as an excuse. Privately he had had his fill of dealing with a union who had no interest in progress. The team of 1991 was breaking up and he couldn't see the point of sticking around.

Gerry Murphy had stayed in regular contact with him and coaxed him back. He had continued playing club rugby with Blackrock. It was hard to pass up the prospect of playing in a third World Cup, of becoming Ireland's record try-scorer. At the time I mentioned to Mullin about the inference that would be drawn from the prodigal's return. He came out with some lame line about the whole operation "heading in the right direction". Not quickly it wasn't.

There were fundamental changes too in the management set-up. Noel Murphy was back in the manager's seat, having missed the tour to Australia, but assistant coach Willie Anderson had resigned. As ever with Willie, it wasn't straightforward. And it involved Pa Whelan, one of the national selectors.

In the preparation for the autumn international against USA, Noel Murphy invited Whelan to work on the Irish scrum. Gerry Murphy had no problem with it. It was more likely that Anderson would have had issues, but he didn't raise them. In his day Whelan was a notoriously abrasive hooker with Garryowen and Munster. He had played 19 times for Ireland; he had coached Munster for five seasons, and this was his third season as a national selector. His ambitions extended beyond sitting on the committee that picked the team.

Anderson had ambitions too. He wanted to be Ireland coach, but he couldn't be an IRFU employee and national coach at the same time. In amateur land there was no room for mixing a paid position—in effect the hired help—with an honorary role such as national coach. And Anderson was hired help. He had joined the union in 1988 as a development officer. That's why he was always referred to officially as a "technical advisor", when de facto he was Gerry Murphy's assistant.

In the week of the USA game Whelan was on hand again and the squad session in Merrion Road descended into near farce as Anderson vied with Whelan for the attention of the players. "It was like musical whistles," one player told me at the time. Anderson was running one way and Whelan running the other, and the players were unsure who to follow.

Sure enough Anderson resigned the week after the game. Lo and behold, Whelan stepped in as forwards' coach. It had all the hallmarks of a tidy removal job: crowd him out in the first place, and in the second, make pointed criticism of the forwards' display, which is exactly what Noel Murphy did in the wake of the poor performance against USA. "This mania coming into rugby—popping balls to forwards—is something that players must realise when to do it and how to do it," the manager said at the post-match press conference. "That was not our plan, as I'm sure Gerry will tell you." Could it have been Willie's plan perhaps?

Anderson cited family reasons for leaving, which we didn't believe for a moment. He wasn't displeased at the conspiratorial spin I put on his departure in the *Sunday Times*, which cast him in the role of victim. But maybe that cover was too convenient. In fact he did need to spend more time at home. Also, he needed to get off the IRFU payroll where he had become an unhappy employee, likely to explode in the face of someone higher up the food chain. The departure of Willie Anderson was bad news for the squad because as a technical coach he was on a different planet to Whelan. Moreover the players liked him and he had inspirational qualities. Unfortunately for him, he was in a different stratosphere to the Limerick man when it came to politics.

The other change behind the scenes saw the introduction of Giles Warrington to put some manners on the fitness drill. Warrington was a physiologist with the National Coach and Training Centre in the University of Limerick (NCTC). Noel Murphy was on the board of NCTC and asked him to help out—on a part-time basis. It wasn't the full-time appointment recommended by Frank Sowman in his end of tour report the previous year, but this was how the union operated.

Warrington got started before the 1995 Five Nations, meeting up with the players mostly at Sunday squad sessions. Immediately he had to make the adjustment from dealing with full-time athletes, as he did in his day job, to part-time rugby players. The attitude of the two groups was polarised: the athletes devoured the work; the rugby players moaned about it. Well, most of them. The Ulster crew were a different breed. Moreover they were comfortable with weight training, the disciplines of which had been instilled up north in the mid 1980s by coach Jimmy Davidson when his Ulster side dominated the land.

I remember the same Jimmy D selling the message of strength conditioning on a course for club coaches in 1988. By then he had become Ireland coach, and had Olympic decathlete Colin Boreham with him, preaching the gospel of plyometrics. And here we were, seven years later, with a national squad whose conditioning was unacceptable.

Warrington and Boreham were good friends. Soon enough the new fitness advisor was picking up the phone to call the old one. "I talked to Colin when I took on the job. He was recounting some of the issues he had gone through. After my time we sat down and had a good discussion about these things but it was interesting: a lot of the issues he was experiencing in the 1980s were still the same."

Warrington decided to cut his cloth. He couldn't squeeze into six months what had been ignored for as many years. And he didn't have the time to get around the country, or across the water, to cater for individual programmes. He concentrated on getting the group fitter. And he warned them that playing at altitude in South Africa would be as big a challenge as the opposition itself. It was an important message.

The Five Nations had been no fun. In January England wheeled out a gargantuan pack which killed stone dead any notions of Ireland conjuring a hat trick of wins over them. In Murrayfield, the next month, Brendan Mullin made a try-scoring return to the Championship, but

Paul Burke missed a clatter of kicks and Ireland managed to lose a game that was begging to be won. Next came France, and despite winning plenty of primary possession Ireland couldn't retain it. You needed power to be able to do that for long periods. And that was a problem. Finally Wales duly obliged in Cardiff and Mullin became Ireland's new record try-scorer, with 17.

Over the four games there were six new caps, ranging from long-term prospects like scrumhalf Niall Hogan to short-term merchants like 35 year old Ulster second row Davy Tweed. Paul Burke, Anthony Foley, Ben Cronin and Eddie Halvey were the others, of whom Halvey was comfortably the most talented. He had an interesting career ahead of him.

Six weeks after the win over Wales in Cardiff Ireland were on the road again. This time it was to Treviso, in that northern pocket of Italy where rugby is a passion. This was to be their dress rehearsal for the World Cup.

The Italians weren't shy about bending the rules on either payment to players or preparation time. They had assembled a good team; an enthusiastic and knowledgeable coach in Georges Coste; and would have a camp for a couple of weeks to prepare for the test. They had twin goals: warming up for their own World Cup campaign, and taking another step towards joining the Five Nations Championship. Taking their first ever scalp from the top table of international rugby would feed into both. They were all set.

For Ireland it was just about keeping things ticking over before their own training camp prior to departure for South Africa. They didn't reckon on being beaten. So their preparation was poor. Then it was further compromised by an unfortunate series of events. These started with the outward journey.

The squad assembled in London on the Thursday and trained in London Irish. They were to fly out the next day. The flight from Heathrow was delayed. For some reason the squad was shown to a room with no ventilation and only tables to sit on. They struggled through a few hours there before being called for their flight. That part of the journey was uneventful, and they got to their hotel in Treviso in one piece. That's when things started sliding. There was no room for IRFU president Ken Reid. They had to find lodgings for him in another hotel and he wasn't best pleased.

The players dropped off their bags and changed for training. They were led off into the countryside to a farmer's field that back home would be the subject of EU grant aid. The Italians are good at this sort of stuff. The session was abandoned as players gingerly side-stepped the potholes. Back to the hotel. Kick-off the next day was in the early evening. The bus was due to collect them at five. At 5.05 Noel Murphy was already anxious. By 5.20 his blood pressure was rising. By 5.30 the taxis he had called at 5.10 still hadn't showed. So he risked life and limb and set about trying to flag down any passing bus. As it happened, that strip was a haunt for prostitutes, so motorists wouldn't have known what to make of an excited man in a green blazer waving a fistful of cash.

At last transport arrived and the players got to the stadium with less than 40 minutes to kick-off. Referee Tony Spreadbury wasn't interested in delaying the start. They were in no mental state to play a test match and performed accordingly. It didn't help that the Italians were very good. The home front row of captain Massimo Cuttitta, Carlo Orlandi and Franco Properzi Curti were serious customers. So were the half-backs, Alessandro Troncon, and a little Argentinian named Diego Dominguez. That quintet alone did a lot of damage.

Ireland were minus Simon Geoghegan and Neil Francis and both scrumhalves, Michael Bradley and Niall Hogan. So they gave a first cap at number nine to David O'Mahony from Cork Constitution. There was a doubt beforehand however about his fitness. He started, and had to come off inside the first quarter. He would never get another cap.

The final scoreline was 22-12, and the Italians were delirious. The Irish retreated to their hotel where Guinness had kindly laid on a barrel of stout. Everybody—players, press and whatever supporters were there—tucked in. The bar was soon hopping and I was struck by the speed with which the players were able to put the defeat behind them. They had just become the first International Board country—as the world's top eight were called—to lose to Italy. When I stumbled up to bed the joint was still jumping.

The next morning I appeared down to reception, somewhat the worse for wear, to see Noel Murphy remonstrating with staff behind the desk. He was waving what looked like a printout in his hand. "This can't be right, this can't be right," he wailed. It seemed there was a fairly large bar bill to be settled. "Perhaps it was the press," suggested Philip

Browne, then the union secretary. No Philip, it wasn't the hacks. This one was down to the players.

The night porter was called. After some time, he arrived and gave a description of the individual who was responsible for bottles that had disappeared after the barrel ran dry. The description encouraged Murphy to settle the bill hastily. That wasn't the end of it.

Before the bus could pull out of the carpark the manager was out again, looking for items that had been—perhaps inadvertently—taken from a few of the rooms. Some bags had to be emptied and property returned. This scene was played out a few paces from the front door of the hotel. Had there been a photographer on hand it would have been catastrophic. Instead it was just embarrassing. The bus pulled away and off to the airport.

The mood on board was sombre. None more so than the coach. After breakfast there had been a team meeting to review the shambles of the previous evening, and Gerry Murphy had taken some flak from players who felt they had been led blindfolded into a minefield. He embarked on what was developing into a valedictory speech, but before he could get to the pay-off line, Noel Murphy jumped in. "No one is getting off the ship," the manager said firmly. Onwards then, towards the rocks.

——

The fact that Ireland had their pre-World Cup training camp in Kilkenny was a source of amusement in some circles: "The Irish prepare for altitude by training sub sea level!" But there was never going to be a jaunt to a camp out of the country. At least there was a track in Kilkenny, and it would allow Giles Warrington to get the running done in quality conditions in the morning before the rugby sessions at the local rugby club in the afternoon. He worked the players as hard as he could without missing the point of the exercise.

That was lost on Noel Murphy, however. In a bizarre scene at training one day the manager intervened to take the warm-up. Effectively this was committee man over-ruling a physiologist on how best to prepare the players. He had them making little circles with their arms; then bigger ones; then even bigger ones. By the end of it the arms were falling off them. Warrington stood there, gobsmacked.

The players were bemused, but said nothing. "Normally, I'd have said: 'Noisy, fuck off will you?'" says Neil Francis. "But everybody wanted to start against the All Blacks and everybody sort of went along with what they were told to do."

Why didn't Warrington pack up there and then and go back to his day job?

He wouldn't comment.

ARRIVING IN SOUTH AFRICA

The squad had only dropped their gear in the Sunnyside Park hotel in Johannesburg when there was a problem. In the previous evening's *Belfast Telegraph,* rugby correspondent Jim Stokes had run a story saying Gerry Murphy had effectively been sidelined. He wrote that the coach would remain in situ but the show would be run by Noel Murphy. After the first training session a press conference was called to rubbish the article.

The two Murphys denounced it as destructive and untrue, and IRFU president Ken Reid climbed in as well. "I must say I'm furious at these suggestions," the president said.

The rest of us were intrigued. Stokes had been writing on rugby for many years and was unlikely to fly such a colourful kite if there wasn't a wisp of wind. He had been given the story from what he considered to be a good source. He supported it with off the record remarks from two players who reckoned all was not well with the management. Stokes referred to a meeting that took place in the wake of the Italy trip on which, seemingly, a disgusted Whelan had threatened to resign. Stokes also threw in the involvement at the Kilkenny training camp of Ray Southam, the IRFU's director of rugby, as being indicative of a power shift away from Gerry Murphy. Southam didn't see it that way.

The meeting Stokes wrote about took place in Dublin and involved the two Murphys, Ken Reid and Tommy Kiernan, the former Ireland captain and coach, and an IRFU heavyweight.

"The gist of the meeting was: what help did we need?" Gerry Murphy says. They needed lots. Ireland's pool opposition were New Zealand, Japan and Wales, in that order. Unlike the previous two tournaments when it was harder not to qualify for the quarter-finals, this was fraught with danger. They would have to combine a win over a minnow—

Japan—with one over a bigger fish. Realistically that would mean winning against Wales.

"Tommy's interest in these things was in Ireland winning matches, and he was one of the few people—other than Noisy and myself—who understood that we were going to have to beat Japan and Wales, or else New Zealand," says Murphy. "We had a long conversation about what we could do. Tommy was giving it the: 'Have ye worked it out, what are ye going to do?' Now the only thing I can think of is that somebody might have got the wrong end of the stick."

That somebody passed the story on to Stokes. If you ran the sequence from the lead-in to the Treviso debacle, to the meeting in Dublin, to Ray Southam's appearance at Kilkenny where Noel Murphy was doing his warm-up routine, it didn't seem far-fetched that the coach could be in trouble. He was. But with Noisy riding shotgun, Gerry Murphy ploughed on.

The manager had a lot on his plate. Prop Nick Popplewell and wing Simon Geoghegan had picked up injuries and Ireland needed everything to go absolutely right. So Noel Murphy was pretty jumpy when he took his seat in the Sunnyside Park for the announcement of the team to face New Zealand. Michael Bradley was back in at scrumhalf for Niall Hogan, in a reversal of the Five Nations finish, and David Corkery was picked somewhat out of position on the short side of the scrum. It wasn't earth shattering but it was worth mentioning. Mark Jones of the *Sunday Tribune* questioned Noel Murphy about the positioning of Corkery. It was like he had sought deeply personal information.

The manager cornered Jones as soon as the conference ended. He was apoplectic. "What are ye doing asking that for?" Murphy screeched. "Sure there could have been New Zealand fellas there!"

We imagined the consequences: that a Kiwi hack would hotfoot it over to the New Zealand team hotel with the news for the All Blacks' coach, Laurie Mains. "Jeez Laurie, you're not going to believe this. They've selected Corkery at blind side!"

Noel Murphy had good reason to be nervous. The All Blacks were a scary prospect at the best of times, but there was a particularly clinical look to this batch. Statistically the previous 12 months had been bad for them, winning only three of seven tests, but they arrived to South Africa in great shape and with a few players of real promise.

The night before the game both teams had a light run out at Ellis Park. The Irish boys were wrapping up, skitting about the place, when the All Blacks arrived. They appeared from the tunnel in a group, walking in almost total silence to the side of pitch where they sat down and changed their track shoes for boots. Every one of them looked like he had been sculpted in the rugby factory. And their giant left wing had taken longest to put together.

We knew very little about Jonah Lomu. A New Zealand colleague explained that the 20 year old giant was lucky to be there at all. Laurie Mains had to send him off on the Sevens circuit to get into condition after he had failed miserably at a training camp earlier in the season. It looked like time well spent. Nothing quite prepared you for seeing him at close quarters. My Kiwi pal pointed him out in the way you would warn the new boy about the school bully. You got the feeling that a whole lot of lunch money would be coming his way real soon. The All Blacks cast a few withering glances over at the Irish boys who were still in high spirits. Then they went to work. We went back to the hotel fearing the worst.

I was walking through reception in the Sunnyside Park when a journalist comes up to me: "Richie have you got a few minutes?"

"Yeah sure, what do you want to talk about?"

"Well this fella you're up against on the wing."

"A typically fast, powerful All Black no doubt."

"Yeah, yeah. He's 6.4."

(Jesus that's tall.)

"He's about 18.7st."

(The colour started draining from my face.)

"And he does the 100 metres in about 10.7."

(Holy shit! How am I going to keep a straight face here and pretend I know this? My brain was doing somersaults.)

"Ah, you know, the bigger they are the harder they fall." I didn't realise he was going to be falling on top of ME.—Richie Wallace

NEW ZEALAND

It wasn't quite as spectacular as the start against Australia in Sydney a year earlier but nobody was complaining. The Irish forwards were fired up to fever pitch. They hunted the All Blacks about the place, wading in with their feet at every breakdown. It was working. New Zealand were rattled, and after eight minutes they had conceded a try.

Ireland prop Gary Halpin had adrenaline coursing through his veins. From a short penalty move he burst through the tackles of the entire opposition back row to score. Then he reversed from the scene, giving the finger to Sean Fitzpatrick, the New Zealand captain, as he went. There were only eight minutes gone. It was sensational, but even if there were only eight seconds left you wondered about the wisdom of Halpin's sign language.

"I remember the incident but we didn't really make anything of it," Fitzpatrick says. "Props don't score many tries so maybe he was just excited."

Ireland refused to let their opponents settle. If they had kept it like that we might have got an early glimpse of this Kiwi side under pressure, but a deadly two-try burst in the space of three minutes, late in the half, settled the favourites. Both scores were gift wrapped.

Hello Jonah: NZ have a great attacking position in the Ireland 22 only to lose control. The ball pops out of the ruck at Michael Bradley's feet. What a result! He could pick it and run, but he doesn't. Instead he fly hacks it. It goes straight to Jonah. There was a split second in which the gravity of the moment set in. Especially for Richie Wallace.

"I'd say there was a 15 metre blind side. There was me, and there was him. And I'm going: 'This guy is going to run right over the top of me, so I'd better just go for it.' So I went for it. I went to tackle him on the basis that he was going to run over me, and I'd already decided this in my brain which is not a good thing to do in football anyway. So I went low to fall back with him. Suddenly there was a hand on my head or shoulder or wherever, and I'm going: hang on, this is not going according to the script?"

When he looked up Jonah was already making a right turn for the posts. "Thanks Brads," said Wallace.

A couple of minutes later Ireland nicked a lineout 22 metres from their own line and shifted the ball to Brendan Mullin. Instead of moving it wider he opted to kick, and took an age to do it. Frank Bunce couldn't believe his luck, and blocked it down. Try New Zealand. Game over.

Ireland pulled back a fine try from Denis McBride and another one late in the game for the combative David Corkery, but they weren't able to cope with self-inflicted damage. They would sustain enough as it was. They lost Jim Staples with a broken hand and somehow Jonathan Bell continued after suffering a hideous looking thumb injury.

As the game wound down, Sean Fitzpatrick chose his moment to chat with Gary Halpin who, along with the Irish front five, was struggling to cope with New Zealand's scrum. "Where's the finger now mate?" asked Fitzpatrick. Halpin didn't have the breath to answer.

Predictably, Noel Murphy read him the riot act in the dressing-room. One-fingered gestures were bad for business. But overall the management were proud of the performance and the vibe around the tournament was that Ireland showed up well. When they flew up to the less than beautiful Bloemfontein the next day, the decision had already been made to play Nick Popplewell against Japan. Three games in eight days was a terrible toll on any squad, especially one with Ireland's limitations in conditioning, and it would be especially hard on Popplewell who had a lot of weight to drag around.

The alternative was to start Henry Hurley who had joined the squad late in Kilkenny when Young Munster's Paco Fitzgerald had to cry off injured. Hurley was called aside before the team was announced. "Not even getting a bench spot was an even bigger pain in the arse for me personally," he says. Being left out altogether meant he was likely not to play at all in the tournament.

JAPAN

They scored seven tries, the champagne Irish, and the most spectacular concluded a blistering 14 point haul inside seven minutes of the final quarter. Ireland mauled a lineout close to the Japan line; Eddie Halvey broke free about three metres out and then raced around the front of the maul, over the line, and towards the sticks to make the conversion easier for Paul Burke. In all Halvey must have covered 15 metres. Breathtaking stuff.

The locals in the half empty Free State Stadium booed. Your average Bloemfontein rugby fan knows what he likes: a pack of Winston cigarettes; a steady supply of biltong, boerewors and Castle beer; a hot sun and a rugby game with lots of action. How they bellowed and roared abuse at the Irish that day. Previously there was little to connect the Free Sate with the Land of the Rising Sun, but they were as one for this gig.

Ireland came with a plan and executed it diligently. Daylight was a dirty word and the ball was to see none of it. They stuck it in the corners; they mauled like it was going out of style; they gleefully packed down for scrums close in. They were petrified that shifting the ball wide, where it might break down, would result in a try for the, eh, nippy Japanese. And of course they were right. That it reflected the bankrupt nature of the Irish game was for another day. This was about taking another step towards the quarter-finals.

The Japanese were—with the exception of Tongan Sinali Latu and Fijian Bruce Ferguson—small and quick and desperate to hurry the game up. They treated the tight stuff like it was a radioactive zone. And every time they escaped the clutches of the Paddies the crowd would respond incrementally. The pitch of the roars reflected the scale of the danger.

After getting out to 19-0 inside the half hour the heavyweights in green looked happy, though they had lost Keith Wood with a dislocated shoulder in the first quarter. He tore a tendon in the process. He had had an operation on the same shoulder in 1993, from which he never properly recovered. This setback would be a watershed in his career. For the moment, however, his loss made little impact. The forwards were motoring well, so much so that they relaxed a bit. Outhalf Paul Burke had passed the ball once and gotten away with it, though he wasn't sure if it was worth risking again.

"I got a bollocking from Franno for that," he says. "I remember Franno giving out a few bollockings that day. For example when I kicked the ball out, it only went out 20 metres instead of 50 metres. I didn't kick the ball far enough for him."

The last 10 minutes of the half were painfully quick. And the last five of those were costly: Sinali Latu got the first Japan try and provided the momentum for the second, for Ko Izama. It was 19-14 at half time. You could see this ending up as a quiz question.

At the break the Irish resolved to play it even further into Japanese territory, and turn the screw even more. They got a penalty try off a scrum inside four minutes, with the debutant Paul Wallace buckling his opposite number, but the Japanese pulled off a clever if obstructive backline move to pull it back to 26-21. "It was like a bad smell you couldn't get rid of," says Burke. "One of those desperately annoying games where you'd be glad to hear the final whistle."

Well, yes, if you were comfortably in front at the time. In the end the scoreboard said they were just that—50-28—but it was embarrassing if you dwelt on it. The beauty of rugby as a game was that you could pick up the ball and run with it.

In the lead-up to the Wales game, back in Jo'burg, there was a little presentation to be made. Niall Hogan had just qualified as a doctor, and the Royal College of Surgeons took advantage of the opportunity to fly their flag. Ken Reid also took advantage of the opportunity to promote the cause of amateurism. He made a speech in which he said that Hogan was living proof that pursuing your degree and pursuing your sporting pastime were not just compatible, but the ideal to which all should aspire. It was a hijack, and down the back of the room there were dark mutterings among players who were offended by the president's remarks.

"I knew that the players didn't appreciate necessarily what he was saying in relation to that because there was this impetus that the game was going professional and the guys wanted to take that step, but the union—IRFU and other unions—were reluctant to let it go," Hogan says. "So I know they were a little bit disgruntled at what he said." That was putting it mildly.

WALES

If in doubt, kick it out. And at Ellis Park on 4 June 1995, there was a lot of doubt about the place. For two of the rugby world's guard this was what would define their status in the game. Win and you went to Durban to play France in the quarter-final, still part of the Big 8; lose and you flew home the next day, in shame. There was a boisterous crowd in the stadium that evening, made up of partisans and interested locals. The game had three phases: first was where the tension had everyone gripped; second was the awfulness where the Mexican wave took over in the stands, followed by booing; and thirdly when the tension returned for the endgame. The relief at the end was palpable: for Ireland as victors, and for the neutrals that it was all over. It was a truly awful game of rugby.

The Irish did a lap of honour, which took some neck. It was a spur of the moment reaction, to thank their fans rather than to bask in the quality of the performance. The game was an almost endless battle for territory, waged through the boot. Typically this involved Ireland forcing Wales to drop out, from which they would go long. Then Eric Elwood or Conor O'Shea would hoof it back, and whichever red jersey— forward or back—collected it, would do the same. Back and forward, on and on, the evil spell broken only by knock-ons.

The nadir came in the second half when O'Shea picked up a long Welsh drop out. He almost broke ranks. "I couldn't cope with the aerial ping-pong any more. You say to yourself mentally that this is what I've been told to do and this is the game plan, but in my mind I'd say I'd done it around 14 times in the match. I remember looking to run and a voice from the sideline went: 'Kick it!' So I changed my mind, and the ball sliced off my foot into touch. I just thought: 'What's the point?'"

The crowd howled at him. And they had been on Ireland's side after another rapid start in which they were 14 points up inside the first quarter. They cleverly avoided the 6'10" Derwyn Jones out of touch and it helped them build a head of steam with tries from Nick Popplewell and Denis McBride.

Wales had pulled it back to 14-9 midway through the second half when Eddie Halvey got the killer try. He was only on the field as a temporary replacement for McBride, who was having his head stitched, and he knocked the ball on about a metre at the start of the move. Referee Ian Rogers missed it, and Halvey showed up at the end of the sequence to crash over. A couple of minutes later he was back on the bench. He sat down with a smile on his face, turned to the other replacements and said: "I suppose from now on I'll be known in Wales as that fucker Halvey!"

In the post match interview Ireland captain Terry Kingston was the picture of happiness. "We set ourselves a task of getting to the knock out stages and we've done that," he said. "The world is our oyster now!"

It was far from oysters that the Ireland rugby team was reared. But they were about to enjoy a bit of the good life. After the hard slog they deserved a break, and it came with a couple of days R&R in Sun City. The next day the squad boarded the coach in high spirits, having said their goodbyes to Keith Wood and Jim Staples who were going home. Ireland would play France on the Saturday. Time enough to think about that later, but it wasn't like taking them on in Paris. And the form of the French in the tournament had been awful. If they could combine the right preparation with their soaring spirit, then who knew what might happen?

It was an opportunity for all of us to take a few days' break. I pointed the car for North East Transvaal and five hours later arrived in the small town of Malamulele. My aunt was working there as a community nurse, and it was a unique opportunity to catch up on family and take a look at life outside the World Cup. It was another world. The tournament hadn't quite caught the imagination of the locals who had more pressing issues on their minds. Things like food, and medicine, and securing a decent place to live. There I met an elderly Irish nun, Stella, who was one of those special characters who always figured a way to get things done.

She was working with refugees from Mozambique, and was busy planning a trip across the border to get some farming equipment, which then had to be smuggled back into South Africa without incurring any charges. It sounded a lot more exciting than anything Ireland were up to. As I left the next day I was warned about the speed traps on the road back to Pretoria. It was more like a runway than a road, and it was hard going trying to stay close to the limit.

An hour out of the capital I was flagged down by a black police officer, risking life and limb in the fast lane, who directed me to his white colleague who was resting up in the patrol car set back from the road. He explained the gravity of the situation, and the grief I would have to go through to get out of it. Then he paused.

"Maybe there's a way out of this," he said. "Perhaps you would like to buy a cool drink for me and the guys up there (the ones who had clocked me with the speed gun)."

This seemed like a very good idea. "Would 50 rand be cool enough?"

"Whatever," he said. He told me to be discreet about taking the money out of my wallet, and to throw it on the floor of the car. Then we talked about rugby for a while, and as he tapped my World Cup accreditation against the steering wheel he said: "I know you're a reporter, but you can't say anything about this. It will be trouble for both of us."

"No problem," I replied. "This will be our little secret."

As I walked back to the hire car he wished Ireland luck against the French. "Thanks a lot," I said. "Oh, I suppose a receipt would be out of the question?"

It all started to go wrong early in the week. RWC had told the four teams who were coming down from altitude—England, Australia, Ireland and

France—to travel the day before their games. But Noel Murphy reckoned it was better to go down to Durban a day earlier. He was concerned, he said, that an hour's drive to the airport, followed by an hour in the air, concluding with the drive from Durban airport to the hotel, was poor preparation the day before a game. Moreover there was the prospect of getting out of dull Pretoria and down to Durban where there was the beach and the Irish fan base.

There was a very good reason however for staying in Pretoria as late as possible, and coming down the day before the game. The expert opinion on how to handle a change in altitude—whether you are climbing or descending—is either to get there at least a week ahead of your game, or to come in as late as possible and get out again just as fast. Giles Warrington was the expert. His opinion was to travel on the Friday. He was over-ruled by Noel Murphy. They trained soon after arriving in Durban on the Thursday and were zipping about the place. On match day however they were like flat batteries.

FRANCE

A noon kick-off in murderous heat; you're battling the effects of altitude change; the previous week you've had the toughest playing schedule of your career—it wasn't one of the great Ireland displays. In a way though its conclusion was entirely apt: Brendan Mullin failing to chase down the leggy Emile Ntamack was the closing play of his career, and Ireland's World Cup. Mullin's reappearance from retirement conferred status on the professionalism of the Irish set-up. The truth was that it was little different from the one he had left in 1992. He should have stayed where he was.

France were pretty awful, but good enough to win. They overcame the wretched performance of outhalf Christophe Deylaud who played as if he was in a daze—one that involved a fixation with dropping goals, all of which missed.

Laurent Cabannes made up for him though. It was a mistake to leave Denis McBride at the tail of the line, and Cabannes made hay in the sunshine. It was McBride's foraging and fitness that kept out Halvey, who was infinitely more skilful. And it was Michael Bradley's awful passing that prevented him getting back into the starting line-up. Gerry Murphy couldn't understand why Bradley's deliveries had become an issue on the trip when they had always been poor. It was a factor in Hogan hanging on to his place.

There was a moment in the second half when he desperately needed to whip it away on the short side at a critical moment when Ireland had France under pressure. The scores were 18-12 to France; Eric Elwood's kicking was keeping Ireland in touch with the metronomic boot of Thierry Lacroix. But Hogan couldn't ferret it out fast enough, and then passed to the open side where there wasn't much happening. The sequence ended with a critical penalty for Elwood, which he missed. Ireland never came close after that, and the 36-12 scoreline sickened them.

The dressing-room was a mixture of emotions. Some were gutted at having missed an opportunity to put one over a French side that was playing poorly; others were glad to be going home. The plan hadn't catered for them getting in too deep. They would have been like fish out of water had they gone on to the semi-final. Mind you, the South Africans would have been keen on facing Ireland instead of France at that stage. Before the last of the Irish had left the scene, the French were already en route to the airport to fly back to altitude. In late, out early.

The Irish flew home with a lot to think about. They had been petrified that failure to get out of the pool would banish them to the backwaters of international rugby. But the redundancy of that thinking was tacitly recognised by Noel Murphy before a ball had been kicked in the World Cup. The big three of the southern hemisphere were looking at expanding their provincial and international rugby competitions. There would be no room for amateurs.

"It (professionalism) will almost certainly mean the end of the World Cup, Lions tours, and inevitably lead to a severing of the links between those north and south of the equator, certainly as far as the major southern countries are concerned," he said.

Set against that doomsday scenario, getting to the quarter-final was hardly a hill of beans. It would be put into perspective by the IRB meeting to follow in August. Either his comments were predicated on the idea that the northern hemisphere delegates would wade into that meeting and cut a line along the equator—leaving one half amateur and one half professional—or he was scaremongering.

He had every reason to be afraid, for he understood how far the big players had moved ahead on and off the field. No sooner had we arrived in South Africa than SA Breweries were offering £20,000 to the Springboks' players' pool if they could win the opener against Australia.

Ireland didn't have a pool so much as a puddle. They were lined up to get a few bob for visiting a bar a couple of nights after the Japan game, but had to reverse out of the deal. The gig was in a strip joint. Understandably, Noel Murphy knocked it on the head. For their efforts at the World Cup the IRFU gave the players travel vouchers for £1,500.

The players went home and planned their holidays. The IRFU braced themselves for what would happen at the Paris meeting. If by some miracle the tide turned, and the renegade rugby unions came back onside, then all would be well. And there would be a fly-by of pigs to mark the occasion. It would be an uneasy summer.

Chapter 3 ❧

EXODUS

The Departure of Ireland's International Class, 1996

S ome accounts had the delegates all but stumbling from the room, as if a nerve agent had been released. The Paris meeting of the International Rugby Board on 27 August 1995, was, as it had been billed, momentous. On the face of it the moment had already passed two months earlier. That summer had been dominated by the battle for control of competitions and players in the southern hemisphere. Once Rupert Murdoch won that war, and snuggled up to the unions of Australia, New Zealand and South Africa with a 10 year deal covering provincial and international rugby, there was no amateur game left at international or provincial level in the serious nations south of the equator. So either those north of that line opted to row their own boat, or they got on board.

Still, there was a sense of disbelief inside and outside the committee room that this would force decisive action. That just wasn't the way the IRB did its business. Afterwards, Irish delegate Syd Millar walked across the lobby of the Ambassador Hotel to George Spotswood, the IRFU administrator. "It's gone," he said.

Millar's main surprise was that it was gone lock, stock and barrel. There was a staging post of sorts in that a 12 month moratorium was declared in Europe so that the game could catch its breath. But it was no more than that. There would be no more sub-committees to explore new ways to stem the tide of professionalism. The old guard were traumatised by what had happened. A colleague of mine remembers coming across one of the English delegates outside the hotel. "He had his hands resting on the wall, and was rocking back and forth—not exactly nutting the wall, but making contact with it just the same. He was absolutely devastated."

Overnight the IRFU had to establish a legal relationship with their players. The first test of the new season was just three months away, against Fiji, and some sort of contracts had to be in place by then.

The union's track record on any kind of contractual dealings with the players was troubled. There had been that bitter stand-off over the Participation Agreement during the 1991 World Cup. Then there was friction over a Code of Conduct which they wanted the players to sign in 1992. That process descended into farce at a Sunday squad session in Lansdowne Road before Ireland played Australia in October of that year.

The players felt they were being asked to sign their lives away, and resisted putting pen to paper. Noel Murphy had left a pile of documents on a table and given the players 15 minutes to discuss things among themselves, and then sign them. He came back in to collect them as the players were filing out the door. To his horror, the dotted lines had no signatures. He ran out after them as they scrambled into the carpark: "Boys, boys, where're ye going? They're not signed! They're not signed!"

Three months later, Murphy walked into a team meeting before the squad flew out to Edinburgh for the opening game of the 1993 Five Nations. He made it clear that if the players didn't sign, they didn't travel. They signed.

The IRFU was hopeful that this latest journey down the legal route could be completed without battle lines being drawn. They set up a contracts committee to get things straightened out. Its chairman was Billy Lavery, who had been on the union since 1988. He was the natural choice: a solicitor by profession, he had chaired the amateur status sub-committee, and subsequently the game participation committee, which was put together to figure out what areas needed to be addressed now that the game had been opened up. Contracts were top of the list. Across the table from Lavery was a players' representative group of Philip Danaher, Brendan Mullin and Denis McBride.

"I found my relationship with the players excellent," says Lavery. "They co-operated, and I co-operated with them, and that created a relationship of mutual trust."

Years later, the decision to contract the players would be presented as a master stroke by a group of visionaries. It was nothing of the sort. The summit of the IRFU's ambition at that point was to regularise the relationship between themselves and a group—i.e. the international players—who overnight had become their employees. The contracts focused on the international game, but later would take into account payment to players who represented their provinces in a brand new cross border competition that had been thrust into place as the game was going professional.

Almost as soon as the market had opened up—just over two months after the Paris meeting—the European Cup was kicking off for the first time, driven into place largely by the efforts of Tom Kiernan, Marcel Martin of France and Wales's Vernon Pugh. This competition was the first cashpoint for Ireland's rugby players, though it wasn't a question of popping in your card and waiting for the greenbacks to tumble out. Leinster for example didn't get around to paying their players until the third round of the competition when they played Pontypridd. "And we got into trouble for it," says Sandy Heffernan, then the honorary secretary of the Leinster Branch. "I remember being called to a meeting in Lansdowne Road and being admonished by Dr Syd Millar and the late Ken Reid for paying the players so soon. What did he expect us to do? They were playing against fellas who were being paid." The payment was IR£300 per game.

There were two kinds of contract: one for the Ireland players who lived and played in Ireland; and one for those who were based abroad. Before long, the home-based boys started drifting across the water. That's where the money was; that's where you could live life as part of a full-time rugby squad. There was no prospect of doing that at home. And there was a feeling that the boat was sailing: get on board or get left behind.

Ireland's final championship match that season was against England, on the eve of St Patrick's Day. Of the 16 players who featured in the 28-15 defeat that afternoon in Twickenham, 10 of them were based in Ireland. Eight months later, the 1996/97 season started with a home game against Western Samoa. And of the 16 who were humbled that night, 40-25, only three were home-based players. It had been a busy summer on the Irish Sea.

London Irish was the most popular destination, but from Birmingham to Bristol you could find Irish players who had packed up and were trying their luck. For everybody—clubs as much as players—it was a learning experience. Most hadn't a clue what was required. In one club they copied contracts from cricket, and with a bottle of Tippex turned them into rugby contracts. For the players, discovering this new world would be more fun than they had ever imagined. Wide eyed, they stepped forth.

———

KIERON DAWSON (BANGOR TO LONDON IRISH)

David Humphreys was the connection between Clive Woodward and myself. He recommended me. Plus, I'd had a good game for Ireland under 21s against England in Northampton and Clive was the coach, so he knew who I was. I had a couple of chats with him and he invited me over. At the time I was in Queen's doing accountancy and was one year away from my finals. I was playing at Bangor and had spoken to other clubs around Ulster who were offering me jobs. Bangor were already on the slide. Mark McCall had already left and there weren't any good young players coming through. For my own career I was always going to move.

In those days the only things on offer were travelling expenses and being helped out getting a job. Ballymena and Dungannon had made me offers. Then London Irish came in with a cash offer of £30,000 and a house and a car! To a poor student that was a ridiculous amount of money. I was used to scraping together a few beer tokens and begging Bangor for travelling expenses to get up and down three times a week in the old Austin Metro that my parents had bought me. The IRFU offered me a student contract with the Academy, which I think was for £3,000. It took about two seconds to make up my mind.

Part of my reason for going was to sample something different. When I left school most of my friends had gone to university in Scotland or England, but I stayed and went to Queen's, purely for the rugby. At the time I wondered what it would have been like if I'd gone away and had that experience? There was still a bit of that wanderlust in me when the London Irish opportunity came along. The prospect of living in London with a few mates, playing rugby and having the crack, was very appealing. There were a couple of houses owned by the club and I lived with Malcolm O'Kelly and Ray Hennessy and Kevin Spicer in Elizabeth Gardens, which was down the road from Sunbury. At some stage or another I think most of the players passed through that house.

It was always my intention to work as well as play because in that first year of professionalism you didn't know if it was going to go belly up or not. So on my first day I arrived into Sunbury in a suit with a view to doing some job interviews. Conor O'Shea had a smile on his face when he came to pick me up. I think he was expecting this yokel from Bangor and I rocked up in my suit. And picked up my new Rover 620.

They hadn't got all the Rover 400s sorted out in that first year so myself and Justin Bishop were given these big 620s. The first thing I did was drive it back on the ferry to collect all my gear from home. I'll never forget driving over to Donegal for a going away "do". I had the car stuffed full of people and crates of beer, and on the way we passed the father of one my best mates from school. He was a bank manager, and he was on the board of Bangor at the time. And he had the model below mine! I think the sight of us rammed into this car will stay with him forever. At least it will with me.

I was injured going over after dislocating my shoulder in the Students World Cup, but the club looked after me very well and I made my debut a few months later against Bath. We had a massive squad at the time and as part of the incentive to get into the first team you'd get a pair of Adidas World Cup boots. You knew you'd made it when you got your boots.

In the early days training was a bit haphazard. You did weights in your own time and then the semi pros would pitch up at about five o'clock and we'd all train together then. So it was just one pitch session a day. You can imagine what it was like: picture yourself being on tour and getting paid for it. Those first six months were crazy: it was like a student's life, except with money.

After training we'd head off into town for a few scoops. We'd have various venues for various nights. You'd have a nice lie in the next morning and get up about 11 or 12 and have lunch. Then we'd do some weights and the cycle would start again. It was hard to adapt to the lifestyle because the training was easy and we were left to our own devices a lot of the time. We were young guys, mostly Irish, having great crack. It couldn't continue, and when Willie Anderson arrived it all got a lot harder. Then we had to knuckle down and the professional attitude kicked in.

Dick Best came in after Willie, and it was during his time there that the pressure came on to get the lads back to Ireland. He made it clear that he wanted me to stay, and he came up with a very good offer. I'll never forget one day during that period, talking things over with Mark McCall and Conor O'Shea and David Humphreys about what we were going to do. Should we stay or should we go? And we were down in Richmond, chatting it over. It was a really beautiful day. The sun was splitting the trees and there was just a lovely buzz about the place. It's a beautiful spot. And I said to myself: "I love it here. I'm staying."

At that stage the rugby wasn't great back home—it was pre-renaissance if you like—and I didn't see any point in going back. I felt I was doing well at London Irish and there was no reason to change that. For me it was absolutely the right decision.

Kieron Dawson was the longest serving of the Irish recruits at Sunbury. He stayed there for 10 years before returning home to a contract with Ulster in 2006. He is married with a son and living in Bangor. He played 21 times for Ireland.

DAVID CORKERY (CORK CONSTITUTION TO BRISTOL)

I left in May 1996, at the end of the Irish club season. There was nobody in the IRFU suggesting I stay. I didn't think that was strange because there was no talk of anybody being offered anything by the union, and if there was I would have been included because I got Irish player of the tournament in the World Cup in South Africa in 1995. I was in the shop window.

I had an approach from London Irish and one from Harlequins, and then a guy who set himself up as an agent approached me with an offer from Bristol. I went over to check it out and liked the place straight away. I was never keen on moving to London so that helped make my mind up. Call me a small town boy or whatever but while Bristol wasn't small, I thought it was homely.

I did a bit of research on the history of the club and it appealed to me. I thought that there was a kind of Munster feel to it in that they had good local support. Bristol was a big rugby town. And the grounds and clubhouse were magnificent. It looked a fantastic set-up.

They weren't awash with back rowers at the time so my place was almost guaranteed.

And the deal was good: £50,000 and a Ford Probe, which was a nice little trinket. I had a beautiful apartment on the river that I shared with Paul Burke. It was really scenic and picturesque. I was coming from working in an insurance brokerage and then all of a sudden I'm handed a new standard of living, all prepared and ready to go. To get paid for doing something you loved, it was just incredible.

I had no difficulty adjusting, but unfortunately the club had. The big issue for Bristol was that they weren't prepared for professional rugby. They had this incredible talent to work with—the team sheet was unreal: Simon Shaw, Martin Corry, Robert Jones, Paul Burke, Mark Regan, Kevin Maggs, Fraser Waters, Mark Denney and Josh Lewsey. All in the one club. There was the makings of a world class club side there.

I think the training regime was probably different to any other professional set-up in the world. We were given fitness programmes, and whether you did them or didn't do them was basically up to yourself. Nobody checked up on you. Nobody seemed to really care. It was as if they were caught completely on the hop: the game went pro and they went along for the sake of it. They bought players left, right and centre but there was no structure there to support them.

It wasn't as if you had to show up at the Memorial Ground every morning at 9 a.m. for work. Our coach was Alan Davies, who had coached Wales, and he used to come along twice a week for field sessions, and then at the weekend for the game. We had a semi-professional fitness guy who was very good, but he couldn't believe the way things were run either. In fairness, we worked hard. We'd go down to the gym in groups of six or seven but you weren't pushed as hard as you should have been.

The quality of rugby was superb, even though we were getting beaten most weeks. It was like playing an international every week because you were up against so many test players. There were players from all over the world coming into that league then. I described it at the time as being so fast that there wasn't time for a fight. I loved it, though there were some awful days.

The worst was playing Bath one day at The Rec, and they had a superb team: Henry Paul and Andy Robinson were there then. It was packed for this local derby—Bath and Bristol was fairly intense—and we were beaten 70 something points to six. They were the tough times. Incredibly there was nothing said to us afterwards. It was just back to the normal routine, with little or no pressure put on us. I don't think there could have been because of the way the whole thing was run.

In the first year there I came back to play for Munster in Europe but in the second year I played for Bristol in the Challenge Cup or whatever it was called then. The travelling back and forwards had become too much so I was happy enough with that arrangement.

Looking back I have good memories of living there. It was a university town and we were the only rugby team there, so we were treated like soccer players. We had a good lifestyle, probably too good at times. I suppose it was inevitable the way things were run that the club got into huge financial difficulty. But we always got paid, even if it was late a few times.

I came back to Ireland in 1998 when most of the other lads were moving home as well. And a year after that I was finished. It was the fourth provincial game, against Connacht, after the 1999 World Cup. I ruptured my Achilles. And then when I came back from that a year later I ruptured the other one straight away. It was a freak that something like that could happen, and to be honest, it broke my heart. That knocked the stuffing out of me.

My only regret from my couple of years away was that I went to the wrong club. With the players we had it could have been a "Leicester". Instead it was a badly run Bristol.

After retiring through injury, David Corkery worked for the IRFU as a development officer for three years, and coached with Bandon, Clonakilty and Cork Constitution. In 2006 he was working in the family's ceramic tile business, married with twins and living in Cork. He has 27 Ireland caps.

DARRAGH O'MAHONY (LANSDOWNE TO MOSELEY, BEDFORD, SARACENS)

We were training with Leinster in Old Belvedere one night in October 1996, and Trigger (Martin Ridge) pulled me aside and says: "What would you think of playing professionally?"

"Fantastic," I said. I was working in a finance house and was having difficulty trying to play rugby at a decent level and be worth my place in an office. I was trying to do both and doing neither effectively. In my job I was always looking for time off for this, that and the other and at the same time I didn't feel I was doing myself justice out on the rugby pitch. It was in my head that when the game did go professional I would have to make a decision one way or the other. I had promised myself that if a chance came along I'd grasp it.

So Trigger says: "It's with Moseley." He had just signed for them a week earlier. They were second division but ambitious and they had a good history. I knew none of this. But I'd just found out they were looking for wingers. "Great," says I. And about five minutes later I was going: "Eh, where's Moseley?"

"It's in Birmingham," he says. OK I knew where Birmingham was. Roughly.

That was the level of my ignorance at the time. But it was hard to pass up the offer, wherever it was. At that stage we were getting match fees with Leinster—about £500 a game, depending on the competition. That nearly kept people happy when it was introduced first. And then English clubs said they'd pay you a living wage. For me with Moseley that was £35,000.

The whole wage structure was hard to comprehend, and it was typical of those early days. By the time I got to Saracens a few years later clubs had either copped on or gone to the wall, but at the start they were throwing money at you. The basic was good—but not outstanding—but then there were appearance fees just for turning out, and win bonuses. Then they paid for your accommodation and your car. They even paid for some of the house bills! I rang home a lot. They paid for that. If they could have started again I'm sure it would have been different, but for some of them it would be too late, including Moseley.

They even let us come home and play for our provinces in the European Cup. That arrangement stopped after the first year, but in my case it was Leinster who pulled the plug on it, not Moseley who were the ones losing out. Incredible.

I pulled a sickie in work to fly over and meet them and see the place. We had lunch and went to the club—which was nice but nothing special—and then I got this tour of Villa Park which I thought was strange. I think Doug Ellis was a very silent investor in the rugby club and somebody thought it would be a good idea to include that on the itinerary. After all the shadow boxing I was looking at my watch and wondering when we'd get to the nitty gritty. The offer was fine and I jumped on the five o'clock flight to Dublin and went training with Leinster that night.

I lived with Trigger and Henry Hurley and Alain Rolland, who came out for a few months after that. It was a good enough house out in Solihull, about 10 miles from the centre of Birmingham, but we knew nobody, and at first you felt pretty isolated. After six months Roller left and Trigger was let go and Henry looked like he was going but ended up staying. After the first year I got my own place and got on my own feet.

The groundsman in the club was a Welsh guy who liked his pints, and on Monday mornings he'd be wrecked. So we'd all be sent off on a run with him so that he could sweat the beer out of his system. That was the start of the week, running around the roads of Moseley, which probably wasn't too good for our legs. Then it was: "Right we're doing weights!" I'd never lifted a weight in my life and I suspect a lot of the others hadn't either. So we'd be sent off to the gym on our own, with nobody monitoring us. You could have smoked 10 cigarettes and gone away after your hour. Some of us worked at it and others didn't really bother. Luckily we had a rugby league guy who had joined—he wasn't much use at rugby but he knew his weights. It became a lot more organised the second year, but by then they'd missed out on promotion to the first division.

The big two were Newcastle and Richmond, and once they were promoted we thought we'd romp home the second year. But it didn't happen. There was always another few clubs with the same ambition and the same drive, and towards the middle of that second year everything started falling to pieces. They basically went bust, but they honoured the contracts as best they could. I'd done well on the field and Bedford made me a decent offer.

They were a good club in a rugby-mad town, but the end wasn't long coming. The financial trouble started in our first year in the Premiership and there was a problem on a few paydays. One day a guy turned up and said: "OK lads, here are your cheques, everything's fine." And they bounced all over the place. Christ almighty!

But I remember I wasn't that stressed by it all—when the Moseley situation was getting serious, or then with Bedford. I was young and single and there were lots of clubs out there, and my star was still rising. You wouldn't wake up in the morning worried about what was around the corner.

I was glad to leave and sign with Sarries who were much more serious about everything. It was strange though: in Bedford you were being asked for your autograph in the streets, but you could be walking around Enfield with Richard Hill, England star, and you'd be anonymous. It was a professional rugby club without a real home and without any tie in to the local community—like, Watford was a soccer town and they didn't give a toss about rugby. It was a great club, and we belonged to Saracens, but at the end of the day who were Saracens?

I had five great years there and never really thought of coming home. That said, it wasn't as if the IRFU were beating my door down. Any time they rang it was after I'd sorted a new contract with Sarries. And that suited me, to be honest. I embraced the game over there. The experiences were fantastic. The variety of people I met was fantastic. The different cultures in everyday life was something I really enjoyed. I had eight great years of professional rugby from the bottom up, and I'm so grateful for that. I miss it, I have to say. And I'd be sorry if I didn't.

Darragh O'Mahony was let go from Saracens in August 2004 and came back to Ireland to start a career in business. With his brother he set up Ontap, a drinks service catering for home entertainment. In 2005/06 he was playing amateur rugby for Dolphin, married, and living in Cork. He has four Ireland caps.

——

Life went on without the cream of Ireland's crop, but it would never be the same again. When the player drain started, the All Ireland League was still the dominant force in domestic rugby. It took up a disproportionate amount of space and time in the national media. Remove most of the international stars from it and the glamour went too. The space receded and the time shortened.

It presented a whole new difficulty for the national management as well. Instead of the players hitting the road after an AIL game for a Sunday squad session in Dublin, now they had to fly in and fly out again. That cost money. Where once there was no issue about having them released for these sessions, now there was a whole new vista opening up: the club managers of England. They had some pressing questions. Like when would the players be back? What condition would they be in? Would they be insured? Would the clubs, who were paying the wages, be compensated if a player ended up missing league games?

The European Cup was a different story again. In October 1996 London Irish agreed to release their contingent to the provinces, but it would be after the first three rounds of the pool stages. There were only four rounds in the pool stages. Relations between the exiles and the parent body were worsening, fast.

Having sat out the first year of the tournament, the English clubs and Scottish districts had got on board. Overnight it became a tougher gig. The IRFU needed the provinces to do well in Europe if only to keep the Irish clubs, who were developing grand plans, in their place. They had already watched the best and brightest take flight across the channel. The last thing they needed was a power struggle with their own rank and file. Club before province? This was getting really messy.

Problem was, if they wanted to boost the provinces they had to assemble squads of full and part-time players. That was the minimum. In September 1996 I spoke to Tony Russ (Ulster coach), Jim Glennon (Leinster manager) and Jerry Holland (Munster coach), and all were calling for workable squads, contracted to the IRFU. "I think that's really got to be seriously addressed," Russ said. "My view is that it has to be sorted by Christmas."

In August the union had announced the setting up of a working party to look at the whole question of retaining players in Ireland. They had set aside a day in October when the union committee would focus exclusively on the talent drain. I asked IRFU president Bobby Deacy if the working party might have an interim report in time for the day-long brainstorming session.

"Not at all," he said. "The issue is much more complex, much more detailed and much bigger than that."

Fair enough. How were they getting on, this working party? He wouldn't say.

And what about the provinces looking for contracted squads?

"I have no comment to make on their opinion. I don't know what they mean by provincial contracts, and I don't know if they know what they mean by provincial contracts."

Meanwhile Philip Browne, the IRFU secretary, said that he didn't know who was on this working party. Tony Russ stood a better chance of finding a winning lotto ticket under his Christmas tree than a squad list of contracted players. But Deacy dispelled my cynicism with a reassuring message for the rugby world.

"We take this matter very, very seriously," he said. "So seriously that we're looking at it, and looking at it in depth, and in its broadest context."

Murray Kidd had looked it up and down and from every angle and for him it came down to two issues: get the players home and get them fit. He had been unveiled just over a year earlier as Ireland's new coach: no international experience; limited and unhappy provincial experience in New Zealand with King Country; and not first choice for Ireland. Never mind. He went at the job full throttle and attacked the fitness shortcomings at the core of the squad.

He was playing catch up from the start. He flogged them in training, so much that they couldn't move on match day. And they hated him for it. That wouldn't have worried him unduly for he wasn't a very social animal.

"How could you endear yourself to some fella who used to greet everybody with: 'How's it going, Fuck Knuckle?'" recalls Eric Elwood. "That's my abiding memory of him."

In January 1996 Ireland had gone to Atlanta for what was supposed to be a week of warm weather training, concluding with a test against USA. It rained. All the time. And Murray coursed the boys through the puddles, and out the other side, and back in again. "Down and Ups" were the most hated exercise in rugby: you'd run five metres; hit the deck full length; get up and run back; hit the deck again. Repeat. They did more down and ups than a whore's drawers.

Kidd could have coped with the lack of popularity if the results were good. They weren't. In nine games in charge Ireland won three of them: Fiji, USA and Wales. It was the losses to Western Samoa and Italy that did for him. All the while he told the union that they needed to get the players home, and to carve out a season comprising international matches, inter-provincials, European games, and an All Ireland League with the top players spread across eight teams in the first division. He didn't just want to get the wild geese back, he wanted all the exiles to set up here. Murray Kidd was a limited coach who made more sense off the field than on it. They turfed him out just before the Five Nations in 1997.

Chapter 4 ～

| TRAUMA

Ireland's Development Tour to New Zealand and Western Samoa, 1997

I arrived in late—it was the first time I got the call up. To be honest I wasn't sure where Limerick was, just about knew where the hotel was and arrived an hour late. Walked in there and the boys were already on the bus. "Right Bishy, I'll give you two minutes to get your bags." I was rooming with Maggsy. It was the first time I ever met him and he was already on the bus. Came back down and they were gone. I didn't even know where the university was. I discovered it was across the road. The lady on the desk grabbed a taxi for me and when I got there they were already running around as I pulled my boots on. I just thought: "Oh my God, not a good start. Not a good start at all."

Justin Bishop recovered. Despite the late start he got through the rest of that first session without drawing too much attention to himself. He didn't miss any more deadlines over the next few days. There wasn't much room left for error. The Ireland A/Development Squad assembled on the afternoon of Monday 12 May, and flew out of Shannon just three days later. They were in high spirits. Certainly Brian Ashton would take a bit of getting used to but it would work out. This was tour time. And for this mixed bag of experienced internationals, and prospective internationals, and those whose only chance of getting to Lansdowne Road was with a match ticket in one hand and a DART ticket in the other, the adventure was about to begin.

This was to be Ireland's first tour of the professional era. Ashton had made his name with Bath, and had been drafted in when the union decided that one Five Nations campaign with Murray Kidd was enough. The Championship had concluded against Scotland in Edinburgh and a press conference was called in Dublin airport as they were flying out. Eddie Coleman, chairman of the IRFU's all powerful elections sub-committee, had some important news for us. They had just given Ashton a six year contract. And Pa Whelan was confirmed as manager until after the 1999 World Cup.

This development trip would be their first chance to get away together. Ashton had been thrown in initially on a short-term basis, and hardly had a chance to do anything other than match preparation. Now he had an opportunity to lay down a marker for how he wanted things done, to identify and develop a few new players for the World Cup. I went down to Limerick to interview him before departure, and when I walked into the appointed room he was busy poring over videos of Super 12 rugby. He was upbeat about the tour. We all were.

Even then however there were warning signs. The traditional avalanche of new gear was reduced to a trickle. Nike were going to revamp their kit range the following season so the tourists would have to make do with what was left of the current stock. The alarm-bell should have rung when the players read through the full kit list.

"Wet suit (if available)". They were flying down to a New Zealand winter.

There was a problem too with the captaincy. Gary Halpin was a risky choice to begin with. His fitness was a bigger factor than his age (31). After a fraught season London Irish had been forced to play off over two games against Coventry in order to maintain their first division status. "I'd missed a whole chunk of the second half of that season," he says. "I'd been injured with a knee ligament for about nine weeks before the tour so they must have known that. My first reaction was: 'I'm not really fucking ready for this.' I'd played in the two games against Coventry but was really on shaky ground. I wasn't at all fit." Great.

This was Ireland's second spin in the development stakes. In 1993 they had gone to Zimbabwe, Namibia and South Africa. The grounds had been hard and the weather glorious. The results too were impressive. They lost just one of seven games, and back then there was no shame in losing to what effectively was the full Namibia side. It was a precedent of sorts but not one that you could rely on. Even the financial arrangements were different this time around. In 1993, for example, the host countries were keen for action, and so they picked up the tab for the tourists once they landed. The Kiwis would be doing no such thing. This trip would set the IRFU back IR£300,000.

Of those selected, six would be ruled out before the off. Five of them were internationals. Another two test players would be gone after the first game. In the context of this trip, where war veterans would be a priceless asset, these were serious setbacks.

Immediately it had implications for the status of the tour itself. This would become an issue as the body count rose. In New Zealand it was billed as the Ireland A side, and the locals were sorely disappointed at the spectacle that unfolded. Sky television would be beaming the pictures into homes from Invercargill up to Manganui. Within a couple of weeks they revised their programme schedules. The measure of the tourists' importance came a week into the trip, at Eden Park in Auckland. The squad had gone along to watch the Super 12 final between the home team and Natal Sharks. Before half time Brian Ashton and Gary Halpin were asked to trek to the other end of the ground for a live TV interview. They were standing there, ready to deliver, when New Zealand Academy coach Ross Cooper appeared. Sky went with him instead. The lads went back to their seats.

In Ireland the tour was played up as another learning curve, even though the original selection had a handful whose developing years were far behind them. No less than eight of the 1993 party were selected as latent developers in 1997. Seven boarded the plane for what would be a whole new experience. Paul Wallace was the lucky one. Running around with the lads in Limerick, he got a late call up to join the Lions who were in London preparing for their tour to South Africa. Peter Clohessy had failed a fitness test on a back injury and Wallace was in like a shot. To this day he looks back and wonders what good deeds he must have done in a previous life.

The others who came close to the edge were Paddy Johns (replaced by Brian Cusack), Denis Hickie (David Coleman), Jonathan Bell (Kevin Maggs), Ross Nesdale (Shane Byrne) and Mark Egan (Dean Macartney). Out of that lot you'd imagine Hickie breathed the biggest sigh of relief. New Zealand would be a hellish version of death by defence for the Irish wingers. He was well off out of it.

Yet nobody predicted the scale of the horror. Back then, when you looked at the itinerary, you saw the likes of Northland and Thames Valley and Bay of Plenty and King Country. All second division sides. The obvious muggings were against the New Zealand Academy, the Maori and, finally, Samoa. In all their years of picking up Samoan players not once have the All Blacks reciprocated by playing a test in Apia, the sweltering capital of the south sea island nation. Ireland would close their tour there. It is a battle first against the elements and second against the opposition. Seven months earlier the Samoans had come to Lansdowne Road, and on a cold, damp evening, ran Ireland off the park. Thoughts drifted to what they would be like with the sun on their backs and an ocean of moisture in the air. The tour would finish with an uphill climb.

What stunned the senses was the carnage before the tourists got to the foothills of that mountain. Nobody really talked about this beforehand, because they didn't want to dwell on the cultural change that the professional game now demanded. In describing what the tour was about, both Pa Whelan and Brian Ashton spoke of settling on a style of play that would suit Ireland; about giving players the freedom to make decisions on the field. With the 1999 World Cup on the horizon these were things that needed to be sorted quickly. Most important though was the lifestyle stuff. Ashton was really big on that. Rugby was now a job and you had to get your head around that or you were doomed. Reading the job spec and living the life however were different tasks. For the players it was an alien lifestyle.

For the next five weeks they would come to understand what was expected of professional athletes. It became an endurance test. There was the length and frequency of the training sessions; the crap weather; the towns that shut down at tea time; the towns that never opened at all; the speed and strength and skill of the opposition; the laughter of the locals who felt cheated that they had paid in to watch a contest and instead saw a team who played like pansies. In Rotorua one day a few of the tourists were walking downtown when a man on a motorbike fired a kiwi fruit at them. "Here lads, see if you can beat that!"

The atmosphere inside the camp wasn't great either. Early on the coach was lambasting them for their short-comings. Brian Ashton came from a background of unbridled success at Bath. It had taken years to achieve. It was hard for him to go back to square one. Then there was a manager, Pa Whelan, whom many were happy to avoid. And it didn't help that himself and Ashton evidently were not close. This was what rugby could be like when it was your job and you weren't very good at it. For some it would be the end of the beginning. For others it was the beginning of the end.

――――

Northland's second division status started to lose its appeal in the few days before that first game in Whangarei. It is a sleepy, picturesque town of 40,000 souls, a couple of hours drive north of Auckland. Like many places in New Zealand, it was hard to reconcile the statistic of how many people lived there with the evidence of bodies on the street.

Pa Whelan was more concerned with the chill running down his spine. He noted how the goal-posts had shifted since the touring party was selected: he was minus a clatter of selected players and the opposition seemed to have struck a rich vein of form. Northland had opened the season by knocking over three first division sides: a depleted Auckland, Counties and North Harbour. They were ambitious. They were unfazed at facing the Irish without the second row pairing of All Black Glenn Taylor and All Black in waiting Norm Maxwell. They were looking forward to giving the tourists a bit of hurry up. Oh, and they had Norm Berryman on the wing. Had he been born in Ireland he surely would never have escaped the front row. Did a lot of damage out wide did Big Norm.

Gary Halpin could feel it in his bones. He had been to New Zealand in 1992 when ritual hammerings were standard. "It's not about winning or losing," Halpin said this time around. That kind of comment invariably precedes a drubbing.

Oh well. The selection policy was to get as many players as possible involved in the first two games, so inevitably there were a few fellas struggling for air. Even those who were supposed to be up to it were hopelessly off the pace.

Niall Woods suffered acutely. He was one of the most balanced attacking wings Ireland ever produced. Frequently this ability was undermined by porous defence. The only reason he was on the trip was because Ashton went in to bat for him when the other selectors didn't want to know. The coach reminded him of that fact at the earliest opportunity. He went out and played like a drain.

Under Ashton's painful programme of therapy, kicking the ball away was something you would contemplate only in a life-threatening circumstance. This was a radical policy shift. At a stroke it wiped out Ireland's traditional mode of progress: kick and chase. Difficult to contemplate at the best of times, in the circumstances of this tour it was extraordinarily demanding to effect. Kicking the ball was so much easier than working your backside off trying to retain it. Ashton's idea was that if you didn't give it away you didn't have to win it back. But you needed huge self belief, never mind technique, to go for it.

Woods's nadir came when he screwed a kick into the path of Big Norm, who had three tries to his credit at that stage. "He trucked over two people and then trucked over Crow (Woods)," Justin Bishop remembers with glee. "We just looked at each other and laughed. It was just ridiculous."

Ashton was a long way from seeing the funny side. "It was a massive culture shock for everybody involved," he says. "We got blitzed big time. The pace and the physicality and the general rugby knowledge. They were so physical. You have to remember that a lot of the players who were out on this trip weren't full-time pros.

"So we were sending out a bunch of amateur players along with one or two pros—some of them just turned pro—and they're faced with this bloody side who played the game at 100 miles an hour and were incredibly physical both in defence and attack. It was something that our players had never experienced in their lives before and they just couldn't handle it. Once you got over the hammering with 69 points it didn't half clarify for everyone exactly what we needed to do on the trip—otherwise every bloody game was going to be the same."

That sameness revolved around attempting a tackle only to see it broken with disdain; or taking the ball into contact only to have it whipped away. To cap it off there was a tour-ending injury. Outhalf David Humphreys had contributed three penalties to Ireland's unlikely 16-14 lead, which they enjoyed for all of six minutes late in the first half. By 45 minutes, when Norm had "trucked over" for his fourth, Northland led 45-16. Irish sides would struggle to do that in training. Then Humphreys hobbled off with an ankle injury that turned into a plane ticket home. Even at that stage of the trip there was a realisation that they had been parachuted into a combat zone in their pyjamas. "I remember Humph got injured and he wasn't the saddest man in the world to be going home," recalls Andy Matchett, the Ulster scrumhalf. "And I was going: 'You bastard!'"

Richie Governey came on thinking he was just filling in for the last quarter. A couple of days later he realised he had become the first choice number 10 on the tour. Well, the only choice number 10. "We just assumed once Humphreys had gone that they'd call somebody else in," Governey says. "But they didn't. Or maybe they did, but the flights kept arriving and there was nobody with an Irish track suit getting off."

He was 21. He'd never been beaten 69-16 in his life before. There were six games to go.

The high flying stars of the New Zealand Rugby Academy were waiting in Auckland. And Eddie Halvey was preparing to go home. He had been diagnosed with a bacterial ulcer and would leave the day after the Academy game in the North Harbour stadium. It was wet, which didn't seem to bother the home team, who ran in 12 tries, two more than Northland. The team was stuffed with Super 12 players. Of their starting xv, Jeff Wilson was already an All Black—he was getting a run out to prove his fitness—and only four others (Matt Carrington, Remi Ropati, Blair Feeney and Ace Tiatia) did not go on to wear the silver fern. So the New Zealand Rugby Union were getting a good return on their investment. They were awesome.

Given the direction of the traffic, Governey was getting plenty of opportunities to display his drop out skills. None of them was reclaimed. "They were going terribly and at half time Ashton just said: 'These drop outs are killing us; if the next one isn't fucking right you're off.'"

It wasn't, but Humphreys was already history and it was a bit early in the tour to press Mike Lynch, a centre, in at number 10. In any case Lynch would be needed to replace Marcus Dillon who was called ashore after 55 minutes of flapping about on the wing.

Centre Alan McGrath recalled a moment from training in Limerick before they had set out. "Marcus took off like a rocket and Ashton looked at him and went: 'Oooh, we're in business!' Ten days later he was lambasting him for being brutal."

On the other wing Niall Woods wasn't having it much better. It was after this experience that he started thinking home might be a nicer place to be. Ashton reminded him beforehand that his display against Northland wasn't what he had in mind as a repayment for selecting him. Now would be a good time to deliver.

Woods was done for the first try after a chip behind him that he seemed to have covered. Then his opposite number, Jeff Wilson, scored the first of his five tries. "He scored four of the tries nowhere near me," Woods recalls in mitigation. "Then he scored one where he rounded me. He did well actually. I don't mind getting done like a kipper. I think it's about the only time I ever was. It was at the end: him full of confidence with four tries already; me not a lot of confidence, not having touched the ball in the pissing rain."

Walking off the field the players knew that the match was only the first part. The inquisition was imminent.

"I must admit I did lose it a bit in the dressing-room after the game," Ashton says. "I remember saying that we'd sat down after the first game and said that this was a level of rugby new to most of them but after the second game I said: 'Look, there's two ways this bloody tour can go now: it can either start to get better, in every respect, in terms of preparing to train in that every time you cross that white line in training it's as if you're playing a game and we don't go through the motions. In a professional world this is your job, like going to the office where you work through the day to the best of your ability. Or it could get worse, that the next guys we'd meet would be licking their lips at the prospect of playing you lot. So anyone who couldn't step up to the mark in training or off the field behaviour or anything like that, either you take the plane home or you never play again on the trip. You'll be like a little boy in the corner, on your own.'"

Lots of coaches had made threats like this before without intending to carry them out. Ashton was true to his word. Those in the firing line didn't even have the nous to fake injury and escape. "They were still inexperienced enough to stay there looking like fucking lemons," says the coach. In time, Marcus Dillon would try to make a break for it.

———

It is mid afternoon on 20 July 2004, a dull Irish summer's day. Richie Governey is relaxing in his comfortable apartment at the foot of the Dublin mountains. He is thinking back on what might have been. What bugs him most is the empty feeling: your name's on the team sheet; this is the business end of professional rugby; but the guy who turns on the showers has a better chance of getting a run. The scene was Welford Road, and Leinster were under the cosh against Leicester in the quarter-final of the 2002 Heineken Cup.

Their Australian outhalf, Nathan Spooner, was patently lame, having carried a leg injury into the game. He should never have played. It had sparked a crisis in the camp: it was like there was an epidemic striking down anyone in the province with a 10 on his back. They called Governey a week before the quarter-final. He was playing club rugby with Terenure at the time, and jumped at the chance. Training had gone well. He knew most of the lads anyway, felt comfortable with them and knew he could make a contribution.

"I was sitting on the bench with Spooner's leg hanging off and I was wondering why the fuck I'd been brought there. You still feel: 'I was here once,' but then when you're sitting there with two minutes to go and all the subs are gone and the old fellas are off the pitch, or breathing heavily, and I'm fresh as a daisy. It was so embarrassing. I was annoyed after it. I came back home thinking I shouldn't have done that. I was trying to get back or do something I probably should have done years ago. The only thing I gained from the experience, possibly, was that if that had been the way it was regimented back in 1997, when I came back from New Zealand, I could have done all right."

It wasn't. If the tourists of 1997 were feeling the pain at the sharp end, then back home there was a country still in its comfort zone. The effect of this torpor would have immediate implications for Brian Ashton, 12,000 miles away, but it was later that it hit the young outhalf. Having survived the slaughterhouse that was the tour, Governey somehow fetched up back in Dublin full of energy and good intentions. He had proved his durability in dire straits. He had taken the grief heaped on him by Ashton and come up smiling. A professional career stretched out ahead of him, starting with Leinster. He'd played eight times for them in the season before the tour.

For 1997/98 he got a full contract. Back then they were in short supply, so the work environment was surreal. "There were maybe six or seven of us training every morning and I just didn't get into it. I was enjoying myself too much maybe. Between training and playing and studying I thought it was great but I wasn't taking it as seriously as I should have been.

"The thing in New Zealand was that you'd no choice. And that probably suited me, to be directed from hotel to gym to pitch to whatever. Then I came home and there were these other things going on. It was professional rugby but I was still at college and meeting up with all my pals. When I went back to Leinster for that week in 2002 it was a real eye opener. I came away from it going: 'Jeez, I'd have loved that to be the norm when I came back.' It's a regret that I didn't give it a lick. At this stage all the professional lads are pals and realise that this is their career. With me I'd wanted to remain with my friends in college who were just normal students. But I've learned that you can't do that. I tried to do too many things and still be friends with the lads. It was naïve and it caught up with me. Mike Ruddock was the Leinster coach then and he'd seen that. At the end of the season (1997/98) the contract wasn't renewed. The whole time is pretty hazy and I was kind of pissed off from the get go. I didn't really have any good period when I came back from the tour. I had all this energy and I really wanted to cement a place with Leinster and then it just didn't happen. I was . . . I suppose lazy is the word. I loved playing rugby but . . ."

Governey had gone to Clongowes, one of the top rugby schools in the country. He played Irish Schools and Leinster under 19s before stepping up to Ireland under 21s. It was from there that he was chucked into an Ireland A game, against Scotland in February 1997, when Killian Keane was forced to withdraw at the last minute. So he was clearly visible on the radar. He expressed genuine amazement at his inclusion in the squad for New Zealand, but he should have seen it coming. Especially given his confidence in his own ability.

Like many of his school-mates Governey came out of Clongowes in two minds: in one he had a well developed sense of his own importance as a rugby player; in the other he struggled for direction and motivation when his days weren't mapped out for him. Years later he would warn his sister not to go out with any Clongowes guys until they'd had a chance to settle into the real world.

"They're like mice at a cross-roads. There was still a bit of that left in me: I was still exploring. For that five weeks in New Zealand I guess I was back in Clongowes."

The regimen may have had common ground but the atmosphere was unrecognisable. Mention his name to colleagues from '97 and they remember the grief he got from Ashton, and his ability to ride it out. He recalls one tortuous session which couldn't conclude until he had performed a punt the way Ashton wanted it done. Throughout the tour—from restarts to cross-kicks—Governey's unreliable boot had driven the coach to distraction.

"So he says: 'This is the way I want you to fucking kick it; now kick it. And we're not going fucking in until you do it.' I'd no problem staying out on my own and doing it until I got it right but when the whole squad was waiting? And it was probably pissing rain again. So the ball would be popped back through somebody's legs again and the lads were standing around and you can imagine the scene. I thought that was cruel. It's one thing I do remember quite distinctly because it was harsh. I put up with a lot of stuff and was quite happy to do that, but when the rest of the lads are looking at you going: 'Fuck's sake, when's he going to do it?' And eventually I got it and it was: 'Now we can all fucking go in.' You see, he can fucking do it!'"

From the moment he ran on to replace Humphreys on the first night in Northland, to the last steaming moment of a hectic game in Samoa, Governey took the criticism and got on with the job as best he could. Remarkably, off the field he was the life and soul of the group.

"I think if I'd been more mature or more qualified or had more experience I probably would have reacted differently to Ashton, but because I wasn't, and I was so keen to actually make an impression, I probably would have taken anything."

He went on taking it right to the end. He played in every game. He was a better player for it. Then he came home to a regime that hadn't picked up on the lessons the tour had handed out. He started to sink. He went to Oxford for a year—Clongowes with girls—hoping it might kick-start his career in the way it had benefited David Humphreys. It didn't. He was 23 and his representative career was over. He hooked up with Terenure and played club rugby, and went to work on the marketing side of the family firm: designing golf courses, a job he loves. He looks back on the experience, and Brian Ashton, without bitterness.

"Ashton didn't get involved socially with the players, so every criticism he had of you therefore was based on your technical ability and not on your personality. And that's what I took from it. I couldn't hate him, because he was judging me on what he saw of me and that was his job. I jest when I say he was a little shit because you're obviously going to look at this little man and the little voice and there was obviously a caricature there, but I would have to say that that's the type of person he was. It wasn't a personal criticism: it was for you to develop your game and as it happened I did. I did get better. He was brilliant for me. He was just what I needed and the more I think about it that tour was what I needed. What happened after that—over which he didn't have direct control—was where it went wrong."

——

Tuesday 27 May: All aboard the bus for Rotorua. It was early days but the road trips were becoming a grind. Given the increasingly fragile mental state of some of the players lots of things were problematic. Like the weather. And the hotels. And trying to dry your gear before going out to train again. And the absence of anywhere to hide from the horrendous match statistics that were following them around.

There were other things to be considered. Like the prospect of not getting any more game time. What if Ashton was serious? Or worse still, what if you were given your big chance and blew it?

In the team room of the Princes Gate Hotel the team is announced to face Bay of Plenty. They are another second division outfit but with less menace than Northland. Still, there were a heap of Maoris in their line-up, and unless you smashed them early you would suffer as the game wore on.

In the first two games Ashton had used 28 of the 32 players. Already he knew that the passenger section was full to overflowing. Nevertheless, against the Bay he would start three of the remaining four: Andy Matchett, hooker Shane Byrne and second row Rory Sheriff. That left Alan McGrath as the only man with one arm as long as the other.

"To be honest, I was on the tour on the back of performances for Shannon—I hadn't even been involved with Munster before that—so my attitude was that even if I didn't play at all I would still be going home with experience gained," McGrath says. "I remember when the team was announced, Gary Halpin came over to me and said that he knew I hadn't been involved, and to hang in there. After what I'd seen in the first two games I was like: 'Hey, I'll just take the experience! At least if I don't get involved I can go home and say it had nothing to do with me, I wasn't on the park!'"

This day holds a unique place in Irish rugby history: never has an adult Irish side conceded so many points so fast; and never has a coach reacted so dramatically. The least Ashton had expected was that his players would climb into the opposition. The Bay lashed them out of it. "The first 20 minutes were worse than the previous two games," says Woods, who was on the touchline. "They were certainly perceived as the weakest side we'd played. Mind you they did have Caleb Ralph. They ran riot for 20 minutes. I was sitting there going: 'Thank fuck I'm not out there.'"

Second row Gabriel Fulcher was sitting nearby. One of the few veterans of the squad, Ashton had told him the previous week that he could forget about rest and relaxation. "The good news was I was in form and playing well; the bad news was that when the crappy game came along I'd have to play," he says. "My one day off was against Bay of Plenty. Watching that first 20 minutes I just thought: 'Oh my Jesus.' It must have been the smell of sulphur in that place, or else it was the lads shitting themselves, I'm not sure. I just remember four guys coming off after 20 something minutes. It was phenomenal. People asked how a coach or manager could just whip people off so quickly? There was a lot of criticism at the time that they never got a chance, but after 25 minutes it was about 35 nil. You can't argue with that. You were staring down the barrel of a hundred."

In fact it was 45-3.

At that stage in the tour—over the two and a quarter games—Ireland were conceding a point a minute. Ashton had had enough. He hauled off Matchett, Bishop, Sheriff and Anthony Foley. Five minutes into the second half Shane Byrne followed suit. For Foley this was one of those bleak days in the yawning gap that spread from him being a schoolboy star to a respected international. He picked up an injury in the next game, against Thames Valley. By then he was already out of the running.

For Byrne it was another entry on what was then an unimpressive CV. He had cornered the market on making late arrivals—Australia in 1994; the World Cup in 1995—without coming close to picking up a cap. This experience brought him no good. He didn't feature again on the trip.

Bishop's recovery was the quickest. He had the mentality to put it behind him and played in three of the last four games. Matchett got only another half a game and that was it for him. Of the three scrumhalves he was comfortably the best passer, but even that deserted him when he needed it most.

"I remember missing Richie Governey with a pass off a lineout and I couldn't believe I'd done it," Matchett says. "I don't know whether it was confidence or whatever but that was the thing that annoyed me about Ashton: he didn't instil any confidence in me in terms of my ability. That day wasn't even wet. I don't know if I felt I should be doing more to get noticed, but it just fell away. Then being taken off was the last straw. It was a fucking disaster."

Steve McIvor came on for him. Standing on the touchline, waiting to explode into the game, he painted the picture for centre Rob Henderson (on for Bishop), and back rowers David Wallace (Foley) and David Erskine (Sheriff). The impact was immediate.

"I almost sent the whole fucking bench on, and suddenly the game changed just like that," says Ashton. "If we'd started with the team that finished we'd have beaten them. It was a real turning point on the trip, and the guy that really stood up to be counted that day was Rob Henderson.

"He'd been playing at London Irish at the time and I'd always known he had the ability but mentally he was so bloody weak and away with the fairies that he would only show up on his terms, when it suited. But that day when the shit hit the fan, and it hit the fan big time, to his credit he stood up in both attack and defence. He made massive hits that I'd never seen him do before, but also he took them on with his running. It was: 'OK I'm Rob Henderson, see if you can tackle me you bloody Maoris.' He just transformed the whole team."

They battled back to lose 52-39. The coach could stomach the defeat if it meant a corner had been turned. It had, but not the way he thought. Thereafter there was a clear division in the group: the useful and the useless. "When we got together the group of people who actually wanted to play it was OK," says Conor O'Shea. "At least you felt there were guys who were trying to compete because there were some guys who just could not get out on the park. The one thing I never did in my career was not give a hundred per cent. In fairness to some of the guys on the tour they did give 100 per cent, but 100 per cent of what they had was absolute crap."

With four games left it was a long road if you were excess baggage.
Rory Sheriff had joined Marcus Dillon and Shane Byrne as surplus to
requirements.

———

At 6'7" he was hard to miss. And it wasn't as if he was built like a stick
insect. Rory Sheriff had the type of physical presence that made an
impression. If you were a rugby scout and you saw him in the street
you'd presume he played the game. And next you'd be after his phone
number. That's pretty much what happened.

In 1994 he was working part time in the pro shop at Courtown
Golf Club. A few Blackrock members dropped in before their round
and were gobsmacked by the giant behind the counter. A year later
he was playing for the Blackrock under 20s, and a year after that he was
on his way to Shannon. So at 20 years of age, and with a level of
rugby experience that could be accommodated on the back of a
postage stamp, Rory Sheriff was playing for the All Ireland League
champions. It was from there that he was picked for the New Zealand
trip. A club tour to Scotland would have been more appropriate
for him.

Right off the bat he had an unsettling introduction to touring life.
His first roommate was a guy who knew his way around, and some of
his personal habits made Sheriff uncomfortable. Thereafter he spent as
little time in the room as possible. It became a source of great amusement to his colleagues who remember him as being something of a
character. He got mileage out of it himself.

On the field however Sheriff was so far off the pace it wasn't funny.
In training he struggled to look like a serious rugby player. When it
came his time to deliver on the field he was wiped out. After Bay of
Plenty nobody expected him to get another run.

"I came back (home) and was written off, and I was basically told so
as well," he said in an interview, three years later. "Not by coaches so
much, just things you hear. But being told you're finished at 20 years of
age isn't very nice."

He switched clubs again as soon as he came back from the tour,
heading back to Dublin and Terenure where Gerry Murphy was coach.
"Gerry and my parents built me back up and made me believe in myself

again. Murph gave me confidence in my own ability and I basically got my hunger back."

He was rehabilitated to the extent that he captained the club—to an AIB League semi-final—and then got a Leinster contract in 2000/01. That was as far as it went however. He could never improve his position behind Malcolm O'Kelly and Bob Casey and Leo Cullen. Perhaps the low point came when, in frustration, he slugged Shane Byrne in training one day. Byrne didn't react, beyond shaking his head in bewilderment, and promptly the story went around the province like wildfire. His contract wasn't renewed. It had nothing to do with the incident in training, rather that he wasn't going to make it as a professional player. He gave up rugby altogether in 2004, aged 28. "I was tired of all the shite," he said. He didn't want to talk about the tour.

——

When the win came it was more a case of relief than wild celebration. "Thames Valley: they were called the Swamp Foxes," recalls Justin Bishop. "I remember Jarrod Cunningham (a future team-mate at London Irish) telling me that if you don't beat them you may as well pack up." If only it was that easy. The packing up bit.

A late change in the itinerary saw the squad shifted up the road to Whangamata instead of Paeroa. It would mean their staying together—rather than be split between two motels in Paeroa—but it would mean a trek on match day. And it was another contender for Dullsville NZ.

Niall Woods felt ill when he saw the place. His form was wretched and he was struggling to find any positives. "We were getting beasted in training," he says. "We'd be out for like two hours at a time. Then back to a motel in some fucking shit hole. Whangamata. You couldn't find a bar in the town. Nothing. No one around. And you'd to go home and sit in your bed for a few hours—the food was crap—and then go back out in the rain in the afternoon to train again. In wet gear half the time. I just thought: 'Oh Christ.' I've never been on a tour where I'd seen so many people want to go home. I've never been on a tour where people wanted to go home anyway."

Nobody wanted to go home more than Marcus Dillon. At the end of one session he had been knocking the ball around with Woods when he stopped and said: "I'm going to kick this ball as hard as I can and hope-fully I'll pull my hamstring and I can go home."

He tried and failed. Woods wasn't sure how to react. "What do you say to a bloke who's saying that, to get him to want to stay? I knew they weren't going to pick him again. I wished they'd pick him instead of me, but fucking hell!"

Matchett had similar dreams. "I remember myself and (hooker) Stevie Ritchie going out in one of those decrepit wee towns and you'd be sort of putting your ankle down over the kerb: 'Go for it, Stevie!' It shouldn't be like that but that was the general feeling. There was no fun on that tour at all."

At least they got out of there with a win. And Alan McGrath got to play, and did well. The only thing special about the 38-12 perform-ance in another downpour was a length of the pitch try started by scrumhalf Brian O'Meara and finished by full back Ciaran Clarke. And both Mike Lynch and David Erskine had big games. Erskine had been in doubt for the tour having broken his nose in the English cup final the week before departure. He was up there with Fulcher, prop Gavin Walsh, Malcolm O'Kelly and David Wallace as the best forwards on the trip.

Monday 2 June: Another long bus journey and the bandwagon rolled wearily into Taupo, picturesque adventure capital of the north island. The players were given their first completely free day. It rained. The news from home didn't do much to lift the spirits of the embattled coach.

From the early days of his involvement with the IRFU Brian Ashton had understood that there was a commitment to establish a fully professional structure feeding into the Ireland team. Mike Ruddock and Warren Gatland were already set up in Leinster and Connacht respectively. Welshmen Clive Griffiths and John Bevan were to be their counterparts in Ulster and Munster. Ashton had sat down with them on 30 April where he outlined his plans. The meeting had gone well. He expected all four to be ready and waiting when he got back from the tour.

My own schedule involved picking up the last three games of the development gig and then heading over to South Africa for the Lions tour. The week before I arrived in Taupo I had written that Griffiths and Bevan had changed their minds. When I walked into the reception of the team hotel Ashton was one of the first people I met. He was still reeling from the news.

"I was absolutely appalled," he says. "I remember when I'd initially spoken to Noel Murphy, Syd Millar, Eddie Coleman and Pat Whelan in Dublin, about doing the caretaker's job, I'm almost certain that one of the things I'd been promised was that there would be four full-time directors of coaching in the provinces. That was one of the reasons I took on the job. And here we were, five months down the line, and suddenly we'd still got only two. I was bloody furious. We were getting thrashed left, right and centre on the other side of the world with two provinces without full-time coaches."

It undermined everything he was trying to achieve Down Under. What was the point of banging on about a professional lifestyle and the changes it demanded if the players would return to the old comfort zone back home?

Around the next corner was King Country. Ashton had been hoping it would be the test of how far the tourists had travelled on their road to self discovery. Not that far as it turned out. They lost again. "I remember being really disappointed because I thought we'd turned the corner after Rotorua with some of the players—not all of them. I knew some of them would never see a green jersey again unless they bought one in Woolworths. That game knocked me back again: I started thinking: 'Jesus, am I wrong?'"

It was a hard night for Gary Halpin. He had struggled all tour with his knee. The pace of Ashton's game didn't suit 31 year old heavyweights with dodgy knees. The decision-making on the field had already been switched to Gabriel Fulcher when he was there. Halpin had no problem with that. He was hauled off half way through the King Country game for Gavin Walsh. He wasn't wild about the idea but what alternative could he offer Ashton? Walsh would remain first choice tight head for the remaining two games. As a bit-playing captain, Halpin did well to keep it together.

Mike Lynch too had an evening to forget. First and foremost he was an inside centre, but Governey needed some sort of break. "They asked me to play outhalf and like an eejit I said yes because I had played a little bit for the club there," Lynch says. "But stepping up to that level? It was shocking. I'd been split in the game against Thames Valley after

getting a boot in the head and I had two staples over my eye going out
to play King Country. In the very first minute didn't I get another boot
in the same place. I'm not excusing it but that's the reason why I played
so poorly. So I was taken off and Richie came on."

The bonus for Lynch was a bout of blood poisoning from his
eye injury. The tour moved on to Palmerston North the next morning
and he got to spend three days there with his feet up in hospital.
Glorious! It was warm, and dry and comfortable. There was nobody
queuing up to kick him. Nobody shouting at him. He got lots of visits
from team-mates and management alike. They brought him food
and other goodies. There were phone calls from home wishing him
well. He thoroughly enjoyed it. "It was the highlight of my tour," he
says. A few miles away Barry McConnell was having the direct opposite
experience.

——

He was a good thing: mobile and strong and durable. He had switched
from loose head prop to hooker and was making a go of it. Bristol rated
him highly. He wasn't Jocky Wilson with the darts but he was prepared
to work at it. With any luck he was heading for a collection of Ireland
caps. This is what he had in mind when Barry McConnell was a kid in
Garvagh, Co. Derry.

His older brothers were rugby players: John had played for Llanelli,
and Brian had captained Bristol University. So Barry took the same
road and made good progress. He was well suited to the game. In 1992
he played on the same Schools Cup winning team as Jonny Bell. They
beat Methody, and Jeremy Davidson, in the final. He had two years with
Ulster Schools; one with the Ireland squad. When he went off to study
civil engineering in Bristol University rugby was a big part of his life.
He signed up for Bristol RFC, then a serious outfit. He had two seasons,
winning eight caps, with the Ireland under 21s, and just before the call
up to the New Zealand tour Bristol had contracted him full time. It was
looking good.

The tour wasn't working out too badly either. Like the rest he was
fed up with the slog, but of the three hookers he was first choice. He
had been selected for what was being classed as the first of their two

"test" matches: the New Zealand Maori. The next day his career was virtually over.

They were playing a rugby league style game across the width of one of the back pitches when he launched himself to tackle Alan McGrath. He got hold of McGrath's shorts but the centre kept going and McConnell's momentum swung him through the air. He stopped when he hit the post—in effect a thin metal pole—at full tilt. His knee took the full force of the impact.

"It was agony and I thought: 'I've really done something bad here.' I was lying on the side of the pitch with tears—I wasn't crying—welling up, and Brian Ashton just said to play on. Malcolm O'Kelly came over to see how I was and he could tell it was something really bad. But Brian Ashton, in the mood he was in at that stage you couldn't do anything right. I could see the funny side of hitting the post but a year later I couldn't see the funny side of it when you're running up the steps of Bristol rugby ground trying to get better. The way he reacted to it was typical of him."

It wasn't one of the coach's more compassionate moments. He was utterly dismissive of McConnell's plight. Strange as it may seem, immediately there is something comical about somebody colliding with a rugby post. Then the humour should evaporate when you see the state of the victim. "Nowadays if that happened to someone you'd get medical attention immediately," McConnell says. "I had to crawl to the side of the pitch. Obviously it turned out to be a really bad injury but they didn't diagnose it. They sent me home with a note saying I had a bruised knee. I didn't get X-rays; I didn't get MRIs. The Bristol physio couldn't believe it when I got back. I'd even been stuck in economy class on the way home with my knee in the worst possible position to improve, while all the tall people and Brian Ashton were sitting in business class. I remember sort of hinting to the management at the airport that it might be better for my knee if I could get some sort of upgrade. That was greeted with the same hilarity that hitting the post had generated."

Bizarrely he was asked to attend a full Ireland session out in Westmanstown at the end of the summer. Clearly Pa Whelan—with whom McConnell had a good relationship—had no idea of the damage that had been done. Bristol organised for him to have surgery to repair his anterior cruciate ligament. After a year of rehabilitation he made a comeback of sorts. Then his back caved in at a buckled scrum. He didn't play again. He was 23.

"I kind of couldn't care and really couldn't face a 50-50 chance of recovering properly. I had psychologically turned against rugby and I stopped following it totally, to the extent that I barely watched a game or took any form of interest for about three years."

At least the injury meant he had to sit still and study for his finals which he had postponed in order to make the tour. He got his degree and works in London now in a property investment company. He got back his love for rugby. He'd love to meet up with the lads from that tour again.

———

Conor O'Shea remembers the Haka pretty well. He picked out Jarrod Cunningham to focus on because he was the only one who didn't intimidate him. There were some grizzled characters in the Maori line-up. Norm Hewitt was the best known of the forwards but captain and number eight Errol Brain was your prototype New Zealand forward from another era: all muscle and sinews and big hits.

For much of the contest—the fourth game out of six washed down by rain—the Irish played tremendously well. Governey scored a lovely individual try to stay in touch in the first half, and had they put away a four to one overlap, with Bishop spilling the final pass a few metres short, they could have led midway through the period.

For much of the second half it was desperate defence with David Wallace and David Erskine doing really well. Ultimately they ran out of steam, as always happens to the side making all the tackles. It finished 41-10 but was light years ahead of the standard shown four weeks previously. The players themselves could feel the improvement, which they allowed to overshadow the result.

"The one thing that will always live in my mind was after that game," says Alan McGrath. "We'd played well and were only beaten by 30 points. And we were going home on the bus afterwards and we were laughing and joking and singing. And Brian stood up: 'For fuck's sake you're a national side, development or not, and you're after being beaten by 30 points, and you're fucking happy? You should be quiet as mice, going home to your room, sitting in your fucking room and nobody coming out until we go training.' That summed it up. This was professional rugby."

There was nothing too professional about the accommodation. The next day the party headed down to Wellington—to another kip of a hotel in the less than delightful Lower Hutt—before flying out to Samoa. It afforded an opportunity for IRFU president Bobby Deacy to hold a press conference to update us on the saga that was the provincial coaching positions back home. Twelve days previously I had reported that Andy Leslie was in line to replace John Bevan in Munster. At a little get together in a bar in Lower Hutt, Deacy announced that the deal with Leslie was "80 per cent complete". In time Leslie would withdraw his 20 per cent.

"I spoke to Andy in Wellington and told him what my plans were and he was really interested and wanted to be a part of building something like this up and was impressed that we had a clear vision of where we wanted to go," Ashton says. "That was it. I thought: 'Fantastic!' Then it disappeared. I don't know what happened. The strange thing was that it wasn't long after that that his sons came over to play for Scotland and you would have thought it was a great chance for the whole family to come over."

Yes it would. But the business difficulties that prevented Leslie taking the IRFU offer occupied him for a while after that. He had enough on his plate.

Thursday 12 June: Flight PH820 climbs above the long white cloud. There is palpable relief to be leaving New Zealand behind. Ahead lies Western Samoa, and no one is too sure what to expect. Even the itinerary is ambivalent. On one side of the sheet it told the players they would be staying in Aggie Grey's, part of the fabric of the South Pacific. Apia is a piece of the third world but Aggie's, originally a club for US servicemen stationed in Samoa during the Second World War, is charming and comfortable. It held out some promise after the drudgery of New Zealand. The blurb tells you of the royalty and movie stars and diplomats who have rested up there. On the flip side of the itinerary there were details of some place called the Hotel Insel Fehmarn. Compared to Aggie's it was a concentration camp. The Samoans got to stay in Aggie's.

Up the road the Irish settled into their quarters. It was a dump. You could have turned a fire hose on in any room and not worried about damaging anything. It was all coming together nicely: crap tour finishes in another crap hotel. But there was hope in the weather forecast. There was a storm on the way. Well, a hurricane, to be more accurate. And we would be on the edge of it. So the rain threatened to drown the players as they sloshed about in training. Then the wind whipped up. The day before the game the pitch at Apia Park was under water. I remember sitting in the car with colleagues Tom English and Gerry Thornley, drawing lots to see who would hop out, run over to the locked gates, and peer through the gap to see how much water was on the pitch. I lost. You couldn't see the pitch under the lake. "Good news lads," I reported triumphantly. "There's no way they'll play on that."

The pitch was grand. The sun was blazing high in the sky and temperature reading showed 33 degrees. It was inhuman. Pa Whelan had been trying to downgrade its status by reiterating that not only was this not a test match—unlike the defeat in Dublin the previous November—it was well removed from an A international as well. Samoa coach Bryan Williams hummed a happy tune when hearing of Pa's pleas for leniency. It was a rare day they got to entertain one of the International Board's top countries. For their legendary wing, Inga Tuigamala, it was his first test at home. They were going to enjoy it.

For this last stand Ashton opted not to give Niall Woods another chance. Kevin Maggs was switched to the wing and Mike Lynch came back to the centre. In the pack Malcolm O'Kelly started ahead of Brian Cusack in what was a full strength unit. It would be a draining experience. And it could have produced a stunning finish had the recurring theme of the trip not been replayed in glorious technicolour.

From the time they came together in Limerick to the final team talk in Apia, Brian Ashton had warned of the consequences of giving the ball away. Whether the transfer was made by hand or foot it mattered little: there would be a price to pay. And it was as likely to be exacted a mile from your own line as within a few metres of it. The illustration of the point would come later. Before that Ireland made a fantastic start. Tries from Gabriel Fulcher and David Erskine had them ahead 12-3 after 17 minutes. And even though they had fallen behind 22-15 at the break, they came out and dominated the first 10 minutes of the second half.

Governey knocked over a penalty and then O'Kelly got a great score to give them the lead. It was hard to believe: half an hour left and an Irish side who started with just four test players were leading a full strength Samoa in their own hot house. Then the mistakes crept in and the punishment was cruel.

Gerry Murphy assisting with Ireland in New Zealand, June 1992. Later that year he was appointed as coach.

Keith Wood under pressure from Ilie Tabua and Phil Kearns, with Garrick Morgan in the background, in the second test against Australia, in Sydney, 1994. (*Dallas Kilponen/Fairfaxphotos*)

RWC 1995, South Africa: Gary Halpin celebrates his try against the All Blacks in unique fashion.

Jonah Lomu occupies the minds of (*from left*) Eric Elwood, Maurice Field, Denis McBride and Paddy Johns in the New Zealand game.

RWC 1995, South Africa: Niall Hogan is supported in his graduation by Gary Halpin and Nick Popplewell with Eric Elwood (*front*).

Darragh O'Mahony: "It (Saracens) was a professional rugby club without a real home and without any tie-in to the local community."

Kieron Dawson playing for London Irish: "I said to myself, 'I love it here. I'm staying.'"

David Corkery in action for Bristol against Wasps. "There was the makings of a world class club side there."

Gabriel Fulcher secures lineout ball in the searing heat of Apia Park against Western Samoa in 1997.

The Development Tourists in Whangarei, New Zealand, 1997: (*Back row*) Richie Governey, Niall Woods, Alan McGrath, Dean Macartney, Malcom O'Kelly, Anthony Foley. (*Fourth row*) Barry McConnell, Darren Molloy, Justin Fitzpatrick, David Coleman, Mike Lynch, Rob Henderson. (*Third row*) Gabriel Fulcher, Shane Byrne, Marcus Dillon, Kevin Maggs, David Wallace, Andy Matchett. (*Second row*) Stephen Ritchie, David Humphreys, Stephen McIvor, Eddie Halvey, Gary Halpin, Brian Cusack, Brian O'Meara, Conor O'Shea, Ciaran Clarke. (*Front row*) David Erskine, Kieron Dawson, Justin Bishop, Gavin Walsh. (Not pictured: Rory Sheriff)

New Zealand, 1997: Richie Governey with Justin Bishop on hand against Bay of Plenty.

Pa Whelan and Brian Ashton, poles apart at a squad session in Sutton in 1998.

Donal Lenihan, Warren Gatland and Philip Danaher, feeling the pain in Lens, 1999.

Paul Wallace, Eric Miller and Kieron Dawson, moments after the final whistle against Argentina.

Conor O'Shea took a big hit in trying to stop second row Potu Leavasa and Samoa got the lead back. The full back was concussed, and played on. That proved costly. It was only four points and Ireland came again. They were scorching into the Samoan 22 when Junior Paramore read an inside pass from O'Shea and took off. Somehow O'Kelly managed to chase him down only to see the ball popped off to the supporting Joe Filemu. It was the sickener. That put 11 points between them. They would concede another three tries, two of them from Irish attacking situations. Ashton didn't look best pleased.

"I nearly killed Conor O'Shea in the dressing-room afterwards," Ashton says. "It was the end of the tour and I went in and said that normally at the end of a tour the coach comes in the dressing-room and thanks the players, which I am doing, but there's one or two other things I want to fucking say before I see you again, that's if I see any of you again. And that was about having a look in that bloody mirror and think what you've done for Irish rugby on this trip, and what you've done for yourself and your mates around you. And I looked at him all the time I was saying it. I reckon we could have won that if it weren't for the interception try. We should have scored and it would have taken us a couple of scores up." It finished 57-25.

It was ironic that O'Shea should take the brunt of the coach's anger for they could sing from the same hymn sheet. O'Shea was a genuine professional. Later that night when I pointed out the irony to Ashton he dismissed it as being utterly irrelevant. O'Shea had cocked up and that was as deep as it got. It didn't surprise Gabriel Fulcher.

"His psyche was very different," Fulcher says. "In Ireland we tend to put a lot of emphasis and a lot of respect on getting stuck in. Then when someone does something stupid we say: 'Well look at his tackle count,' or whatever. Ashton wouldn't be like that. As far as he was concerned if you threw a bad pass or dropped a ball you might as well have funked out of a tackle. It's: 'I don't care; if you made a mistake you made a mistake.' I think guys get a lot of respect for being physical but what winning teams do is they're absolute perfectionists. If ever I met a perfectionist it was him. He just would not allow a session to go on without it."

Governey had direct experience of exactly that scenario. McConnell too knew how blind Ashton could become if something got in the way of his training session.

"His immediate response to Barry's injury was quite harsh but I felt that was his frustration in general coming out," says Fulcher. "If he was a happy, contented man with better results he may have dealt with that situation differently."

That's not much consolation to McConnell, or to Marcus Dillon who was traumatised by the experience. Ashton would look at him and say: "Are you still here?" He made no allowances for the fact that a raft of his squad were boy scouts trying out for the Hell's Angels. Hence they slaughtered him behind his back. One of the crossword kings among them came up with "Shaton" from his surname. Many of them couldn't wait to get away from him. Or indeed Pa Whelan. And they struggle to remember assistant coach Davy Haslett. He was a late draft for the position and was a peripheral figure throughout.

On that last night they drank the Evening Shade nightclub dry. In Samoa there is a tradition of *fa'afafine*, where boys take on the role of women from a young age. Even allowing for the fact that in that neck of the woods sometimes the women are as big as the men, and the dress code is not that different, there are tell-tale signs. They eluded some of the Paddies that night. My enduring memory of the scene is of one of the less successful tourists slow dancing with a *fa'afafine* who had an Adam's apple the size of a rock and hands like shovels. He thought he was sorted. Brian Ashton wasn't dealing with quick learners.

The next day the bandwagon rolled out for the last time. Suitably it was a nightmare trip, numbed by as much alcohol as possible: Apia to Wellington, to Auckland, to Los Angeles, to Frankfurt, to Heathrow. Dublin was as far as the itinerary covered. The Limerick crew hired a car to get themselves home. At last it was over. I went to South Africa and tuned into a different wavelength.

———

Had it been in Australia then certainly the tour would have gone off the rails. If only they had been able to find more towns open for business they would have waded into the grog. That's what makes New Zealand such a tough destination: there is no respite from the rugby. And there are more sleepy hollows than you can shake a stick at.

That temperance is considered one of the more remarkable aspects of the trip, yet it was simply down to the itinerary. Chance would have been a fine thing. More notable by far was the determination of Brian Ashton not to compromise. He had a vision of how the game should be played and he ploughed ahead regardless. Consider the number of times on that trip when it would have been easier to put boot to ball and perhaps slow the flow of points. He had a shallow relationship with Davy Haslett and a worsening one with Pa Whelan, so there was only himself to consult on this. He never wavered. Perhaps the effort took it out of him because that stubborn streak would weaken when his dealings with the IRFU got worse.

By then the players were still coming to terms with their five weeks at the other end of the world. The trip is remembered as an embarrassment now. It shouldn't be. Mike Lynch would not be alone in this assessment.

"At the time I'd rather have been anywhere else, and Ashton wasn't a very popular guy with the players, but it has to be said that there's a certain amount of credit due to him for bringing in the whole notion of professionalism. Not just the word, but how you carry yourself, what you do, how you train, how you rest—all of these things. He's very much responsible for an awful lot of that. Some people will just retain the memories that they didn't like the guy. But he has to be acknowledged. It's not the easiest thing to do when you're looking back at memories which weren't the rosiest but you have to take your hat off to the guy: he achieved something. He made people think about what they were actually doing and why they were doing it, and that if they wanted to do it well they were going to have to change their attitude."

At times it seemed like he was on a one man crusade.

See Appendix 1, Development Squad, 1997, page 225.

Chapter 5 ⌒

DIVORCE

The Separation of Pa Whelan and Brian Ashton, 1998

I've got a great love of Irish rugby and over the years was living in hope and disappointment really. Suddenly here I was with, at the time, the greatest coach in the northern hemisphere—and probably the world—and Ireland didn't have a coach. I was getting more and more despondent. And I thought: "Bugger this—Brian hasn't got a job and Ireland haven't got a coach." And I rang directory enquiries and asked for the Irish rugby union.

Actually Ireland did have a coach at the time. His name was Murray Kidd, but from Tim Drohan's office in Bristol he could see that there was about to be a gap in the market. And he knew just how to fill it. It was sweet: Brian Ashton was his client; Ireland was his passion. One needed a job and the other needed a boss. The girl in the IRFU gave him the number for Pa Whelan in Limerick. He rang it straight away.

"Hello Pat, my name is Tim Drohan. I'm an agent."

Before he could continue, he got a long blast from Whelan who believed agents lived under the same rock as leeches and assorted bloodsuckers.

"So what do you want?" asked Whelan, when he'd delivered his rant.

"I have the best coach in the world," Drohan replied.

"We already have a coach. So who is this guy you've got?"

"Brian Ashton."

"Oh."

A few days after that conversation, on 4 January 1997, Ireland played Italy in Lansdowne Road. They lost. Kidd got a call to come to Dublin on the Tuesday. He brought his lawyer with him, and left with a severance package. On the Wednesday, Brian Ashton made the same trip with his agent. When they flew back to Bristol that night he was Ireland's new coach. That's how it all started.

Pa Whelan was quite pleased with the way it worked out. He had come across Ashton three years earlier when Garryowen played Bath to mark the opening of a new clubhouse in Dooradoyle. Garryowen went to the Rec the next season and the connection between the clubs has continued over the years. Bath put on a brilliant show that day in Limerick. Afterwards the two men chatted, and Ashton expanded a bit on how rugby could look so good.

Brian Ashton is, as he described himself, a proud Lancastrian. He was born in Leigh, rugby league country, in 1946. By the time he was five he was a season ticket holder at Wigan's Central Park. He tells you this with some pride. He grew up understanding professional sport, that it was a job. But it was rugby union that took him to Tyldesley, Fylde and Orrell in the north of England, and then abroad to Montferrand, Roma and Milan.

The peak of his playing career was to tour Australia with England in 1975. Mercifully for him he wasn't called off the bench for the only test. That battle in Sydney remains the most brutal test match in the history of the game. It was as close to a cap as Ashton would get. In the circumstances it was close enough.

If he underachieved at the top level as a player he made up for it as a coach. He was involved with Orrell first before moving to Somerset in 1987 to take up a teaching post in King's School, Bruton. That was where Bath found him. From 1989 to 1994 he assisted Jack Rowell at the Rec as they blazed a trail around England. Bath had started accumulating silverware five years before Ashton came on board, but he gave their back play a whole new dimension, and the trophies kept coming. Rowell was a pragmatist, and Ashton was fascinated by the relationship between risk and reward. With a terrific squad of players they produced great rugby.

When Rowell left to run England, Ashton took over. He left in 1996 after falling out with manager John Hall. Among other things, Ashton felt his own influence over the running of rugby at the club was being undermined.

Initially the deal with Ireland was to see out the 1997 Five Nations Championship, and then assess where both parties stood. But before they got to that stage Ashton and the IRFU joined hands and jumped into the deep end with a six year deal. At the time it seemed like a strikingly bold move: here was the most conservative of rugby unions making a positive statement about their appetite for the professional game. In retrospect it was madness, for even by then Brian Ashton had doubts. He had doubts about the players he was working with; he had doubts about the manager he was working with; he had doubts about the union he was working for. And he had doubts about himself.

"I couldn't work out at the time—and I didn't say anything—was this good news or bad news?" he says of the contract. "There was an escape clause as there always is, but it was still a massive thing to take on board because my family were still living in England. My daughter was at Bristol University and my son was doing A levels at Lancaster Royal Grammar School. My wife was teaching in Bruton. And suddenly I'd committed the next six years to Irish rugby."

Did he not think it through?

"No, not fully."

On day one Ashton's vision for Ireland was clear, and there didn't seem to be any ambiguity about his role. He would coach the national side and have a major say as part of a five man selection committee that comprised team manager Pa Whelan, Donal Lenihan, Joey Miles and Frank Sowman. Beneath that level would be four fully professional provincial squads. He would have a critical input to filling those provincial coaching roles; he would open his playbook to these men and get them to share his vision of how rugby should be played. It was simple and it was beautiful; and in an Irish context it was radical because it involved a cultural shift. We had been reared on kick and chase. Now we would be reincarnated as runners and handlers. There wouldn't be just the national team doing it: the four feeders would play the same way; and below them the message would go out that there was a structure and pathway that not only led you to water, but showed you how to drink without spilling. This was exciting!

On paper it couldn't have been simpler. The structure was even ready-made. The history of provincial teams went back to 1875/76 when Leinster and Ulster first played each other. And the four provinces had been in official competition since 1946/47. You didn't need to merge or liquidate or create new identities. It was all on tap. All you had to do was fill it up and let it flow into the national side. All this was discussed with the IRFU. Everyone was happy.

The problems started early. In fact, at the first training session in Limerick. Ashton had been introduced to the players in the week of the opening Five Nations game of 1997, against France in Dublin. That's when he discovered that many of them struggled passing the ball from left to right. He had come from an environment where the motto was: "Good enough for England, but is it good enough for Bath?" The required adjustment shouldn't have surprised him, but it did. In those days access to training didn't involve a background security check, so we stood on the sideline and watched his reactions. There was a fair bit of: "OK, we'll try that again" going on.

As well as Whelan, Ashton inherited Mike Brewer as assistant coach. He had an immediate rapport with the former All Black who was equally forthright and demanding of high standards. By then Brewer had a good handle on the rawness of the material, and the system that produced it. "I think he was surprised at the lack of ability, particularly in the backs," Brewer recalls. "I remember after that first week he said to me: 'Jesus, I don't know if I've made the right decision here.' And he was looking at it purely from a professional point of view, probably as far as his cv was concerned. But I remember saying it was a matter of profiling the team and deciding on a game plan that best suited them."

There were other issues. Like why they trained in Limerick. Dublin was much easier to access for players coming from the UK or further afield. It meant that by the time everybody showed up on the Monday of test week, the day was gone. The hotel was fine and the facilities in the University of Limerick were good, but on the occasions when the bus didn't show up it meant lugging all the gear over by foot. It cost time. It dawned on Brewer and Ashton that the person best suited by the Limerick arrangement was Pa Whelan, even if that wasn't his priority in making the decision. It was a battle for him to combine his thriving property business with managing a professional rugby team. It was eased somewhat if they trained in his backyard.

If it seemed anachronistic to have an amateur running a professional operation, then there were other examples to come. After losing 32-15 to France in the first Championship match, Wales were next on the list. In the early hours of the morning of the game in Cardiff, the fire alarm went off in the team hotel and the players were rousted from their beds.

"It was almost like a scene from the Titanic, running around making sure everyone was out of their rooms," remembers Jim Staples, who had taken over as captain from the injured Keith Wood. "The most notable fact was that the only person who wouldn't shift was Mo Field, who was a fireman. The bizarre image that will always stick in my mind was from outside the hotel: Syd Millar, dressed in his dinner suit, talking through the finer points of scrummaging with Nick Popplewell who was standing there in his boxer shorts. At the time there were all sorts of conspiracy theories going around that it was Welsh supporters who had set the alarm off. But it wasn't until the next day that we realised who the culprits were."

The night before Championship matches the respective union committees get together for long, sumptuous dinners. It's part of the tradition. The IRFU boys had arrived back to the hotel and carried on into the night. The alarm was triggered by their cigar smoke. Ashton was apoplectic. "There was one guy in particular who strolled out and his attitude was: 'What's all the fuss about?' As if this was normal preparation for international rugby. Stood in the bloody street at two o'clock in the morning!"

The team recovered from the interruption to their sleep. In the first half the next afternoon they stuck it to Wales, but by the end of the game another pressing problem had arisen. The default mode for Irish players was to kick the ball, whether they were behind or ahead. In the first half they ran a simple pattern that caused havoc in the Welsh defence. Brewer had pointed Jonathan Bell to the channel between Wales outhalf Arwel Thomas, who looked and played like a choirboy, and Scott Gibbs, a hard nut with explosive power. There was no way Gibbs would trust Thomas to keep his end up defensively, so he would have to cut back to make the tackle for his outhalf if Bell attacked that channel. And that would open up the space for Maurice Field to exploit. Despite conceding a try in the first minute Ireland recovered really well, and everything was going according to plan. By half time they were 20-10 in front.

"They came in shocked, as if they were losing 20-10," says Brewer. "And I remember saying to them: 'Just keep on doing what you're doing, and we'll win this game comfortably. Keep attacking and keep doing what we've trained to do.' Well from the start of the second half we started to kick the ball and to defend the lead. And we won the game 26-25 in the end. And they came in absolutely delighted. And I was ropeable [fit to be tied]. We'd just chucked away an opportunity to put 40 or 50 on them."

At first Ashton thought this struggle to change the habits of a lifetime was about overcoming a reflex, that if they could get accustomed to a new range of movement then the old impulses would wither. As time went on he began to believe there were other forces at work, that his orders were being countermanded. He never unearthed any evidence of this.

England were next, and the game was presented as a match up between Rowell in the England camp, and his erstwhile club assistant in the Irish one. Ashton had hardly put pen to paper with the IRFU when Rowell was bemoaning his loss to English rugby. Yet he had lots of opportunity to get Ashton on board before he hooked up with Ireland. Anyway, the game went the way it was expected, and England were able to spring a powerful bench that ran Ireland ragged in the last quarter.

It was around that time that the IRFU gave the go ahead to reduce the selection panel from five to three, which Ashton had wanted. Subsequently it dawned on him that he should have stuck with the old system a while longer, for he simply didn't know enough about the players, and could have done with the extra selectorial input. Typical of the time however, what in theory was a progressive move was delivered as an incendiary device.

It was the day Ireland were flying to Scotland for the last game of the Championship. Before the squad departed, there would be a specially convened coronation in Dublin airport to crown Ashton as the six year king. Donal Lenihan was in the building, but not in the loop.

"The press conference was upstairs in the VIP area, and we were downstairs in departures—myself, Joey (Miles) and Frank Sowman—and the committee came down and they were all talk. In effect they had scrapped the selection committee. It was to be a three man committee, and Pa and Ashton were already there. Nobody had told the three of us. Somebody made a comment to me: 'Well you're out the fucking door!' And I didn't know what they were talking about. And I said to Joey: 'Do you know what's going on?' And I went up to Pa in the Balmoral when we got over to Scotland. 'Come here,' I said to him, 'will you ever tell me what's going on?' And he says: 'Oh, the five man committee is gone.'"

Lenihan was livid. He had no problem with the operation being streamlined, but was insulted that nobody could have told himself and the other two that they were surplus to requirements. As it turned out he would, much later, become the third man. He wasn't the only one running a temperature that day.

For the squad, the day had started with training in Limerick, before dashing to Shannon to catch their flight. Mike Brewer thought there was something odd. They were scheduled to leave in 40 minutes and the only aircraft on the tarmac was a 767. "So with about 15 minutes to go I said to Rala (Paddy O'Reilly, the bag man): 'Rala, where's the fucking plane?'

'It's out on the runway.'

'There's no fucking plane out there; there's just a 767.'

'Yeah, that's it.'

'What? A 767 for us to go to Edinburgh?'

'What do you mean just for us?'

'But we're going from here straight up to Edinburgh.'

'Ah, you haven't been told.'"

The plane stopped in Dublin. By the time the press conference had been held, and the committee and their wives and the various other Irish teams had boarded, the players had been hanging around for an age.

"We left Shannon I think at one, and we got into our hotel room in Edinburgh at 9.30 that night," says Brewer. "As soon as we got off the plane I was ropeable. And I said to Pat: 'Are you serious about winning this game on the weekend?' And he sort of looked at me as if I had 10 heads, and said: 'Why?' And I said: 'Well, what should have been a 45 minute trip has just taken us eight and half hours. It's less than two days before the match. We may as well get on the plane and go back to Ireland.' And the response was: 'Well that's the way we've always done it.' And my response was: 'Well that's why you've always lost.'

"After that I pretty much knew that was the end of me, but it didn't bother me because unless those things changed Ireland would continue to lose games when the first team was waiting for the seconds and the committee and the universities and all the rest of it. They played really poorly and I remember there was quite a discussion after the game."

Brewer left the next month to take up as rugby director in West Hartlepool. His departure would rob Ashton of the man he had come to know best in the Ireland set-up. There was a further loss that weekend. Jim Staples hobbled off with a pulled hamstring after 24 minutes. It was related to a back injury which would require surgery. That was his last game for Ireland. Keith Wood had been Ashton's captain in his first game in charge, against France, only to fall over Thomas Castaignede after 15 minutes and pop his collar bone. So Ashton had pushed away selectors he could have done with, lost his assistant coach, and finally his new captain had to be helped away from the scene. Ashton had just run out of moral support, for Staples was more than a stand-in captain, he was also was something of a confidant.

"I'd played against Bath a whole number of times for Harlequins," says Staples. "So when he got the job, if himself and Pa were from different planets then I'd be just down the road from Brian in terms of how I thought the game should be played. We spoke quite a lot, not just about the team and the games but also about certain players."

Not any more they didn't. Brian Ashton's first Championship season had just concluded with him already feeling isolated. It would get worse over the summer, with the development trip to New Zealand. For that tour Ashton turned to an unfit Gary Halpin. "When I spoke to him, when he asked me to be captain, he spoke to me in terms of: 'I kind of need a guy like you there because I don't know Pat Whelan,'" Halpin says. "He was very, very sceptical of Pa from the start."

That trip only deepened the scepticism. The players were too busy keeping body and soul together to be bothered about the quality of the relationship between the coach and the manager. If they'd looked closely they would have seen it was worsening.

"We had one or two fallouts on tour," Ashton says. "I just felt that he (Whelan) was paying lip service to professionalism and it rankled with me, and I made the point on a number of occasions that I felt slightly isolated, that I was the only professional on the management side of that tour, and all the rest were amateurs. So it didn't really matter despite the noises they made about: 'Fucking hell we're not doing this and we need to be doing that.' I was thinking: 'Well ultimately to you guys it doesn't matter because you'll go home and go off to work. This is my job, my livelihood. And I've been in rugby too long to know that people talk a hell of a lot and nothing gets done.' In the (English) RFU things went through committee after committee and it was the same in the IRFU. And the same fucking people sat on all the committees. So if there was a dispute on one committee there was no chance of it getting through. How much of this are they going to push forward and how much aren't they?"

Whelan recalls those five weeks as an endurance test. He had the speech off by heart well before the end of the tour, the one about the learning curve. If Ashton felt his manager was paying lip service to professionalism, then Whelan felt his coach saw only fault in everything. Finally he lost it with him on one of the coach journeys from one sleepy hollow to another.

"I stopped the bus in the next town to let the whole thing cool down," says Whelan. "Like, no-one knew that now—the players, nobody knew it—as far as they were concerned we were getting a break. I hauled him into my room when we reached our destination and I seriously told him: 'Never fucking try and do what you did there again.' He was giving out about the training, about the fact that all the gear wasn't there lined up on time and this kind of carry on, but I was only learning my fucking trade the same as everyone else."

Next came a balmy autumn, but it didn't bring any warmth. There were big issues; then there were smaller ones that added up to big issues. In the first category was Andy Leslie pulling out of the Munster job. "All I know is that relatively recently I had four (provincial) coaches and now I have only two," Ashton said at the time. In the second category were logistical errors: flights not booked; too many players turning up for training because the right letters had been sent to the wrong people.

The manure that bonded all this stuff together was the results. In the three internationals between the end of the development tour and Christmas 1997, Ireland lost to New Zealand, beat Canada, and then lost to Italy in Bologna. Whelan called an early morning meeting in the wake of what was Ireland's second defeat by the Azzurri in 12 months. "We were all there and there was no sign of Ashton," says Donal Lenihan. "And Pa nearly blew a fucking head gasket."

There was a lot about their new coach that Whelan and the IRFU couldn't understand and didn't like. He had been provided with an apartment in Dún Laoghaire which he hardly ever used. Had he come over to watch All Ireland League games then the neighbours might have seen him, but he didn't. Repeatedly Whelan and Lenihan advised him that it might be good for business to check out the local talent, but Ashton never deviated from the English circuit. It was a higher standard of rugby, unquestionably, but that he couldn't see the value in fetching up at an Irish ground every so often was instructive. And if he wasn't going that far then a permanent move—as was suggested to him by IRFU secretary Philip Browne—was never going to happen. In which case the teaching post they had sorted for his wife wouldn't be taken up either.

"He really didn't do what he should have done and we weren't strict enough in saying: 'You're employed here, you bloody well live in Dublin,'" says an IRFU source who didn't want to be named. "We let him away with it."

Ashton had a different take on it: the IRFU was the horse and he was the cart and there was a logical sequence to how they would go forward.

"As time went on I thought with all the amateurism surrounding it there was no way I was going to put myself or my family into a situation like that until things drastically changed," he says. "To uproot all that lot would have been totally unfair, certainly in the short-term future which I couldn't see changing dramatically. I was in an uncertain situation and one I didn't particularly enjoy, so I wasn't going to move from England to Ireland in a situation like that. The other thing was that 10 out of the starting 15 were still playing in England. So to watch these players et cetera, living in England was a logical thing to do. That was about to change significantly, so whether that would have swayed me or not I really don't know."

The change he was referring to was Operation Repatriate: Bringing the Boys Back Home. That would have given him the numbers he needed to work with. Yet had that come to pass, you wonder would he have come up with another reason to be unhappy.

And that issue—professional players for a professional game—had been his recurring complaint: the union's reluctance to deliver on the number of contracted players around the country. The process of appointing provincial coaches had turned into a farce, and every time he asked about the squads of 25 professional players in each province he was fobbed off. The only legitimate reason for the IRFU not following through on this was in how they could keep four squads active.

Coming up with enough games to sustain those numbers was a challenge, but not a mind-bending one. If the IRFU had, for example, delivered on Whelan's proposal to scale down the 14 team first division of the All Ireland League to eight—it had first been mooted by Murray

Kidd—then the professional players could have filtered into these clubs when the international, European Cup and inter-provincial matches were complete. But that would have involved acute pain for some committee men who would have to cut their own clubs out of the picture. And they couldn't hack that.

Interestingly, Whelan was more agitated by Ashton's demands than the IRFU's reluctance to run with his plan. "As far as I was concerned it was going to happen—it might have been delayed but it was going to happen," Whelan says. "The man wanted the whole thing done overnight."

By then the man knew he had made a mistake. The only issue was how he could extricate himself from it.

On 10 January 1998 Cork Constitution played Shannon in the AIL game of the day. Coming off the Cork train that night, I stopped off for a pint in the Horse and Tram on Eden Quay with my colleague Tom English. The relationship between Whelan and Ashton was the main topic of conversation. The standard position—among the Sunday hacks—was that Whelan was invading Ashton's space, refusing to slip into the background and allow him get on with the job. Incorrectly we all presumed that the manager was dominating selection, and at the time Ashton did nothing to dissuade us. We talked a bit about what we had written for the next day, and I left thinking that the temperature was coming nicely to the boil. When I opened the *Sunday Times* the next morning the lid was blown off. The headline on Tom's piece read: "Pa must be put out to pasture." The key line in the copy was that the relationship had broken down "irretrievably".

Things kicked on from there. The daily papers asked Ashton to clarify the position, and for two days he chose not to comment. It was the equivalent of adding a gallon of kerosene to the mix. He explained this by saying that he wanted to speak to Whelan first. Could he not find a phone?

Whelan had come back on the Sunday morning from a short break and walked into the storm. He got a call from Tim Drohan telling him what the papers were already screaming—that Ashton had issues—and they needed to meet. It was arranged for the hotel at Dublin airport on the Tuesday night. Subsequently it would be reported that Donal Lenihan, who by then had become the third man, sat in on it, but it was only Whelan, Ashton and Drohan who convened at 9.30 p.m. It went on for four hours.

Whelan should have been the man under pressure. His media profile was horrendous: we had portrayed him as the playground bully who wouldn't let the other lads get on with the game; that all Ashton wanted to do was play. In fact Ashton wanted to take the ball and go home.

Beforehand he had sat down with Drohan, who reduced the list of grievances to a manageable level. "I said: 'Look Brian, this seems to be an ongoing whinge—can you write down—let's be specific—tell me everything that's wrong.' And he came up with 30 things and we cut it down. Some of them were repeats, and some of them were—'I don't like the milk over here.' Not that, but silly stuff. And we got it down to 20–24, something like that, and Pa agreed to 23 of them. Or if it was 20 he agreed to 19. The one sticking point was when Brian said: 'And I want to train in England.' Pa said: 'I can't do that. I'd do anything for you Brian—I'll put it by the bloody airport but I cannot ever say yes to Ireland training in England.'

"And I'm going: 'This is obvious stuff!' And as far as I saw it there were 20 odd yeses and one no, and to be brutally frank on some of the yeses he was very unreasonable to ask for them—and the fact that they (Whelan) had said yes was incredible. And we're walking up the stairs afterwards and I said: 'Brian, you should be really pleased with that.' And he said: 'Pfff, no.'"

Ashton was unhappy because he was staying when he wanted to go. The training issue had been hugely important and he knew that Whelan couldn't agree to it. In the lead-up to the game in Bologna the previous month, the Ireland team had trained for the week at London Irish's ground in Sunbury. In the micro climate around 62 Lansdowne Road, a storm raged. This was the grim illustration of the extent to which they had lost control of their own game: the players had left and now they weren't even coming home to train? In those circumstances the logic of location meant nothing.

But Ashton couldn't walk because of that. It would have appeared utterly unreasonable. Had it been combined with Whelan refusing to concede on other issues, then maybe. But the manager was far from belligerent. And there had been another key moment in the meeting. Early on, Whelan offered to stand aside altogether.

"I felt I'd missed an opportunity because he'd offered to resign and

I didn't take it," says Ashton.

Why didn't he grab it with both hands?

"I don't know. Maybe I just didn't have the confidence at that time to [do so]."

Drohan worked all night writing up the minutes and flew back to Bristol first thing on the Wednesday morning. It was freezing. A few hours later the squad were training in the Suttonians ground, which was the nearest usable venue. Photographers scurried around trying to get Whelan and Ashton in the same frame. "It was a nightmare," says Patrick Bolger, who was on duty for the INPHO photo agency that day. "Every time you set up it was like the two boys would run off in opposite directions."

The session was preceded by a squad meeting where the players were told that everything was grand, and that Pa and Brian would be marching forward together. Ashton didn't sound like he believed it; neither did Whelan; and the players certainly weren't convinced, though it's questionable to what degree it bothered them. Keith Wood was back as captain by then, but it was before the time when he infused power into the role. He was too occupied sorting out his injuries and his commitments as captain of Harlequins to get involved in this battle. "There's trouble in Paradise—where's Paradise?" Wood says.

It wasn't in Suttonians. In an effort to promote the idea of solidarity, Whelan put the finger on Lenihan to join himself and Ashton at the top table for the press conference that followed the session. Lenihan looked almost as uncomfortable as the other pair. Whelan batted on, trying to claim it was a media conspiracy, but the killer line was delivered by the little Lancastrian beside him. "Pat's Irish; I'm English. Pat's an amateur; I'm professional." And this was the *rapprochement*?

Brian Ashton had one more classic delivery which confirmed his departure before it became official. Three weeks later Ireland played Scotland in Lansdowne Road. They lost by a point. Just as Brewer had been frustrated by what had happened in Cardiff 12 months earlier, Ashton was going mad at the same thing unfolding before his eyes. "I'm not quite sure whose game plan that is, but it's nothing to do with me," he said afterwards.

That summed up his predicament. A year after he had started, the players were making the same mistakes. When the pressure came on, they resorted to kicking the ball away. He railed against this lack of composure when the heat intensified, but the irony was that he had failed his own test when Whelan offered to stand aside.

"The actual answer was he was looking for a reason to leave," says Drohan. "That's all. That's the real answer. The reality was, when he said: 'No, I'm still not happy,' that the whole thing had been a bloody waste of time . . . really and truly he didn't have the balls to say: 'I don't like this job.' And in that sense I don't think the IRFU could have done any more."

The stress of that time induced a bout of shingles in Ashton. Before the next squad session he rang up Connacht coach Warren Gatland. Along with Leinster's Mike Ruddock, Gatland had been helping out at Ireland training runs. Ashton asked him to fill in, saying that he should be OK for the next one ahead of the France game. He wasn't. He resigned the next week, citing personal reasons. Gatland was installed in his place until the end of the season.

Brian Ashton was recovering back in Bruton, building a mental barrier between himself and his 13 months in the Ireland job, when the IRFU announced they would be offering 25 professional contracts in each of the provinces. It was as if they had been waiting for him to leave. He looks on it as his legacy. Certainly his agitation had helped bring that about, to push the IRFU into resourcing the template for the professional game. In different circumstances, and at a different time, he would have been able to do much more. But Ireland was no more ready for Brian Ashton than Brian Ashton was ready for being a head coach of a national side. He had no problem highlighting the first bit, but took a while to accept the second.

Pa Whelan found Warren Gatland easier to deal with. The New Zealander was less ambitious in his game plan. His focus was on tightening up what they had, and blocking the revolving door which had seen 45 players through the Ireland team in Ashton's eight games. In the remaining matches, Gatland's team lost to France, Wales and England, but such was the depth of resistance shown on his opening day, at Stade de France, that the honeymoon lingered. And he had wasted no time in showing up in Thomond Park for the AIB League. He got a stirring welcome. This was no absentee landlord.

In mid April 1998 that competition was down to its last four. On the Saturday, Shannon played St Mary's in Thomond Park; the next day Garryowen took on Young Munster in Dooradoyle. It would be an all

Limerick final the following Saturday, and Whelan's club had booked their passage. By early the next morning that bit of light in his life had gone out.

Over that weekend, Whelan hosted meetings in his house with Gatland and Donal Lenihan to discuss the South Africa tour which was coming up the next month. Lenihan was due to travel in his capacity as selector. They took in both AIL games and assessed the form. Sometime on the Monday, Lenihan got a call from Noel Murphy. Whelan had resigned as manager; could he step in? "What do you mean he's resigned?"

Lenihan had driven back to Cork after the Garryowen game. Whelan went into the clubhouse and climbed into a few pints. By the early hours of Monday morning he was the worse for wear and occupying the same general area as Tom English in the Brazen Head sports bar. Both were aware of each other's presence.

Although English's parents lived less than 100 metres up the road from Whelan on O'Connell Avenue, there would have been precious little contact between them. There was no history; it's just they weren't friends as such. English's assessment of Whelan's managerial talents wouldn't have altered that for the better. In the interim, English had got a mouthful of abuse from a friend of Whelan's, which didn't surprise him or upset him greatly. What happened next did.

At roughly 2.15 a.m., sober enough having been drinking relatively little, English went to the gents. It was empty. He was standing at the urinal a few moments when Whelan came in. The manager unloaded some verbal abuse, and then unloaded a few punches which sent English's glasses flying across the floor. Whelan left and rejoined his friends. English followed a minute or two later, badly shaken. He left the nightclub, went home, and wrote down what had happened.

There was no way the story would stay under wraps, and English's boss in the *Sunday Times*, Rory Godson, made the most of it. He went on national radio while the IRFU went into legal mode. Whelan's resignation was announced on the Wednesday. It was a public relations disaster for the union.

Pa Whelan said his reasons for leaving were down to pressures of work. Given that he had just slugged a journalist in the jacks of a night-club, it was a hard line to sell. It did, however, substantiate much of Brian Ashton's unrest: how professional could this be when an amateur was struggling to manage the operation? And he was struggling.

"Ah, I was getting out anyway," he says. "I was going to get out after the South Africa tour. I was running a substantial business at that stage and it was suffering, and it needed me, and on the other hand I also realised that the position of manager of the Irish team was full-time. The one regret I had was that I didn't have enough time to devote to the man management and one to one situations."

It was a one to one situation that moved things along for him. "No, I won't talk about it at all," he says of that night. "It's just something that's better if it remains left where it is."

He never apologised for the incident. Initially this would have been for legal reasons, but subsequently that was no longer an issue. More likely he said nothing because that's the way Pa is. It was a pity, because Tom deserved an apology, and Pa's image could have done with a positive touch. In our rush to understand the pain of Brian Ashton, we ignored that the manager wasn't having much fun either. Genuinely he was passionate about Ireland being successful. But he was the wrong man in the wrong job at the wrong time.

Chapter 6 ∿

LONG NIGHT IN LENS

Ireland's defeat by Argentina, Rugby World Cup, 1999

It was embarrassing. It came at the end of what was a very difficult transition for us from '95. Our period from '95 up to Lens was an absolute fuck up altogether. It was sort of a catharsis point where everybody said: "OK, we've reached it, now we can either play around with the professional game or get seriously into the professional game."—
IRFU *member*

We were staying in Villeneuve D'Ascq, near Lille. It seemed that everybody had difficulty getting flights and accommodation. And everybody's accommodation was awful. France must have more travelling salesmen on miserable expense accounts than anywhere else in Europe, because around the country they have built any number of cheap, soulless stopovers for them to pause before moving on. Typically, instead of carpets, they have rice paper laid straight onto bare concrete. Stand in the same spot long enough and you can feel the cold work its way up through your body. Everything in the bathroom is plastic and grubby. The televisions are tiny and bolted to the wall. There is no room service, and the food is so wretched that having it in your room would be no better than having it in the restaurant which is always dark and grim. They usually plonk these places in industrial estates, tucked up beside a motorway: not great for sleep, but good for a quick getaway. And we were desperate for a quick getaway.

We had returned to our hovel in near silence on the night of the game. Everything was closed when we got back. It was still closed when we left early the next morning to get down to Beauvais, where nearly everything was closed. It was raining hard, and we were on a mission. In France, drivers make no concessions in the wet: it was hairy stuff, trying to eat up the kilometres and see through the windscreen at the same time. The headline in *The Irish Times* the previous day had read: "Losing is not an option." Forget that. Making the flight was life or death. The only other one was 12 hours later, and we were flying Ryanair. We made the flight. And when we got home we cleared the desks and started the post mortem. God, it was depressing stuff.

Our standing joke when things would go horribly wrong in Irish rugby was to blame somebody on the periphery. It reflected our opinion of an organisation that hired and fired without ever disturbing the inner core. With the IRFU, accountability was always an issue. So blame the bus driver, or the guy who turns on the showers, or the man who makes the soup and sandwiches. The bag man—or baggage master to use the official term—was Paddy O'Reilly, or Rala as he is known. "Rala must go," we decided, as we sped back down the motorway. And for a while he did.

It was the most apposite footnote to this traumatic episode that the bagman should be loaned out to the enemy. He's not even sure how it happened. He thinks it was "some guy from the IRB" who asked him to give the Argentinians a dig out with their kit for the quarter-final in Lansdowne Road, where Ireland were supposed to be. So as the Irish squad broke up and went their separate ways, dragging their chins along the floor, Rala was humping gear for the Pumas. "I was numb from the previous thing—I kind of floated through it," he says of the defeat, and what followed. And then, just in case you think he got any professional pride out of it, he adds. "Me heart wasn't in it." Well fancy that.

THE BACKGROUND

It wasn't supposed to finish like this. Two months earlier, after an interprovincial match in Donnybrook, Warren Gatland had been urging us Sunday journalists to get on board the World Cup bandwagon. "I just think we could finish up in a quarter-final in Lansdowne Road against France, and it might be a bit late for you guys then," he warned. We were in the bar in Old Wesley after a provincial game. Gatland was good in those situations. Unusually for a Kiwi he knew where his pocket was. There had been the odd late night drink on the South Africa tour soon after he came on board in 1998, and then in Australia in the summer of

1999. They were invaluable sessions for us because he was good with off the record information, and better company than his sometimes dour demeanour suggested. He was fairly bullish that night in Donnybrook. The way he presented it, we had to sign up soon or risk being Johnny Come Latelys.

The whole togetherness thing was very much part of Warren's plan. Perhaps it was his New Zealand background, but it used to bother him that the media weren't automatic card carriers. The way he saw it, he was working hard to sort out a mess he had inherited, and we needed to do our bit as well. Certainly he was doing his best, and it helped that his relationship with the new manager was a good one.

Donal Lenihan and Gatland resolved early to keep things simple on the pitch, and simple off the pitch. They wanted the team to be difficult to play against and fun to play for. They wanted training sessions to be attended by players who were happy to be there. Ultimately they wanted them to be filled with players who didn't have to travel from clubs in England. There would be continuity and stability and self respect across the board, and they'd see how far that took them.

It wasn't part of Lenihan's career plan to step up so soon, but circumstances put a bit of pace into it. He had massive experience as a player, as an Ireland captain and a Lion, and when he took on the manager's role he made a point of approaching it from the perspective of the players, not the IRFU. It was a significant shift in how things were done. He involved the senior group in decision-making, and wanted them to be treated with respect. He soon ran into problems.

The tour to South Africa in 1998 saw Ireland lose the series on a points aggregate of 70-13. If the first test was nasty, the second was nakedly violent. Lenihan was incensed by the treatment off the pitch as much as on it: the squad were jerked around by stadium staff and then shown zero hospitality at the post match functions. After the second test they left in disgust and had a meal back at their team hotel. Lenihan wanted to reciprocate when the Springboks came to Dublin in the autumn. Instead the IRFU saw to it that the South Africans were treated royally.

"They sound like irrelevant things but in many ways they affect your standing, because what you're saying is that they're better than we are," he says. "From the perception of a player it's a case of: 'Will we accept them kicking us when we're down? That they can get away with treating us like pigs, but when they come to us we treat them like kings?' It's a psychological thing with players. That really annoyed me."

It was a struggle all round. Gatland was trying to get more structure into the team, and improve their physical conditioning, but there was always some crisis around the next corner. October brought a story that burned the union to its core.

In his *Sunday Tribune* column, Neil Francis ran a piece alleging that players in Irish rugby used illegal substances. The union reacted with outrage, demanding that he substantiate his claims. Next thing you knew they were calling a press conference admitting that they had two cases to deal with. And, eh, that there had been a third which they already put to bed without telling anybody. There was uproar. It was a shambles.

They held the conference in the Berkeley Court, in a packed room with the heat turned up full blast, and where the opening gambit was a long monologue from their legal advisor which had the effect of intimidating anybody who was still awake. Union president Noel Murphy ran the show, and ran it into the ground.

"That was the problem with the IRFU at the time," Gatland recalls. "They had paid people in positions and they were still rolling out the amateurs to do the job. Those were some of the frustrations. You employ people in certain positions with skills to handle those situations and hopefully do damage limitation, and that definitely wasn't damage limitation. I remember Noisy (Noel Murphy) making a comment like: 'Come on lads give us a break' sort of thing. Well hang on, you don't get a break in this sort of situation; you've got to handle it professionally."

The drugs fiasco was followed by a public stand-off with Keith Wood, who wouldn't sign his contract because of the rights it gave the IRFU over use of his image. Wood hadn't been Ireland's first professional rugby player, but he was the first to grasp the enormity of it all. He understood what the game needed from him and he gave it. In return he knew what he was owed, and had the balls to stand up for it.

"I had a tiny (Irish) contract because I had one in the UK where I was getting paid by Harlequins, which was fine, but I didn't feel I should give away all my rights for little or no money," Wood says. "Basically I was assigning my intellectual property rights to the union who in turn could assign them to sponsors, or whoever, who wouldn't have to pay me. And I couldn't assign them myself to people who *would* pay me, because of the exclusive contract with the union. That's acceptable if you're being paid an awful lot of money. It's not acceptable if you're being paid a pittance. My contract with the IRFU was for £5,000."

For Wood it was an issue about control, so to emphasise the point he offered to play for nothing, but to retain the rights over how his own image would be used. Naturally enough the union wouldn't wear that, but to underline the point Wood gave his match fees for that season to charity.

"In the end I signed the contract because I didn't want my own stubbornness to get in the way of me playing for my country. Ultimately it became a tacit victory for them, but a victory for me in that I lost the battle but kind of won the war. I just ended up doing what I wanted to do, oblivious of whether I could or couldn't according to the terms of the contract. But none of it was done with two fingers to the union."

Although he was butting heads with Lenihan over it, they never fell out. But Lenihan didn't restore him to the captaincy, which had passed to Paddy Johns for the summer tour to South Africa. After his exploits with the Lions in 1997, Wood had come straight back into a season as captain of Harlequins. He desperately needed a summer off. The plan was to leave him out of the South African trip, but then hooker Ross Nesdale cried off and Wood was asked to play just in the tests. He did that, and Johns led the tour. After the contractual wrangle it would continue that way. "I didn't mind," says Wood. "I'd made a few bad mistakes: I was captain of Quins and captain of Ireland at the same time which just wore me to the nub. And we hadn't been successful with me as captain—quite the opposite." Nevertheless, this was an issue that would have to be addressed soon enough, for Johns wasn't a long-term option.

The next crisis came in April, by which point Ireland had beaten Wales in Wembley, but lost to France, England and Scotland. They had rounded off with a win at home against Italy, who in 2000 would be breaking new ground as part of a new Six Nations tournament. Two weeks after that game I got hold of a report written—but not leaked—by Craig White, the national fitness advisor. One section read:

There are no leg strength results. Initially, at the first testing session on 23 March, I was appalled that only two people were "so called" able to perform this test. Because of this I didn't perform it at yesterday's session. This test is extremely important and it seems to me that players are frightened to do it.

It was damning stuff, not so much of the frontline players who were making the 22 man match squads for Ireland, but of the professional ranks that fed into that level. Brian Ashton's demand for four professional provincial squads had been realised the previous year, but the players were slow to understand what that entailed. Given the preamble to their introduction in the first place, it followed that the union didn't have the first clue about getting some bang for their buck. Privately, neither Gatland nor Lenihan was too upset that this had tumbled into the public domain because, despite the further damage done to Irish rugby's reputation in the community, it put acute pressure on their players to shape up. The next month they would take the squad to Australia, where the serious preparation for the World Cup would begin. They couldn't wait to leave.

THE BUILD-UP

There was the Australia tour; then a test against Argentina in Dublin in August; and finally a round of games against three of the provinces. That would carry Ireland into their pool games and, hopefully, their base camp of a home quarter-final against France. For the 1999 World Cup the competition had expanded from 16 teams to 20. This time there would be five pools, which involved a play-off stage in between the pool and the quarter-final. Ireland had USA, Australia and Romania in that order. So we would most likely be coming out as runner up. That meant a play off in Lens, which was somewhere in northern France where they didn't play any rugby. The opposition would be the best third placed team from the other pools. Sweet eh?

Despite all that had gone before, the 28 man tour squad was confident they could get something useful from the Australia trip. After the opening game against New South Wales Country, confidence ran a bit too high. It didn't help that Steve Merrick, the home team's scrumhalf, and a former Wallaby, was effusive about the tourists. "We thought we might catch them first match, but that was unbelievable," he said. When the line was replayed to Gatland, his chest swelled. "That's nice to hear," he said. But this was New South Wales Country, or to give them their full title: The IAMA New South Wales Country Cockatoos. The next weekend Ireland were facing New South Wales proper. Donal Lenihan talked it up, and then watched in horror as the Irish defence was carved to shreds.

They were back where they started. It was like the old days, except
that off the field there was no party culture. The bit I couldn't understand was the incredible workload they took on in training. The line
was that they needed to build up reserves to see them through the
autumn—remember, we're going all the way to the World Cup semi-
final here—but with time on their hands and glorious sunshine to
work in, it seemed strange that they didn't do more technical stuff. Like
how to defend against the likes of New South Wales who were stunned
that the same code kept getting them past Ireland's security.

Between Gatland and Philip Danaher, who was coaching the backs,
and Stephen Aboud—who had been drafted in as an advisor during the
Five Nations—they had enough grey matter to brainstorm a better way
forward. Danaher seemed to be the link between Gatland and Aboud,
who were from different planets. If the coach wasn't overly concerned
about planning every aspect of training from the bus to the field
and back again, then Aboud thrived on detail. Some thought he was
usurping Danaher, but that wasn't the case. The two got on well, and
Danaher—whose modest ego meant he didn't have a problem asking
for help—was more than happy to have Aboud around.

Aboud had been part of the IRFU professional staff since 1990. He
could be technical to a level where every point came bound in hardback. He is not a social animal, and I remember when the management
played the media in a soccer match on the green across the road from
our hotel in Perth—it was an opportunity for Lenihan and Gatland to
wade into us—Aboud disappeared early, saying he was injured. That
kind of gig just wasn't his thing. Had you asked him to debate the
minutiae of turning a traffic jam on the rugby field into freeflow,
he would have been there till the death. And wiped the floor with all
comers. But socially he was a challenge.

That was at the tail end of the four match tour. And having been
milled in the first test in Brisbane the previous weekend, we expected
more of the same. And then they came out and played tremendously
accurate rugby, before losing 32-26. It papered over what had gone
before, and we focused on the positive aspects. Tom Tierney was
emerging as a very useful scrumhalf, and at outside centre there was a
20 year old who appeared to have everything.

Brian O'Driscoll made his debut on that trip, playing for Ireland
ᶜore he played for Leinster. Straight away he made a positive impact,

and even the Australians marked him out as worthy of attention. They weren't that bothered about Matt Mostyn however. He hadn't cut it in Australia but was drafted into the Irish system towards the end of the season along with another overseas back, Mike Mullins. Mostyn had pace but there wasn't much else to enthuse about, though Gatland had a lot of time for him.

Three tries from the leggy wing against the Argentinians in August would make the coach happier still. The fixture hadn't been pencilled in as a confidence booster for Ireland ahead of meeting them eight weeks later in the World Cup, but we reckoned that if it came to it, there wouldn't be that much to worry about. Argentina were pooled with Wales, Samoa and Japan. It was the most open group, and there was a good chance that the best third placed team would come from there. If it was the Argies, then bring them on. That's where the complacency set in.

For an hour in the August game Ireland played a brand of rugby more open and varied than anything they had managed all year. Midway through the second half they were 32-3 ahead. The Pumas looked like a side with problems on and off the field. Agustin Pichot was clearly their best scrumhalf but Hector Mendez—who coached the side along with Alex Wyllie—favoured Nicolas Fernandez Miranda, a decent player who had been around since 1994, and, as it happened, was also a friend of the family. Eventually Pichot came on, and was instrumental in the three tries they scored in the last quarter, which transformed the contest. It finished 32-24, with Ireland looking pretty tired. Gatland put it down to the heavy training they had done earlier in the week. That night he named his World Cup squad, a day ahead of schedule. No need to wait: it was full steam ahead.

There was a still a fair bit to get through before the tournament kicked off. Ireland had a mini series lined up, taking them to Connacht and Munster and Ulster, and the inter-provincial series was continuing. In fact the week after that Argentina game, Munster won in Belfast in a match that was a benchmark: it was their first win up north since 1979, a huge step in their development, even if the game was at Upper Malone instead of Ravenhill which was out of action. This all happened just a few weeks before Ireland opened their World Cup campaign, but it was as if there was no World Cup at all.

The calendar year 1999 had opened in spectacular fashion with Ulster winning the European Cup in unforgettable scenes at

Lansdowne Road. It had been a good campaign for Munster too: they qualified from their pool for the first time. Leinster had come bottom of a tough group, but the previous season they had beaten Leicester on a dramatic evening in Donnybrook. The competition had caught on in a big way in Ireland. The national side weren't the only show in town. Sometimes they were not even the main attraction.

There was a feeling among the national management that resources from head office would flow into the provincial channels before the Irish one. Nor was the tie up with the provinces as close as it should have been. There was an opportunity, after that second test showing in Perth, to map out every waking moment for the players so that they were using their time exclusively towards the World Cup. But the case of Tom Tierney, one of the successes of that tour, was indicative of the differing agendas: he was the starting scrumhalf for Ireland, but wasn't even first choice in Munster.

It was some months later that Gatland ran into another obstacle, but it illustrated perfectly the attitude of the era. He needed a new scrum machine for his squad sessions, and had to go to London to price the one he wanted. "It was £3,000," he says. "I had to fly over to see the machine and come back with a price, and then I had to go to a full committee meeting to present that I wanted a new scrum machine, and then I had to meet with (treasurer) John Lyons to convince him that I wanted a new scrum machine. And the next week the committee fly to Italy on the Thursday with all the ex-presidents and wives et cetera and it costs £150,000. Those sort of things I used to go: 'What?' Why couldn't I just go to the chief executive and say: 'I need a new scrum machine.' 'OK, no problem at all, go and organise it.'"

To cap it off, the tour of the provinces was awful, with struggles against Connacht and Ulster, and defeat by Munster. After the Munster win, their coach Declan Kidney said: "At the end of the day we're all under the same paymaster so it's good for us to help them (by winning)." He managed to keep a straight face while he said it. Neither Gatland nor Lenihan found it particularly beneficial, but as an early example of Kidneyspeak it was instructive.

POOL E: AUSTRALIA, IRELAND, ROMANIA, USA

Occasionally Warren Gatland liked to hop a ball. He bounced one the qualification route to see where it would end up. Maybe

Ireland wouldn't play their full strength side against the Aussies—conserve a bit of energy—and concentrate on that runner-up spot that would take them to the play off for the quarter-final? It bounced back at him fairly hard. It became a hot topic, even on New Zealand talk radio where his compatriots wondered what the hell he was up to. He let the air out of it quickly enough. Of course Ireland would be giving it everything against the Wallabies. No question.

Minding the bodies was an issue however: four games in 18 days wouldn't be easy; and it would be five in 22 days if all went according to plan. His point was that the downside to winning the pool was a trip to Cardiff to play the winner of the group with Wales, Argentina, Samoa and Japan. The upside to being runner up was that the play off was against handy enough opposition, and the reward for winning that would be a quarter-final in Dublin, most likely against France. Over the previous two seasons Ireland had lost to France by two points and one point respectively. The pool would be all about Ireland and Australia.

After the drama of 1991, when Gordon Hamilton's try looked like causing a sensational upset, only for it to be cancelled out a few minutes later by Michael Lynagh, this was a fixture everybody wanted to see. The positive finish to Ireland's summer tour Down Under only whetted the appetite. Ireland had gotten USA out of the way and the Wallabies had looked after Romania when Sunday 10 October rolled around. All week Gatland and Lenihan had been building up the importance of the crowd involvement. The manager longed to see green around Lansdowne Road the way he had seen red when Ulster were winning the European Cup. He saw red again.

If you cared to look closely at the Wallabies you could see how far ahead they were of everybody else in the tournament. They were skilled, very well conditioned, and highly cynical. The notion that they were a wholesome bunch of honest to goodness entertainers was rubbish. They defended better than anybody else, and when they attacked, they didn't just obstruct, they obstructed with menace. Also they could think quickly on their feet.

Towards the end of the first half, with Ireland playing badly into the wind but only trailing by a score, they laid siege to the Australia line. They were on top in the scrum, and here was a platform all ready and waiting. The Wallabies had injury issues however: hooker Phil Kearns and then his replacement Jeremy Paul both had to go off to the blood bin, and on came prop Dan Crowley as their last available front rower, just as the pressure was becoming acute. Straight away Crowley tells referee Clayton Thomas that the scrums will have to be uncontested because he's a prop, not a hooker. Incredibly, Thomas buys the line on safety grounds. Australia get to the break with uncontested scrums and their line intact.

Lenihan goes ballistic, charging down from his seat in the stand to remonstrate with Jim Fleming, the fourth official. Jeremy Paul was fit to start the second half, which got over the scrummaging issue, but first thing from the kick-off, Trevor Brennan clips him in the head with his elbow as he's running past. "I honestly don't think I meant to do that," Brennan says. "I'm awkward at the best of times, all arms and legs. And I just clipped him. I didn't realise until afterwards on the video that that was one of the incidents."

The other incident happened eight minutes later when he got the head thumped off him. A row that started on the ground with Toutai Kefu ended with David Wilson and Jeremy Paul holding Brennan while Kefu used him as a punch bag. Brennan had been off earlier for stitching and the bandage slipped down over his eyes, hampering him even further.

"I think we counted on the replay it was something like 11 times he hit me," he says. "All elbows and stuff. I was going ballistic by the time I did get the headband off. I was like a hoor that night because it was the first time in my rugby career that I got a hiding like it. Personally it was more of a pride thing. Here's this fella who's after getting in as many punches and I'm not after getting one back at him. That's what hurt."

Australia got the penalty. Both players were suspended—Kefu for 14 days and Brennan for 10. It summed up Ireland's day: they had been yanked around by a team that was ahead of them in every facet of the game. You couldn't have scripted a more dispiriting scene.

The Wallabies had put huge pressure on the spine of the Irish team. "It was soul destroying," says Keith Wood. "We were played off the park. I remember I lost four lineouts that day—which was probably the best lineout stat I had. I was under pressure for every single ball. They were inches from every ball."

Numbers eight, nine and 10 were also in trouble, especially the rela-
ship between captain Dion O'Cuinneagain at the back of the

scrum, and Tom Tierney at scrumhalf. O'Cuinneagain had hurt his shoulder in training during the week and needed a shot to play. He was powerless to turn things around, and having become something of a talisman, this was bad for business.

O'Cuinneagain was South African born of Irish parents, and came into the set-up via Sale in 1998. He took over the captaincy for the Australia tour in 1999, by which stage the plan was to ease Paddy Johns out of the picture and pair Malcolm O'Kelly in the second row with Jeremy Davidson. It was a significant departure for Ireland to pick as their leader a man who had grown up in Cape Town. Jim Staples was an England boy with a London accent, and he had led the team in 1997, but at least he had come through the Exiles system. By comparison O'Cuinnegain landed with a pair of shades and a sunny disposition, and the next thing he was practising the phonetics of *Amhran na bhFiann*.

"One of the attractions I suppose at the time was that he was probably the most professional player we had, and at the time we were trying to instil a professional regime in terms of training and nutrition and everything, and if anybody epitomised what being a professional was, it was Dion," says Lenihan.

They expected too much of him. We all did. He was a fantastic athlete, with the pace of a greyhound and a willingness to work all day, but Dion was used to break down doors when his talent was to run through the gap. For that reason he was an easy enough player to shut down, and it was typical of that phase of Warren Gatland's coaching career that there wasn't an alternative plan.

Not all of the squad were convinced of Dion's toughness, but he had to get through that tournament flying on one wing, and he didn't complain. Subsequently he would regret playing in that condition. "Maybe I should have said 'no' to Gatty," he said. But it wasn't in his nature to say no. He was an example of Gatland putting his faith in someone he trusted, rather than someone he needed.

LILLE/LENS

Donal Lenihan maintains that they got the better of the two hotels, the lesser of the two evils in Lille on offer from RWC. To keep a level playing pitch, the tournament organisers don't allow the wealthy unions stay in five star luxury while the paupers stay in a hostel. And Lens was such a kip that they couldn't even come up with a shack to match the ones in Lille. Whatever, Ireland were playing Argentina in the play off for a quarter-final spot. It had panned out as expected. The Pumas had come third in their group, albeit on points difference, and if Ireland could sort them out then we had that quarter-final in Dublin against France. Trevor Brennan's suspension would be up by then. "I remember Gatland saying to me after the hearing: 'You've got your two matches now. After Romania and Argentina you'll be back to play France,'" Brennan recalls. Maybe the coach was just being supportive, but Brennan believed him.

Lens got the gig because of the match facility, and the fact that it ticked the box on taking rugby into unfamiliar territory. As it happened, the capacity of Stade Felix Bollaert could accommodate the population of the town with something to spare. As for Lens itself, the media guide claimed: "As in all of France, there are endless local opportunities for fine wining and dining."

There wasn't much of either in the dump where the team were staying. Andy Ward says he survived the few days on French bread and ham, holding off on the pizzas which tasted like Frisbees. The youngsters Bob Casey and Brian O'Driscoll roamed the locality looking for a restaurant that suited their budget—"You have to remember it was early in Brian's career," Casey says—and found nothing. When someone spotted the golden arches of McDonald's in the distance, the relief was palpable.

It was miserable and it was depressing but it was no fun for the Argies either. And in any case, once the job was done it would be back to Finnstown House and the Berkeley Court and the level of comfort to which they had become accustomed. Selection was an issue, for it was a Wednesday night game and the quarter-final was on the Sunday. Paddy Johns had jarred his knee in training but was available to play. He was told to rest up for the quarters. They put Casey on the bench. Did anyone declare this to be jumping the gun? No. I remember doing a piece with RTÉ radio before the team was picked and suggesting Casey should start!

The Pumas had excelled themselves by getting to this point, farther than ever before in their World Cup history. They had relied on just 20 players to start their three games, and only another three off the bench. They were dipping into the same shallow pool again. They should have been exhausted. They were mostly amateurs for God's sake—

they couldn't keep this up. And anyway, while Ireland were a little conservative, these guys were in a strait jacket that covered eight forwards and the halfbacks—Agustin Pichot and the booming boot, Gonzalo Quesada.

THE BIG NIGHT

It's cold but perfect. The stadium is half full, and those who have made the effort want to be entertained. It's not happening for them. Neither side is prepared to take anything approximating to a risk. The game revolves around referee Stuart Dickinson, with Humphreys and Quesada as support acts. By half time Ireland are 15-9 ahead.

They get out to 21-9 in the third quarter and the management are thinking about subbing in Eric Elwood, and saving Humphreys for France. Quesada pulls it back almost immediately to 21-12, which dampens their enthusiasm. Then Humphreys has a chance to restore the margin with a drop goal. It slides the wrong side of the upright. Ireland have to get the next score. Instead it's Quesada again: 21-15. What the hell is happening here? Why won't they just go away? Why can't Ireland do something other than run into traffic?

Humphreys kicks another penalty on the hour mark but there's nothing comfortable about a 24-15 lead. Finally Jeremy Davidson, who was struggling with a haematoma, and a hand that turned out to be broken, is taken off. Bob Casey runs on for his second cap. "I didn't make any impact when I came on," he says. "The game was turning and I remember taking one ball on and I got smashed. I tried to get involved, but it just didn't happen."

-20

By the final quarter the Argies are becoming more daring. They're two scores behind and they have to chase the game. They remember how uncomfortable Ireland had been in the later stages of the August test in Dublin. They're tapping penalties, running from deep—anything to keep it away from a tie up that will let Dickinson back in. They set up a good position in the Irish 22 but Arbizu throws a loose pass and Kevin Maggs latches onto it.

He gives it to Andy Ward. If the flanker moves it on again Ireland can counter attack the length of the field. He carries it into contact and gets buried. Dickinson surveys the scene and penalises Ireland.

Quesada is 20 metres from the Irish posts. He taps it over: 24-18 and all the momentum is with Argentina.

Paul Wallace has to go off for stitches to a head wound. "I actually ran in to get this done knowing that I had to get back out as quickly as possible," says Wallace. "And Mannix (Donal Lenihan) was panicking and there was no sign of a doctor. Nowhere. We had to wait about five minutes for a doctor to come in. Some French doctor. I think it might have been some ruling to use a local doctor to make sure it was a legitimate blood sub. As you can imagine, we're in there, waiting, and he comes in and starts having a chat! He actually asked me: 'After the game, will you give me your jersey?'"

-10

There are just over eight minutes on the clock and David Humphreys has just hit the post with a drop goal attempt. But it's not all bad. Albanese knocks it into his own in-goal area and tries to get back out again. Brian O'Driscoll and Conor O'Shea tie him down. Scrum five to Ireland. This is it. With a pad and pencil you couldn't sketch a better attacking platform, with acres of room on either side. This was not a good time to have Paul Wallace off the field. The first scrum screws and is reset. The second one goes the same way. As the third one shifts again, Tom Tierney is penalised for delaying the put-in. Andy Ward on the flank is going mad.

"Why would you want to screw your own scrum in that position?" he asks. "It was an unbelievable call. We just wanted a relatively square scrum and to lay a platform from there. Why would we want to give the position away? It was beyond words how a referee could think, in a game of that magnitude, that we would want to screw our own scrum."

Agustin Pichot doesn't hang around. The Pumas are away, running it to the half way line with the crowd willing them on. They're stopped but it's temporary. They're away again on the right hand side, with Arbizu and Mario Ledesma and Pichot combining like it was a fun fixture. The scrumhalf kicks to Ireland's corner. Under pressure, Kieron Dawson ends up conceding a five metre scrum. This can't be happening.

-6

If Ireland's scrum position at the other end of the field had been pretty tasty then this is off the same menu: only one side to attack, but it's a prairie of space. The Pumas try a nudge, and then open up. They spread the ball across the face of Ireland's defence, using two decoy runners to fix the green shirts. It's six attackers against five, and it works beautifully. It all hinges on Gonzalo Camardon getting the ball in front of Albanese so that the winger doesn't have to break his stride. Once he holds it he's home. He holds it and the world slows down. High in the stands we're scanning desperately for green shirts to cut him off. Maybe he'll trip?

"We played four up defence," says Justin Bishop, who was defending out wide along with Conor O'Shea. "We always played the four up, and I kind of came in to hit Conor's man but Albanese just sliced us in half. That was it really." Bishop and O'Shea stood behind the posts, looking at each other, trying to think of something to say. If Quesada missed the touchline conversion at least Ireland had a one point lead. He planted it.

-5

There are less than six minutes on the clock and Ireland are in desperate trouble. They're not equipped for this sort of thing and look uncomfortable keeping the ball in hand under pressure. At a scrum in the middle of the field, Paul Wallace, who is back on, is popped out of the front row. Penalty Argentina. Three points Gonzalo Quesada, and they lead 28-24. Now Ireland need a try to win and normal time is up. The Pumas will do anything to avoid conceding a touchdown. Brian O'Driscoll chips and chases and Mauricio Reggiardo drops him like a stone; just steps in and biffs him without the ball. He gets a yellow card, but it's only a warning—the sin bin hasn't been invented yet. It allows Humphreys to nudge Ireland into the corner. This is finally it. This is what it has come down to.

+5

More than five minutes into injury time and Ireland have to play their get out of jail card. Dion deals the 12 card trick. The snake-like lineout came from Warren Gatland's days in Connacht. You had a hooker to throw, a scrumhalf to clean up any stray taps, and a full back to mind the shop when everybody else was away. That left 12 in the lineout. When Connacht had pulled the stunt on the Australians in the Sportsground in November 1996, the tourists nearly fell about the place laughing. But as the snake of green jerseys worked its way over the line the Wallabies saw the merit of it. Three years later however its value was spent. It should have been binned. Instead Ireland still had it on the shelf, ready to dust off in dire straits.

At last the crowd were getting value for money. This was something to tell the grandchildren. Here was a team that kicked the leather off the ball for 85 minutes and then got into a huddle and stuck it up their jumpers. Incredible! For the next two and a quarter minutes Ireland made 11 attempts to drive over the Argentina line from close range. "Well if they're going to go out, they're going to go out in style!" said Jim Sherwin on RTÉ's match commentary. This was to style what the Morris Minor was to Grand Prix. It was excruciating to watch, a grim illustration of the creative side of the Irish game. And all the while, Conor O'Shea stood out on the wing, unmarked, flapping his arms like a drowning man.

"I remember being out there and all it needed was for somebody to look up, and it just summed up for me my time in an Irish jersey," he says. "I was the only person within 40 yards. There was nobody there. All we had to do was give the ball to Humps, a cross kick, and I was in for a try."

BUENOS AIRES

Florida Street is the main pedestrian thoroughfare in downtown Buenos Aires. Instead of the normal human traffic there were huddles every few metres around those shop windows with TV screens. The action in Lens had caught the imagination of this soccer mad city. As the tension mounted the crowds got bigger. The time difference meant it was afternoon in Argentina, where many were taking a very long lunch. No one was moving. When the final whistle went, the crowds in the street were joined by office workers who had brought portable tellies in for the afternoon. The car horns started up. Rugby had never seen a reaction like this in Argentina. For the next few weeks the game was taken out of its elite social class and shared around. It didn't matter what happened in the quarter-final; they were all heroes. Gonzalo Quesada would win the country's most prestigious sports award, the Olimpia de Oro. The players would all get Congressional medals, and be received by the outgoing president, Carlos Menem, and the incoming Fernando de la Rúa. When it came to the photo opportunity, the squad had to be split evenly to keep both candidates happy. There was a bit of negotiating over who stood in which camp.

The quarter-final against France, on the Sunday, coincided with national elections day in Argentina, and both Menem and de la Rúa would delay casting their votes until the match was over. They weren't slow to tell the players how important they had become, and what they had done for their country.

Journalist Frankie Deges should have been in Lens that night, but instead was back home in Buenos Aires, watching the Ireland game on TV. His work had combined writing about the game and working for the Pumas, and he understood better than most how much it all meant. He had witnessed first hand the deep unrest among the players under previous coach Jose Luis Imhoff, and the reluctance of the Argentine Rugby Union to do anything about it. And when they had come home from their pre World Cup tour to Scotland and Ireland, he saw the next shuffle of power.

"Mendez just slammed the door leaving Grizz Wyllie on his own, which actually was better for the players because they only had one voice of command," says Deges. "So the team had their backs against the wall. And by having their backs against the wall they knew it was up to them. And it formed them into a very tight unit. For that game with Ireland they knew they had already achieved more than any other Argentine team in a World Cup, which was to get out of their pool, so they had nothing to lose and a lot to win. And they went out with that feeling and that spirit. Those final minutes epitomised that spirit."

Initially his own feelings were mixed when the final whistle went. Why the hell wasn't he in France on the biggest and best night they had ever known?

"As soon as I got to the World Cup my missus told me she was pregnant with our first child. It was the day before the opening game. I promised her I'd be back as soon as I could. The way I had mapped things out I planned on going to Scotland (for the quarter-final) and not to Ireland because I felt we were going to end up playing Scotland. Then when our pool worked out the way it did, with everybody beating everybody else, we ended up going to France. It was really awkward trying to change the plans and I said: 'What the hell, I'll go home and then come back if they make it to the semi-finals.'

"It actually worked out nicely, because if I had been told the way the country reacted when the Pumas won in Lens, I wouldn't have believed it. I saw it with my own eyes. For me I got the best of both worlds: I went to the World Cup and even though I missed the biggest game in Argentine rugby history I was here to see how it affected the country. The people went berserk. The country just came to standstill. It was incredible, and for the next three weeks there wasn't any sport other than rugby. I never thought I would see such a thing."

AFTERMATH

"I remember straight away—just as the final whistle had gone—up there in the stands RTÉ were in my face. And I was like: 'Jesus, give us a second here, hang on a minute.'" Too late Warren. In the changing room some of the players were sitting on the floor, others slumped into their seats. Heads were down, already in tears and texting or mumbling into their mobile phones. "You just wanted to talk to someone who'd tell you that everything was going to be all right," says Casey.

Lenihan led the press conference looking like he was about to burst somebody. Gatland sat beside him, empty. "For me personally that really, really affected me," he says. "The funny thing was I thought we could have beaten France, and all of a sudden from a couple of errors in one game the whole thing became the disaster in Lens. And everything was heaped on me as an individual. Everything was my fault."

The squad flew back to Dublin the next day. So did the Argentinians, who moved into Ireland's base at Finnstown House. Everywhere there was evidence that the Irish had been expected back. The Pumas thought that was amusing. It was the day after that when Trevor Brennan got round to collecting the rest of his gear from Finnstown. He lived nearby in Leixlip and the bar manager was a buddy of his. "Jaysus Trev there was a savage session in there last night," he said. With Wyllie leading the charge the Pumas had let their hair down. They were playing France in the quarter-final, and, regardless of the result, they couldn't lose.

This was a new experience for the IRFU. They had been slow to warm to the idea of a World Cup in the first place, and more reluctant still to embrace the professional game. Now the first such tournament of the new era had left them out in the cold, outside the top eight where they had always been. It was unbearable. Something would have to be done. There would need to be a whole new approach to this business, for that's what it was becoming. The limitations on the field reflected what was not happening off it.

"We didn't have an intelligent enough game plan," says Keith Wood. "We could have beaten them. We should have beaten them. And we didn't beat them. The disgrace wasn't that we lost to Argentina—which a lot of people thought was a disgrace—but the disgrace was that we didn't take enough risks. We'd very few risks taken."

Chapter 7 ∽

EUROPE

Munster's March to Twickenham, 2000

It was like someone opened the door and the wind came in and blew the ball around the wrong side of the post. Just like that.

Declan O'Connell is a fan. There was really no such thing as a Munster fan before 1999, but a year later he was one of the estimated 35,000 of them in Twickenham who witnessed Ronan O'Gara's penalty slide past the Northampton post in the Heineken Cup final. Before the explosion, there had always been dyed in the wool rugby people who turned out in numbers to watch Munster against touring teams. Mostly the fascination was with the visitors. Some supporters would fetch up at inter-provincial games in Limerick or Cork; fewer still would go on the road to watch Munster in Dublin or Galway or Belfast. O'Connell could tick all those boxes, and knew by name those who could do the same. By the end of May 2000 that had all changed. A new creature had been born.

It would be a stretch to say that Munster had no support before the 1999/2000 season, for in the preceding European campaign they had qualified for the first time for the knock-out stages. They brought about a hundred to Colomiers, where in a spiteful game Munster were beaten 23-9. When they went back to the same part of the world for the pool game in December 1999 the away crowd was a bit bigger. But it was the semi-final in Bordeaux when it all took off. "That was the first day that we really hit France hard," O'Connell says. "There were red jerseys everywhere in the town. I remember we were drinking non alcoholic lager that they were selling outside the ground. I think they were expecting a soccer crowd."

It was on the way back from that game that O'Connell got talking to Garrett Fitzgerald and Diarmuid Kelly, the chief executive and honorary secretary respectively of the Munster branch, about setting up an official supporters club. There had never been any need for such a thing in Irish rugby. Within a couple of months of that conversation the phenomenon that was Munster's support had become a selling point of the tournament itself: on the road they brought a unique colour and atmosphere; at home they inspired the development of the most feared venue in Europe—Thomond Park. It was an irresistible mix.

The fan factor was critical because it was so unusual in a high-profile professional sport. Everybody knew a player, or a player's brother or sister, or a player's parents. The supporters felt they had a vested interest; they were shareholders. And the players felt a keen responsibility to give value for money, for it was a costly business. "There isn't an airport in the south of France we don't know," O'Connell says. The credit unions across the six counties of the province would sponsor a lot of trips in support of the team. This was becoming an industry. And it centred on a special group of people.

HUMAN RESOURCES

It was when John Langford packed his car for the last time for the drive from Canberra to Sydney that he found himself getting a bit emotional. The ACT Brumbies franchise was set up in 1996, and he had been among their first recruits. ACT had always been the poor relation to New South Wales and Queensland, and when the Super Six competition got under way in the early 1990s, there was a yawning gap between the big two who were a part of it, and the crowd down in Canberra who were not. In filling the Brumbies roster it was inevitable that the cast-offs from the two glamour states would end up in the dreary capital. They traded on that, the idea that they were afterthoughts. By the time Langford left in 1999, they had earned the respect of the rugby world, getting to the Super 12 final in only their second season. "When I was leaving, I was pretty upset that I'd never experience the camaraderie and the spirit we had there again," he says. Then he walked into Munster.

He could have stayed with the Brumbies but he knew his time was up. Younger second rows like Justin Harrison were coming through, and he wasn't getting the game time. He decided to look overseas, but left it a bit late. Not having an EU passport meant he was considered a foreign player in that jurisdiction, and so restricted his chances in the deepest pools: the UK and France. It was suggested he try Leinster, which he did, and things moved along promisingly. Then they stopped.

"I rang them up one day and they said: 'Oh, Malcolm O'Kelly is coming back.' And I said: 'Jeez, well what am I going to do? And they said: 'Try Munster?'"

Mike Mullins took a different road but it had a similar turn. He was an outside centre with a break and a side-step, and was already on the radar screen. A Kiwi with an Irish father, he was already playing in West Hartlepool for Mike Brewer when Warren Gatland picked him for Ireland A. He made an immediate impression, and Connacht coach Glenn Ross called him up. Things moved further than they had for Langford and Leinster. A one year deal had been agreed in principle. Then Ross called back the next day to say it was off—something to do with the IRFU and the number of foreign players. Mullins was confused, because his passport wasn't an issue. While he was trying to make sense of it, Declan Kidney called and offered him terms in Munster. It was the natural move for him. "That's where I got to meet all my father's family," he says. "He had emigrated from Limerick. Making those connections was a real highlight for me."

Langford and Mullins weren't the only changes in personnel that season. Jason Holland was an outhalf from Taranaki who had come to Ireland to help Midleton realise their ambitions in the All Ireland League. That was where Kidney came across him, and drafted him into the Munster squad. He already had the outhalf he needed in the 22 year old Ronan O'Gara, but Holland would make a good 12 with an option as cover at 10. At scrumhalf Kidney had a range of choices, but went for the least obvious. Peter Stringer was chosen ahead of internationals Tom Tierney and Brian O'Meara because of the rapid-fire delivery of the little tyke, just out of UCC. So a season after they had lost to Colomiers in the quarter-finals, the back line had been re-cast, and there was a quality ball winner out of touch. The biggest impact arrival however came in the middle of the front row.

Keith Wood was asked into the office of Harlequins chief executive Huw Morgan one morning in May 1999 to discuss a newspaper article that had appeared in Ireland. The story suggested that Wood might be on his way back home. "I told him there was no possibility of it happening," Wood says. "It wasn't an issue or a thought in any way, shape or form."

It was for Harlequins. Morgan was in the middle of cost-cutting, and to be relieved temporarily of Wood's expense was attractive. It made sense given they would be denied his presence in any case: the World Cup was coming, and between that and the Six Nations the hooker would be on national duty more than club duty. If he was based in Ireland for a season there would be less travel back and forth, and, in theory, fewer games. Moreover there was no relegation from England's Premiership the next season. It was a sweetheart deal all round.

Wood had left Limerick as part of the exodus of Irish players in 1996, having only ever played three times for the province. He had been injured when Munster went into Europe for the first time, in autumn '95, and he had left by the time they were going into their second season. So this would be his first time playing in the Heineken Cup with them. There was a bit of baggage loaded in the interim.

When he returned to Thomond Park leading Harlequins in October 1997, it coincided with some disparaging remarks he had made about the Munster set-up of old. It caused a bit of a stir at the time, and there was some concern about a hangover when he returned. It evaporated quickly enough. "As an experience I thought it would be fantastic, and it was just a good opportunity to play for Munster," he says. "So I went back."

Frankie Sheahan was going into his fourth season with the squad. He had spent the first two behind Terry Kingston, and then one behind Mark McDermott. At last he was looking at a clear road up ahead. Then he was driving home one day when the sports news bulletin caused him to double take before he rear-ended the car in front. The lead item was Wood's homecoming. "I was gutted," he says. "I felt so low because I knew that no matter how hard I tried I wasn't going to be getting my game ahead of Woody. He was a Lion and all that—the best hooker in the world."

Quickly they sorted out that it was better to work together than to tear each other apart, and the pair went forward from there. It was one small example of a camp that was happy and hungry and looking for work. Given the history of the province, this was an achievement.

Munster is unique. No other Irish province is split between two centres, and no other province has the same level of internecine warfare. If there was rivalry between the clubs of Cork it was nothing compared to their dislike of anything from Limerick. Which in turn paled by comparison with the battle within the walls of Limerick itself.

Killian Keane was an outsider to all of this. He arrived in Limerick from Skerries via UCD, and took up with Garryowen when the All Ireland League was the only show in town. He did well enough there to be called up to the Munster squad. It was like he landed on a roundabout, and the circuit gave him a look at the club scene at its height; the provincial scene as it was; and the provincial scene as it would become. Keane was already a fixture when Declan Kidney was brought in as coach in 1997/98.

"If you'd brought in an Alan Gaffney or a Bob Dwyer they'd have taken one look and got back on the plane," he says. "We were an absolute shambles: there were a lot of good points but there were a hell of a lot of bad points. And there was all that thing about old habits dying hard. You had guys coming from Shannon and Garryowen and Cork Con who traditionally had been used to not even talking to each other. They'd come together grudgingly to play a few matches a season for the province, so you had all sorts of difficulties, all these huge rivalries. Professionalism was in its infancy.

"Then you had guys who were behind the comfort zone, they weren't even in it. The whole thing was all over the place and it couldn't have been any other way because that's just where we were coming from."

There was a lot to be done. There was a history in the province of stoic resistance against touring teams, and slovenly preparation against domestic ones. Selection had always been a political minefield. Traditionally, Munster players had a persecution complex about Dublin 4, yet there was enough horse trading in their own backyard to rival Ballinasloe in Fair Week. Their record spoke for itself: the interprovincial championship started in 1946/47, and Munster—despite the stream of quality that flowed through its ranks—had never won back to back titles. When the sun came up on the professional game, they were there to be burnt.

Appropriately enough they were victims even when the IRFU moved in 1997 to appoint the four full-time provincial directors under Brian Ashton. Niall O'Donovan had gone for the job and was beaten by former Wales wing John Bevan. O'Donovan however picked up the role as part-time assistant. He recalls the first meeting with the players.

"They said: 'Dunno why you're coming here, John. We're off to England!'"
And pretty soon Bevan was off to Wales. That's how O'Donovan and
Kidney got together.

They had first crossed swords as schoolboys, though Kidney wouldn't
have noticed. He was a big name, the outhalf on the Pres Cork senior
team that played Limerick CBS in a cup semi-final. Pres was a rugby
institution, part of Cork's old firm. Their opponents that day were
more familiar with hurling's Harty Cup, and were unheard of in rugby.
If Munster legend Ginger McLoughlin hadn't been teaching in the school
there would have been no rugby at all. As it was, they had barely enough
bodies to fill the match day squad. Pres won, and O'Donovan remembered their outhalf. After school their paths would have crossed first as
players, and then as coaches, in games between Dolphin and Shannon.

There was no relationship to speak of. Kidney was a product of the
elite Schools game and set about establishing an excellent record as a
coach with his alma mater, where he returned to teach, as well as
the Irish Schools team. That success didn't easily transfer to the adult
environment with Dolphin.

O'Donovan came from the other side of the street. Shannon was in
his blood; the CBS just happened to be in his path. He started in
Thomond Park as a kid, and went through to the senior team where he
became a fixture at number eight. Along the way he won six Munster
senior cup medals, and three senior leagues. Then he coached the club to
four All Ireland League titles in a row. At one level, he and Kidney were
the perfect match, bringing together the best of two different back-
grounds. Kidney had the order and planning and control that went with
Schools coaching; O'Donovan had the goods on what it took to win dog
fights, to deal with these mongrel men on their own level. It took them a
while to find middle ground where they could both contribute effectively.

"I would have been seen more as a clubman from the club scene,
involved with guys who were doing the hard graft and winning AILs,
and these were the guys to front us with the winning mentality I was
looking for," says O'Donovan. "They were used to winning on a weekly
basis. It's very hard to put guys who aren't used to winning, out at the
level we were asking them to play, and then asking them to win. Declan
probably was looking further down the line, maybe three or four years
down the road, and at times that's great, but it's getting the balance
between the two that was the thing."

They got it right in the end, but at the start it was in danger of tip-
ping over. Kidney favoured younger blood: he looked at the likes of
Peter Clohessy and Mick Galwey and wondered if he would ever win
them over to what was required by the modern game. They looked at
him and wondered whether he would go away quietly, or with a fuss.
The word in that second season, after Munster lost to Leinster in front
of a few hundred in Dooradoyle, was that Kidney was doomed, that the
players couldn't stand his schoolroom style. Then they recovered to win
the championship, beating Leinster with a blistering performance in
the return leg at Donnybrook.

"To say it started off rosy would be wrong," says Galwey. "Declan was
a school teacher from a school background and—he'd been involved
with Dolphin obviously—and I'm not saying we were set in our ways,
but we had our own way of thinking about things. I'm not saying we
were right, but there were certain things. Deccie came in and he had a
totally different way about doing it. We sat down and decided we'd both
change, and we both made sacrifices, for the use of a better word, to get
the thing right."

By the start of the 1999/2000 season the balance had been struck and
the spirit was good. John Langford arrived just in time for a squad
weekend in Kilkee. It was perfect: a keen fisherman, he brought his rod
along and met his new team-mates over a relaxing few days with a few
pints to unwind and open up.

On the second day the choice was golf or fishing. A couple of boats
were hired, and Langford ended up on the same one as Jeremy
Staunton, Dominic Crotty and David Corkery. "It was off Loop Head
and the sea was pretty choppy and rough and the boys all went green
or white," says Langford. "A lot of them were seasick. We were catching
mackerel, and I remember Dominic asking me if you could eat them.

"'Yeah, they're beautiful,' I said. 'We smoke them back in Australia
and they're quite nice that way.'

"And the boat captain says: 'Nah, you just eat them raw.'

"'What do you mean raw, like sushi?'

"And he says: 'No, you just pick one up and eat one.' And he picked
one up and bit the head off it in front of us, and he had blood pouring
out of the corners of his mouth. And the guys who hadn't been sick certainly were after that. He just bit the head off the fish and ate it. And

swallowed it. I'm glad Briano wasn't there because he would have tried to outdo that. I met the captain a couple of years later. He says: 'Do you remember me?' 'Mate,' I said, 'I'll never forget you as long as I live.'"

Briano was the manager, Brian O'Brien. He was 61 years of age that season and his party-piece was to latch on to the luggage racks on the team bus, and swing himself back and forth like a monkey. "Munster are half mad: Briano's totally mad. But his madness made absolute sense," says Keane.

O'Brien was still working for Moremiles Tyres and had just taken over on a part time basis from Jerry Holland, who needed to spend more time with his employers, First Active plc. O'Brien had a lifetime of rugby in him. Like Niall O'Donovan he was Shannon through and through, and had won three caps in 1968 as a hardy centre. Unusually in those days he would have been into gym work, such as it was. He was an outdoor, physical man, and that presence stayed with him through the years. It would have appeared entirely natural to him then to grab Langford under his ribs on first being introduced to him, just to check they weren't buying a "soft craythur". He bobbed and weaved as he did it. "Jaysus, you're not too bad," O'Brien said to the new recruit, approvingly. Langford didn't know what to make of it. "Jeez, who is this guy?"

Typical of the Munster set-up, O'Brien just appeared in the job. "The first day I came out they were training in the University of Limerick," he says. "And Declan was there, and it wasn't official or anything like that, and he said: 'That's your new manager on the side of the pitch.' And I can remember one of the lads saying: 'Who the fuck is he?' I thought it was great! It was John Kelly, and he wouldn't have known me from Adam. So it went on from there. I didn't look on it as a job."

Not only had he a good rapport with the players, but he was the glue that would bind the coaches to each other, and the players to the coaches. It followed that when the team adopted Carmen's "Stand up and Fight" as their anthem, it was O'Brien's doing. Both the song and its first airing marked a landmark moment for the group.

Beating Ulster was a big deal for a few reasons. Ulster were everything Munster were not: they had a culture of hard work, and a background in professional preparation which went back to the mid 1980s. Back then, under coach Jimmy Davidson, they launched the "Club Ulster" philosophy, and it brought them an unprecedented nine titles in a row. They remained unbeaten against Munster for an incredible

13 years from 1980. And now they were champions of Europe, having beaten Colomiers in the final at Lansdowne Road in January 1999.

WORK STATIONS

The game at Upper Malone—Ravenhill was out of action—was high on Kidney's list of things to do. Keith Wood was back, and there was more talent in the side than ever before. The old hands like Galwey and Clohessy were being challenged by the new environment where Wood and Langford—fellow students of the old school, who knew how to unwind—were setting a cracking pace. At his first session back, Wood had lashed Killian Keane out of it for making a mistake. Keane was stunned. Soon after Langford's arrival there was a three kilometre run in which he looked like a greyhound. They were forcing the issue, and the response had to be positive.

"We were well ahead and towards the end of the game we relaxed—the lads relaxed and we conceded a late try and we could have lost it," remembers O'Brien. "There was fierce trauma. The whole place was packed, and I can remember Claw (Clohessy) making a tackle on Andy Ward after some midfield move they did, and I don't know how Claw did it. It was a superhuman tackle. Right round the ankles: Whoosh! Just put fire into his belly. People don't realise how good that guy was.

"We were staying in the Europa or some place and Declan was like a kid afterwards. We had a few pints and Tom Tierney was playing, and he went over to the mic and started to sing. And there was more Ulster guys there than anything. So they said to me: 'Go on, sing a song.' Sure I was half pissed at that stage. So I sang 'Stand up and Fight'. And the whole place stood up. Everyone. So the following week Declan had the words of it given to all the players."

It was the perfect example of Kidney at work: he would spot something that would wash over most others, and he would take it away and dress it up, and represent it as a useful tool. His speciality was in coming up with reasons why Munster would beat the opposition. As time went on, players would look forward to the next instalment: the other lot were paid more than them; or they showed Munster no respect; or a newspaper cutting would be produced, illustrating a terrible wrong that had to be righted. On its own, this stuff wouldn't have counted for much, but in a place where the tradition was to circle the wagons, it carried extra resonance. And if you factored in the quality of the players to begin with, then sometimes it provided that extra edge. They would need that to get out of their Heineken Cup pool.

The English clubs were back. Having opted out of the competition the previous season because they couldn't agree with ERC over participation rights, they waded back in with their top six, eager to prove their strength. Munster got Saracens, a club which had become almost a franchise operation in the professional era. Their wage bill made Munster's look like loose change. The group was completed with Colomiers and Pontypridd. If Munster were to repeat the success of the previous season they would have to do something away from home.

The most likely bet looked like Pontypridd, but the away leg was the last pool game on the schedule. If they were to lay down a marker it would mean winning in England or France. The previous season they had won away against Padova. It had been their first win away from home in four seasons of trying. It was a bit of a jump from there to knocking over a first world team.

The opportunity came before they looked ready to take it. Having been convincing winners over Pontypridd at home, 32-10, next was the trip to Vicarage Road. In time the result of this game would take on a colour that was removed from the reality, in the same way as Munster versus the All Blacks in 1978. There was no army of travelling fans. It was a Sunday game, and at most a couple of hundred went to Watford. They were conspicuous back in Limerick that night, because they wore their Fez hats as proof of their presence at what everybody realised was a watershed moment.

"I always maintain that the day things started to happen was the day over in Vicarage Road," says Declan O'Connell, who was one of the small band of travelling fans. "That was the day we broke the ice. I remember bringing the missus over for the weekend, shopping like. And on the Sunday I mentioned the match. Sure after that she was hooked, like any good Munster woman."

Killian Keane was in the centre that day. It was fitting that he scored a try at a critical moment of the contest, for he felt better going into the game than might normally have been the case. "You have these conversations where guys say they're going to do this or they're going to do that—'we're not afraid of them'—even though you're filling your pants. But I remember Woody turning round on the Thursday or the

Friday and saying: 'I've never lost against Saracens.' To hear someone say that—someone who was on your team—you kind of went: 'Oh, ok so.'"

For 40 minutes it looked like Wood's record was about to be shattered. Saracens opened the game as if on a training run. Their Argentinian prop Roberto Grau scored inside five minutes. Nick Walshe followed up soon after. After half an hour Munster were trailing 18-3 and looking hopeless. They didn't try much, and what they did looked dull. When the Saracens forwards motored it was if they were gliding over the ground, leaving a gift-wrapped ball for Walshe to whip away to Thierry Lacroix at outhalf. Saracens were so comfortable they started to squander stuff, but what did it matter?

Finally, at the end of the half, Munster got their turn to play a bit, and another two penalties from Ronan O'Gara meant that if they could squeeze a try out of this pressure, somehow the game would be on again. You could see Saracens captain Francois Pienaar getting annoyed at the penalties conceded. That period lasted a few minutes but the play never extended further than battering away on a narrow front close to the Sarries' line, and Pienaar was defiant. Munster got nothing out of it. As they trooped off at the break, 21-9 down, you would have put your mortgage on them losing by 30 points.

"I remember Gaillimh (Mick Galwey) was in tears at half time in that match, saying: 'Come on, we can beat these bastards, I know we can,'" recalls Langford. "He was that passionate. He was that worked up in that game there were tears coming out of his eyes and it was pretty moving. That certainly inspired us all to give it that little bit extra. I always slagged him about that . . . he doesn't like it."

Right on cue the second half opened with Alan Quinlan forcing a turnover, Mike Mullins making a break off it, and Keane scampering over. A few minutes later, Mullins hacks a pass he can't hold; it sits up for him and no one else; and he scores in the corner. And O'Gara goals it. They were leading! How the hell did this happen? Normality was restored with Saracens scoring three times in succession to lead 34-23, but then Anthony Foley sickened them, scoring off a tapped penalty from close range. It was a classic example of Foley justifying Wood's description of him.

"We know he's not Mr Atlas, the athlete, and he's not very fast, but he does the right thing at the right time—all the time," says Wood. "And he says the right thing at the right time—all the time. He's very smart, very astute. He brought a level of organisation at the back of the scrum which was vital, and when you have two 12 year old halfbacks you need someone who can make the right decision, the right call."

It finished with a late try from Jeremy Staunton, and a contentious conversion from O'Gara. They sneaked it by a point. "I'll never forget, as we were walking out there was a sign saying it was a criminal offence to come onto the field," says Langford. "And then after we won there was about a hundred Paddies in the crowd and they didn't care."

There was a buzz all over Ireland after the result. Sarries were big business, and nothing illustrated their wealth more than their roster of props: Roberto Grau, Julian White, David Flatman and Paul Wallace. Their captain was one of the biggest names in world rugby, Francois Pienaar, and in Thierry Lacroix they had a French legend who had honed his skills kicking Ireland all over the Parc des Princes. Thoughts of those days drifted into the mind of Mick Galwey as he looked at the next fixture. Munster were flying due south.

FRANCE

He had good times there and bad times. Mostly bad. In fact, mostly horrendous. The better the weather the worse it would be. Mick Galwey's first trip though was something special. It was with Shannon in 1987. At the time the Shannon pack was the most feared in Ireland, and with only occasional cross-provincial opposition to give them some diversion, they embarked on a fixture with Toulon. The game was to be played in Stade Jean Bouin, home of Stade Francais, and next door to the Parc des Princes.

It was typical of trips in those days—pure mad. It was standard practice for example for the host team to ply their opposition with drink the night before the game. Sure enough, with the few snacks that passed for dinner came gallons of wine. Still, it was a cracking game and Shannon—despite losing Colm Tucker and Ginger McLoughlin in the week leading up to it—were good value in a narrow defeat.

"We had done well," says Galwey. "I remember at one stage they were laughing at Pat Murray taking a penalty from the half way line, but he got it. We should have won it, and I was kind of thinking: 'We did ok here.' It was crazy that night. When I think of it I don't know how we ever got home. It was the best tour of all time. Frankie Flynn: we're coming home on the plane and he went around with his cap and made a collection for the pilot. It was like we were on the bus coming from Dublin. 'A few bob there for the pilot.'"

He was back in Paris five years later, but this time it was across the road, and it was for real. He had six caps under his belt by that stage, but nothing prepared you for that gig. "Jesus that was horrific. Were we that bad or were they that good? It was like something out of Gladiator. I remember walking out there and there was a kind of glass screen around the pitch and it was like: 'Fuck it.' You knew you were beaten already. I remember poor Paul Hogan that day, going there with the best of intentions on his debut, screaming his head off in the huddle before the start. What was going through my mind was: 'Shut up or you'll get us all killed!' And looking over at Danaher and thinking: 'Oh Jesus.'"

Going there with Munster hadn't been much different—further south, and just as hot. Against Castres in 1995 they didn't believe they could win until it was too late; against Toulouse the next year he was pleading with the lads to keep it under 50 as the bands struck up, and the sun beat down, and Les Toulousains ran amok. It finished at 60. The next year against Bourgoin it was better, but not good enough. As for Perpignan? A scary trip. Like Young Munster for Leinster clubs in the early 1990s.

And now it was Colomiers. The game the previous season had featured unwelcome crowd involvement. Peter Clohessy was being abused by this banshee in the crowd as Munster were warming up. He turned around and gave her a mouthful. Whereupon her husband tried to climb the fence to defend her honour. It was the prelude to a filthy game. Coincidentally, a year later, Clohessy had to pull out with back trouble the night before the game. When he broke the news to Marcus Horan at dinner, the young understudy didn't believe him. Typical Claw, acting the maggot. Horan played, and looked like he was made for it, bringing an extra verve to Munster's loose game. He even had to switch sides to tight head at one stage as Munster went through a bizarre sequence of injuries in the front row.

The remarkable thing was how straightforward it was in the end. Munster won 31-15. Then they took Colomiers to Musgrave Park in the return leg. On a horrible day where it never stopped raining, the home team won 23-5. It was Christmas, and they were four from four.

THE SARACENS ARE COMING

There were significant changes from the first leg. Dominic Crotty had a broken hand at the start of the season, but had come off the bench in both games against Colomiers. And in the centre Killian Keane had lost out to Jason Holland, who was now partnered by Mike Mullins. The pack was the same, though there had been doubts about Mick Galwey and David Wallace, who was only passed fit just before kick-off.

Saracens were still seething. Pienaar had given them a bollocking after the defeat in Vicarage Road. They were determined to balance the account in Limerick. If they didn't, they were wiped before the last round of pool games which would see Munster travel to Pontypridd with an unassailable lead, and Saracens at home to Colomiers. On the way off the field in the first leg, Peter Clohessy and Saracens hooker George Chuter had exchanged pleasantries. Clohessy made a big deal of offering to shake hands. Chuter made a bigger deal of refusing. Nobody had a greater capacity to upset people than Peter Clohessy.

He first came to national prominence in 1992 when Australia coach Bob Dwyer singled him out for specific criticism after the Wallabies had been beaten by Munster in Musgrave Park. Prior to that, he was well known in rugby circles as a quality tight head with a nasty streak. I wrote a profile of him the week after that game in Musgrave, in which I repeated the joke that he was the only man in Limerick who could leave his car unlocked and not worry about it being there when he came back. He didn't see the funny side of it.

Six months later his club, Young Munster, were heading towards what would be a thrilling AIL finale against St Mary's, and I was off to Limerick to do a piece on the team. The arrangement was to meet Peter, his brother Ger, who was the captain, and blind side flanker, in Jury's Hotel. Ger turned up, but said that the brother couldn't get away from a job he was on. He suggested maybe we—photographer Billy Stickland was with me—would come out to training that night in Derryknockane. The interview with Ger went fine, and we drove out to the session a couple of hours later. Billy had this notion of photographing the two Clohessys in the showers. As in, taking a shower. Artistically this was probably a winner, but he had a better chance of snapping Lord Lucan feeding sugar lumps to Shergar. When he was told to forget about that he got the hump. "What's their problem?" he moaned, shaking his head.

Meanwhile all the Young Munster players had emerged from the changing room, except Peter. It was explained to me that he wasn't feeling very co-operative, and maybe I'd like to pop in and have a word with him. Great. Me and Claw having a tête à tête in private. In I went. He was sitting on the bench, lacing up his boots—an image I found less than reassuring. "Eh, I believe you have a problem with me?" I ventured, keeping a safe distance. "I don't have a problem with you. I have a problem with what you wrote," he said. He wasn't about to accept my line that he should have been flattered to enjoy such respect in a town with a fearsome reputation, and that was that. No interview, no photograph, and a long journey home with Billy giving out yards.

Over the course of his career thereafter Clohessy was twice suspended in high profile stamping incidents, and then was the victim in a biting attack by Castres forward Ismaella Lassissi, who was banned for a year only to get off on appeal. It is beyond doubt that Peter Clohessy did a lot of damage on the rugby field, but those who played with him loved him. They valued his fearlessness as much as his capacity to spread some panic in the opposition. And he had a sense of humour that was infectious.

"He was one of the most important characters in the team," says Keith Wood. "He wears his heart on his sleeve and is the embodiment above and beyond the rest of them of what Munster rugby—and I suppose Limerick rugby—is about."

Thomond Park was stuffed. Maybe dangerously so. Gaining access to the ground wasn't quite like escaping from Colditz. There was a steady trade in legging it over the perimeter wall, and by kick-off the place was heaving. By that stage the bright, sunny morning had given way to a foul afternoon, with dark clouds resident overhead.

It was tailor made for launching bombs at Saracens full back Mark Mapletoft.

Selecting him there was asking for trouble. "He was voted Munster's player of the season," says Niall O'Donovan. Small, and with an aversion to physical contact, Mapletoft was a beacon to the bombs launched from Ronan O'Gara's boot. He dropped the first and the crowd rejoiced. The weather got worse.

Munster were ahead inside four minutes after Galwey scored from a driven lineout. They secured the restart, launched the next bomb, and

Mapletoft failed to dispose of that one as well. For the first quarter it looked like food and drink to the home team, but for the second, Saracens' quality came to the surface. Their pack was excellent, with Danny Grewcock especially relishing the challenge. By half time they had turned it around to lead 17-8.

For the crowd, the second half lurched from apparent triumph to despair. O'Gara was having a good game and hauled his team back into it. Thierry Lacroix wouldn't go away however. And neither, oddly enough, would little Mark Mapletoft. Munster were leading 24-23 with three minutes of normal time remaining when the Sarries full back did brilliantly to hold the final pass in a great move that put them 30-24 in front. If it stayed like that the group was wide open again, with Saracens at home and Munster away in the final round. As Lacroix was adding the conversion, Galwey assessed the situation.

"I remember him as we stood under the posts," says Wood. "The try was partly my fault because I'd made a soak tackle on one of them and let them in behind the gain line. But Galwey just said that we'd work our way down the field and score a try. Simple as that."

There was no panic. At least not on the field. But the tension was acute, and the noise unreal. It was in that endgame that the crowd counted for extra points. "It is a terrifying place," says Langford. "I distinctly remember that match, and they were jammed to the rafters, and I was standing at a lineout down at the Moyross end. The call was made and I didn't have to jump—I just had to pretend it was coming to me—and I was looking at the crowd and I thought: 'Jesus, thank Christ I'm playing for Munster!' because the crowd were so intimidating. They were bloody screaming blue murder—the look in their eyes."

It was from another lineout at that end of the ground that the game was saved. They had done as Galwey told them to do, and worked their way into scoring range. There were 90 seconds left. Sarries opted not to challenge Langford in favour of defending the drive. They dropped it straight away; the ball sat at the back; and Wood picked it up. "I had all of six inches to go," he says. "And I remember being very uncharitable to the guy who tried to tackle me, Nick Walshe. I told him that when I looked up and saw him I knew I was going to score. Which is uncharitable in the extreme."

Then there was the small matter of the conversion. To add to the drama, a couple of Saracens players jumped the gun before O'Gara started his approach. They were sent back by referee Nigel Williams. So there could be no charge of the kick, relieving O'Gara of one strain of pressure, but adding another. "I didn't think about missing it," he says. "I don't do that. Ever. I wasn't as nervous as you might think because I'd hit the previous one well. Then it snuck in off the post! I got a present of a photo of that in black and white from a fella in Limerick. It's an un-believable shot. You see Pienaar and Richard Hill and these fellas, and Paul Wallace, just standing there, hands on hips, staring at the posts from the goal line and not allowed move. There are some great expressions there."

It would take a heroic block down by Langford on Mapletoft in the last seconds to keep the game safe, but when it was confirmed, the place went mad. The result was confirmation that professional rugby could really catch fire in Ireland. It was high drama, and over the two legs an Irish side had beaten the big money team from England. This was what some of us dreamed professionalism could do here: wipe out the one-offs, and close the gap on the leaders. Compete with them. And what Munster offered was unique.

"At that stage, believe it or not, I wasn't aware of the Thomond Park legend," says Nigel Wray, the man whose money kept Saracens afloat. "We got ourselves into a winning position and I remember Francois Pienaar saying years later that he still regretted that day because he cap-tained the last minutes very badly. He should have throttled the game out there and then, and not given them an opportunity to mount another attack.

"But I remember the weekend with enormous pleasure because of the great feel to the game. I think I probably said it at the presentation which they were kind enough to make to me afterwards: it was the sense of community, and the bond between the team and the fans. London doesn't have a sense of community. There isn't a town called Saracens. For me I can still remember with great pleasure a defeat!"

LES ARISTOCRATS

Declan Kidney was in his element. They had lost their last pool game, 38-36, away to Pontypridd, but the home quarter-final already was secure. And it was against the Saracens of France: Stade Francais, the Paris club revived by the investment of media mogul Max Guazzini. On paper it was the toughest draw, but there was an attraction to it as well. Stade's only away win in the pool phase had been in Glasgow, and they had lost to Leinster in Donnybrook. The previous season they had been beaten by Ulster in Ravenhill. Surely Thomond Park would follow suit?

In the lead-up Kidney settled on calling them the Manchester United of rugby. So Man U were coming to Limerick. It was the standard psychological approach. The only surprise came in the team selection where Eddie Halvey was preferred to Alan Quinlan, who had been at number six all the way through.

Halvey wasn't so much an enigma as an infuriation. There was no mystery: Brian O'Driscoll was in a league of his own, and would become the best centre in world rugby, but Halvey too was extraordinarily talented. He was the most skilful Irish forward of his generation, and one of the least prepared to exploit it. He had reverted to virtual amateur status that season, having had enough of the full-time scene. Oh Eddie, where did it all go wrong?

Well, the start of it was in the timing. He was an early bird on the flight out of Ireland, leaving Shannon for Saracens and a £50,000 contract on 1 February 1996. He was home again by the end of that season. Initially he came back to be with his mother, who had been diagnosed with cancer, but there wasn't much chance of Saracens coach Mark Evans ever seeing him again. Shannon ended up paying a £10,000 transfer fee to secure his release. If the professional game was struggling to get a handle on what was required, Eddie hadn't even recognised there was an adjustment to be made. To compound matters, he shared a house with England internationals Tony Diprose and Richard Hill, both of whom had bought into the concept of clean living.

"Hilly was always giving out about me smoking inside in the house so I used to hang out the window for a smoke," he recalls. "I was eating the wrong food. Guys would be loading up on carbohydrates before training and be in the gym. Hilly and Tony Diprose were really serious and I'd throw on a fry here and there, and the lads would be carbing up. I never took it serious over there. But I was still playing well and getting my place."

Eddie could always play well. He had pace and physique and great hands. He was born for it, but preparation wasn't his bag. As a kid in Limerick he played whatever game was going, but trained hard for none of them. The more rugby got into the science of preparation, the more anachronistic his position became.

"Fitness tests—I just can't do them," he says. "I was an amateur and I didn't want to play professional rugby in Ireland any more. I trained my bollocks off for a month—pre-season 1999/2000—to improve. I did a bleep after training my hole off and got to level seven. The thing is I never had the capacity. Once I started hurting in the bleep test I had to go, to give in. It's a different story on the pitch. When a body's tired (in a match) the brain kicks in. But with a bleep test the body gets tired and the brain won't kick in."

So after two seasons as a full-timer with Munster, he decided to get a job. Niall O'Donovan sorted him. O'Donovan had kept an interest in a company that was installing vending machines in pubs. Halvey was only too happy to pick that up, and switch his involvement with Munster to a part time arrangement. Then Kidney dropped Alan Quinlan, and threw Halvey in against Stade Francais.

The plan was to use his athleticism at the front of the lineout to put extra pressure on the French throw. It worked perfectly, adding to the panic in the away team. The other key performer that day was Dominic Crotty.

He was the antithesis of Halvey, the type of player who would be trying to round up a posse to train with. He'd had a high profile career with UCC, and it led to four Ireland caps, but there had been a three year gap since his most recent, against Wales. Against Stade that day, Crotty looked like international material again.

In the swirling wind Munster got off to a flyer, five points clear in as many minutes with a try from Anthony Horgan. Then Crotty appeared outside Ronan O'Gara to create and score a brilliant try. "I remember during the week prior to that, because standing out at full back for Munster can get lonely at times, and I just resolved to get into the game early on," he says. "I said I'd start taking balls off Rog (Ronan O'Gara) if I could. I took that one off him on an angle and through the gap. Conrad Stolz was at full back. He was a big guy and seeing him walking around the pitch beforehand I was going: 'God, I hope I'm not marking him.'

"For the try I said: 'OK, I'll take it up and see what happens.' And the next thing you know you're through, and the crowd are roaring, and you know that you've made a break and you don't feel anybody holding on to you. And the next thing Stolz was there, and I was running around him! It all happened so quickly that before I knew it the ball was on the ground. And it was just such a fantastic feeling when the crowd started roaring. It's something you can't really describe unless you've scored a try in an important game. It was just a brilliant wave of emotion that came over me because I knew that some of my family were at that end of the ground, that they had tickets there. It was just great to score at that end.

"That whole week was one of the most intense I've ever had. I don't know what it was. Maybe it was because it was the first time in the quarter-finals at home and Declan Kidney was playing his mind games calling them the Manchester United of European rugby. He was repeating that mantra all week. And in many ways it was true, when you saw all the stars they had, and here they were coming into our back yard. So it was something that I didn't want to give up or leave inside the dressing-room. Before the game, I was incredibly pumped up. After Anthony Horgan scored I nearly took (Christophe) Dominici's head off for absolutely no reason whatsoever. So I got a great slagging off the lads for a month after that, and I lived to regret it, but I was so pumped that day, I've rarely if ever had that feeling of intensity since then."

Munster were 12-3 up at the break; 27-10 ahead at the finish. The result was never at issue. They were in the Heineken Cup semi-finals for the first time.

Learning of the semi-final draw was one of those awkward moments when you couldn't be seen to be downcast—this was a semi-final—but you knew you'd just drawn the short straw. A group of players were in Anthony Foley's house in Killaloe, celebrating the christening of John Langford's son Conor, when the news came through. Toulouse. Away. "The reaction was: 'Ah fuck it,' to start," says Niall O'Donovan. "And then: 'Ah what the hell?' That kind of attitude. At first fellas were kind of shocked that we were away, and then it was: 'Well why not?'"

Toulouse were the last team you wanted. Winners in the inaugural year, this time they had qualified a bit like Munster, losing only their final pool game, and when it didn't matter. But the quality of their squad was something else: from props Christian Califano and Franck Tournaire, to full back Stephane Ougier, they had class and experience all round. And they would have a hot sun on their backs in Bordeaux. You couldn't see Munster getting past this one.

The game would be at Stade Lescure, where Bath had beaten Brive in dramatic circumstances, and in front of a colourful band of travelling fans, in 1998. Munster's travelling support put that in the shade. Bordeaux is not a big rugby town, but that weekend left an impression on the place.

————

I saw Woody pull up with the injury but I didn't think much of it at the time. He's often having to get treatment and then he'd be grand again. One side of me was saying: "Please, please get back up," you know? And the other side was like: "Jesus, this is your big chance! Go out and enjoy it!" I was probably white as a ghost as usual when I had to go and warm up. It's grand when you're subbing and a fella goes down and you're straight on, there's no problem. You're on and you're in it. But it's the: "Right, you're coming on there in a while." It's those minutes that the negative things can come into your head. "Jesus I hope everything goes OK. I hope I do all right. I hope I don't screw up." It's natural enough. You'd be trying to drown them out obviously with the positive, you know? As you get older you learn to turn them into positive images.

I wasn't sure what was going on at half time. The dressing-rooms were a good five minute walk away so I didn't bother going. I stayed out stretching away with Tom Tierney. I remember Tom saying sure that'll be no bother to you. We'd always be arsing and joking and messing but I remember it actually got serious and him saying "C'mere, you're an Irish player now, go out and play like an Irish player."* And whatever way he said it, it made sense. I kind of pretended it was a small little thing, playing a representative provincial game. I was very positive going out. It was a lovely day and I was going to enjoy it. I'll never forget, at this stage the lads were walking out and I could see the looks. They were kind of looking at me—the rest of the players—and I didn't know what the story was. I wasn't asking, but I wasn't running away either. I was waiting for someone to tell me. And I got a few of the: "Ah you'll be all right." Those sort

* Sheahan was on the Ireland squad. He was first capped two months later.

of looks. Then I could see Woody in the distance hobbling away. So I whipped off the track suit and Deccie said: "You're on."

When Frankie Sheahan came in for Keith Wood, the drama was perfectly poised. Toulouse led 15-11, and threatened to steamroll Munster, but there was another side to the story. Despite the searing heat, Munster did best when they moved up a gear. John Hayes's try, to put them 8-3 up, was a gem. It took 55 seconds, running through five phases and 22 pairs of hands. It was brilliant rugby, the only downside to it being Wood's injury at the start of it. "I took a pass and ran, thinking I was Carl Lewis, ran past (Emile) Ntamack, and he ran back and caught me," says Wood. "And whatever way he caught me, he snagged my foot and I tore my calf."

So you wanted Munster to run, but if they did it too much they might die of heat exhaustion, and be buried far from the final whistle. All the while Toulouse had the menacing look. It turned into the tortured look at the number of passes they dropped. In the conditions, and given who they were, it was incredible.

The lowlight for them came on the hour mark. They had seen the scoreboard transformed to just 18-17 in their favour, when glory beckoned at last. After brilliant interplay by the forwards Munster were scattered, and former All Black Lee Stensness was in space with three players outside him. It was a question of which one of them would score. And he dropped it. Two minutes later O'Gara scored the try of the season.

"It was off a scrum in our own half and I just said to Mikey (Mullins): 'Let's have a go here.' And I hit him (with the pass) wide and he ran an outline, and in to Dominic (Crotty), and then in to Dutchy (Holland). It was probably the most perfect bit of rugby we've put together in years, between forwards and backs. Dominic ended up as first receiver in the 22 and I just ran a support line on him. I just anticipated the pass because he had done really well and attracted two of them in the tackle. Both of them focused on him and it was a clean run in for me. The second I touched the ball it was like: 'Fuck it, here we go!' When I touched it down I did a funny dive, a sort of half a roll, and then up and punched the air. It was like life couldn't have been better at that point. A brilliant feeling. It was the best try I ever scored. I'd say I'll never beat it."

Munster were 24-18 in front; Jason Holland picked up an intercept try soon after, and it was all over with time enough to sit back and enjoy the wonder of it all. It finished 31-25. Three and a half years earlier they had played Toulouse in France, and Mick Galwey wasn't sure whether the colour of his cheeks was from the heat of the sun or the depth of his embarrassment. This time it was all about the sun. He was basking in it.

TWICKENHAM

Northampton were desperate. And they were out on their feet. After a lifetime of empty trophy cabinets, the 1999/2000 season saw them chasing silverware on three fronts: domestic league and cup, and Europe. They'd already lost out on the first two. This was the last chance saloon, and they could barely stand up. The previous week they had to win up in Newcastle in the league to secure their qualification for Europe the next season. They succeeded, but they were shattered. It fastened Munster's position as favourites, and for the first time in the competition there was a different balance to the equation. This wasn't another step on a carefree adventure. It was a European Cup final, against a battered outfit, and there was plenty to be lost.

Soul Mates

"We had what I can only describe as something as emotional as an AA meeting the night before the game," remembers Dominic Crotty. "It felt like it went on for hours and it was incredible. It was a meeting unlike anything I had ever come across. We went from player to player in order, and every one of them said what it meant to them to be in that room at that time, knowing there were thousands of Irish people out-side, knowing the wave of emotion that was going to be there the next day, knowing what it meant to everybody at home. People got caught up in it to a greater or lesser extent. It was new for everybody you know? For a guy like Gaillimh, who had been around the block, to one of the youngest guys like Stringer."

It started off normally enough. Then it was Ken O'Connell's turn. As a 21 year old he had played for the province against Buck Shelford's All Blacks in 1989. The closest he had come to playing in this campaign was as a standby for David Wallace, at home against Saracens. He knew this was his last close-up of a big day out.

Ken is a legend in that part of the world.

"He just poured his heart out," says Ronan O'Gara. "It was incredible. It was one of the most moving speeches I've ever heard, which you would associate with Ken after you get to know him. I suppose there were a lot of young people in the room that night. It's kind of hard to see a grown man cry, but he was so full of passion and emotion. That set the trend. It'll never happen again obviously because it was a first time for a final and the team had gone so well that year that fellas were so close to one another and they had no problem saying exactly what they felt. There was that kind of trust within the room. In hindsight it was like attending a removal, but a kind of happy removal."

Soon after O'Connell came another flanker. David Corkery would have been a part of this but for freakish circumstance, rupturing an Achilles tendon on his return from rupturing the other one.

"He was extremely emotional and many people were extremely emotional for him as well," recalls Crotty. "We just felt so sorry for him that he couldn't be part of it after he'd given so much to Munster and Irish rugby. I was next after him, and I had these word pre-planned and that I'd be stiff upper lip and be rational about it, but I just lost it myself as well. I just blabbered everything out. I was a complete mess. I might as well have been in a bar, drunk, for all the sense I was making. And to be honest, I think that meeting put us over the edge."

That view is common within the group. Northampton reserved their emotional surge until the dressing-room the next day. Andy Blyth was a former Saint who was confined to a wheelchair after breaking his neck on the playing field. He was well known to the Northampton players. He came into the dressing-room beforehand and spoke about how much the day meant to him, and how much he would be behind them. It was the last time that team would play together, and they knew it.

The Plan

"We felt we could get at Ronan O'Gara and really have a go at him and really put him off his game," says Saints flanker Budge Pountney. "We wanted to force him to make tackles, which is not the strongest part of his game. The plan was to do it in the first few minutes. 'Let's get at him!' He was the guy who punched them around the park, so we wanted to make him think of other things apart from where he was going to kick the ball."

They put it into action in the first minute, with Tim Rodber leading the charge at Munster's playmaker. Thereafter there was a queue for the same route. They exploded into the game.

"All week we were thinking: 'We're knackered; we're absolutely screwed; we've got injuries all over the place; we can't put one foot in front of the other,'" says Pountney. "So we wanted to hit them with the unexpected, a team that was on their toes and really battling, really aggressive and energised. Just hit them with something they weren't expecting. That was our mentality—hit them hard in the first 20 minutes and see what we could get done. And then try and hang on for dear life!"

It was working well enough. The swirling wind blew the game all over the place, and wherever it went there was a Saint behaving like a sinner. Gary Pagel and Tim Rodber and Freddie Mendez all were carrying well, and Pat Lam was everywhere. "Lam hit Rog before the ball and after the ball, and hit him on the ground—and we weren't cruel enough with him," says Brian O'Brien. "We had enough to do to think about the game, whereas if you'd played them the following week you'd have quietened him down. In that respect we didn't protect Rog enough."

The Kick

I remember one night in a pub in Cork I went up to the bar and this fella turns round and says: "You're the prick that missed the kick against Northampton." I was a bit shocked all right. I just thought: "He's some beauty isn't he?"

In the end it came down, as rugby often does, to a kick at goal. Munster had recovered from their awful start to lead 8-6 at the break, thanks to Jason Holland's wobbly drop goal, and David Wallace's fine try. They looked in trouble early in the second half when Saints scrumhalf Dom Malone intercepted a pass in his own 22 and took off. In a neat coincidence, Malone, a heavy smoker, was cut down 40 metres later by none other than Eddie Halvey. Soon after, they were in trouble when Paul Grayson kicked Northampton into a 9-8 lead. And more trouble still when Mick Galwey was sin-binned. And still, they recovered to the point where, with a minute of normal time remaining, they had a shot to win it.

John Langford, surrounded by jubilant Munster fans after the win over Saracens in Thomond Park, 2000.

Declan Kidney and Niall O'Donovan in the early days at Munster.

Keith Wood, Mick Galwey and Peter Clohessy embrace after the final whistle in Bordeaux, 2000.

Heineken Cup final, Twickenham, 2000: Ronan O'Gara watches his late penalty kick against Northampton drift wide of the post.

Noel Murphy under pressure at an IRFU press conference, about banned substances, in 1998.

Warren Gatland near the end.

IRFU Rugby Director Eddie Wigglesworth.

Connacht union representative Billy Glynn.

Brian O'Brien (manager), Declan Kidney (assistant coach) and Eddie O'Sullivan (coach) in Terrigal, New South Wales, during RWC 2003.

Keith Wood on the charge with John Hayes and Marcus Horan in support against Argentina, in Adelaide.

Paul Hogan lifts the AIL trophy for Garryowen in 1994.

Paul O'Connell, with Anthony Foley in support, breaks the tackle of Serge Betsen in the Heineken Cup final win over Biarritz in 2006.

Paul O'Connell and Brian O'Driscoll, the most influential players in Eddie O'Sullivan's squad, celebrate the Triple Crown-clinching win over England in 2006.

From 45 metres out on the west stand side of the field, Munster were awarded a penalty. O'Gara stepped up. He went through the standard routine. Then he hit it. Good connection; good direction; depending where you were in the stadium, you fixed your gaze on the ball or the touch-judges behind the goal.

Budge Pountney is rooted to the spot, focused on the ball. "I'm watching it thinking: 'Oh my God, that's going over.'" And just as he feels his innards move south, there is salvation. "Oh no it isn't!"

It was just as supporter Declan O'Connell described it: "Like someone opened the door and the wind came in and blew the ball around the wrong side of the post. Just like that."

O'Gara watched and winced when he realised what was happening. "I gave it as good a shot as I could but there was a bad wind from right to left. Basically it was on target, but there wasn't enough force behind it. When I went back two or three years later I remembered the spot. Nowadays because I've so much experience of kicking I'd probably fancy myself to get it but it was a bloody difficult kick, and I'd still have that opinion today. It was something I just had to live with."

There was a mad, frantic scramble in the dying moments, but the game was gone. It was all over: Northampton 9, Munster 8. They had done to Munster what Munster had done to everybody else.

"You're always hoping for one more lineout; one more play; one more chance to get down there for a drop goal," says Keith Wood. "And it was over and it was awful and because at that stage it was a good journey, you don't recognise it until it's ended. And I'd say 30 seconds later the crowd started singing the Fields of Athenry, and it didn't make it better—it wasn't that at all—but it was going from one of my worst rugby experiences to one of my best rugby experiences. Nobody left. They all stayed. They all sang. Empathy is exactly what it was. I just thought it was extraordinary. It was extraordinary that there were so many people in there and there was a link—and it was that moment, more than any of the other moments, that showed the link between Munster and Munster supporters. That showed there was a level of togetherness there and then. Believe me when I say . . . it was a success."

Chapter 8

BLOODLETTING

The Sacking of Warren Gatland, 2001

*Ladies and gentlemen, boys and girls, would you
please put your hands together and give a very warm
Thomond Park welcome to the new coach of Ireland—
Warren Gatland!*

Tommy Creamer had been doing the PA at Thomond Park since 1975. He liked the job, slipping in the odd extra line, adding a bit of encouragement or rebuke at the right time. When Warren Gatland took his seat in the stand for his first All Ireland League game as the newly crowned king, Creamer called the subjects to attention. "I thought that Brian Ashton's feet hadn't really touched the ground in Ireland," he says. "I have good friends in Galwegians and in Connacht and I knew the good work Warren Gatland had done. People were impressed by his results and his work and I meant it in the fashion of: 'Let's welcome him and wish him well.'" The crowd responded warmly. It was early 1998, and the right man was in the right place at the right time.

There wasn't a dissenting voice when he stepped into the gap left by Ashton. Apart from the fact that neither Ireland nor its rugby supporters were in a position to pick and choose, there were obvious qualities to Gatland that were very appealing.

From the late 1980s through the 1990s a trend developed in the Irish club game of importing foreign players and coaches. I saw this first hand in Clontarf where we had a stream of bodies, mostly from South Africa and New Zealand. Some were good, some were chancers, and our experience was pretty much the same all round. There was a syndrome common to nearly all the coaches from the southern hemisphere: they demanded standards that amateur players were either unwilling or unable to satisfy. And when the players let them down, the antipodeans couldn't figure it out. Warren Gatland was part of that influx, but he was different. He adapted.

He first landed in Galway with Buck Shelford's All Blacks in 1989. There's no such thing as an insignificant All Black tour, but that one was ground-breaking. Like the Grand Slam Australians in 1984, who stunned us with the precision of their handling on the gain line, Shelford's mob burned the place up. They had a thrilling full back by the name of John Gallagher, who opened defences with angles we hadn't considered. It was all predicated on a fearsome pack for whom the maul was their greatest weapon. At this end of the world it was a lie-in affair; for them it was explosive.

Gatland was reserve to Sean Fitzpatrick. The Auckland hooker was the last man in the world you wanted to understudy. It wasn't that you couldn't learn from him, rather you wouldn't get a chance to implement it on test match days. Fitzpatrick was never dropped, and, during Gatland's four years on the squad, never injured. It was before the introduction of bench clearances too, so the door never opened even for a late run-on. Instead, Gatland had to make do with the midweek team. Between 1988 and 1991 he would play 17 times for the All Blacks, but never for New Zealand in a test match. In 1992 he captained a New Zealand xv in two games against the touring England B side— coincidentally when Ireland were in the country on a full tour. But there were no caps.

On that trip to Ireland in 1989 they minced Connacht 40-6, and that was his point of connection with this country. Earlier in the trip Galwegians clubman Michael Heaslip was in London when he happened across two of the tourists out shopping, one of whom was prop Craig Dowd. Heaslip asked if any of the squad might be up for some coaching in the West of Ireland when the tour was over. "Leave it with me," said Dowd. Heaslip contacted him when they arrived in Galway, and Dowd introduced him to Gatland. Galwegians made him a decent offer, an opportunity for a change in lifestyle. So Warren and his wife Trudy packed in their teaching jobs in Waikato and took a chance on the other side of the world.

At his first session at the club there was only a handful of players, and their skills were shocking. For the first league game—away to

Sligo—many arrived in dribs and drabs, after the appointed hour, and he ordered the bus to leave and the stragglers to follow on. One of them was in the toilet in the clubhouse. Instead of getting the hump, Gatland worked with the players and brought them round to his way of preparation, or as close as was feasible in the circumstances. It worked. They won two Connacht League titles for starters, and were promoted into the All Ireland League for the season 1992/93.

It wouldn't have happened without him.

The Gatlands were four years in Galway when tragedy struck. Their new daughter Shauna was born with spina bifida and died aged four months. With the encouragement of Galwegians they returned to their support network in New Zealand. That gesture stayed with him, that a club which had invested heavily in him was prepared to put it aside so he could sort himself out. He didn't know it then, but he would be back.

In September 1996 Gatland was in New Zealand, teaching by day and coaching Thames Valley by night, when he got an sos from Billy Glynn in Connacht. They had just parted company with their coach, Eddie O'Sullivan, and the early season tour to Sweden was about to depart. Could he drop tools and help them out? He caught the next flight out. His coaching career was about to take off.

Gatland transformed Connacht. He had just turned 33, and was more than comfortable with slotting into the front row in training sessions to get his point across. His track record as an All Black gave him gravitas, and he had real drive. He worked the players hard, especially in the gym where the sessions would be painfully competitive. "You'd be on the bench press and the next thing he'd appear over and start leaning on it," recalls Bernard Jackman, Connacht's hooker at the time. "And you wouldn't know when he was going to get off. That was his big thing, and the first year especially he worked us to the bone. I remember one day early the next season he brought us down to Athlone for a video session and it was the bluntest couple of hours I think any of us had ever been through. That was the start of professionalism in terms of analysis. He cut right to the bone with a few guys. That was the first place I'd heard the term 'ruck inspector'. After that we went out on the field for an hour and 'killed' each other. And then we really started to click."

He built a fantastic spirit in the group, feeding off the fact that Connacht was the poor relation of Irish rugby. On the back of their training shirts they had their nicknames, which was not the norm in

Ireland; across the front of their T-shirts they had borrowed from Oliver Cromwell the legend: "To Hell or Connaught".

And as it happened, Cromwell's England, and Northampton in particular, would be the scene of perhaps Connacht's greatest triumph. They had to survive a ferocious assault at Franklin's Gardens before hanging on 20-15 to qualify for the knock out stages of the European Conference in 1997. Along the way they had beaten Begles Bordeaux, becoming the first Irish province to win a European tie in France. This was before Ulster won the European Cup, before Munster even qualified from their pool. In the context of Connacht's history it was phenomenal. The Ireland job would be different.

ALONG COMES EDDIE

There were two parts to Gatland's Ireland career: pre Lens and post Lens. The first part was like a crash course in professional rugby: the IRFU didn't know what they were at, and their young coach was learning as he went. Lens changed everything. It was the electric shock the union needed. Instead of working from one Six Nations to the next, they started to look at the cycle in gaps of four years. The first thing that happened in the wake of RWC '99 was the appointment of a new assistant coach. As far back as the spring, Eddie Coleman, the chairman of the union's elections sub-committee—which was responsible for appointments—and Eddie Wigglesworth, the director of rugby development, drove to the Royal Hotel in Moate where they met with Eddie O'Sullivan. The three Eddies had a cup of tea and a chat, in a little alcove off the foyer, initially about getting O'Sullivan back into the Irish system at some level. By the time they had met for the third time, soon after the Lens disaster, there was an offer as Gatland's assistant on the table.

O'Sullivan had been a development officer in the IRFU, and a fitness advisor on their tours to Namibia in 1991 and New Zealand in 1992. At the start of the 1996/97 season he was negotiating an extension on his contract as Connacht coach when the relationship broke off. That was where Gatland came onto the IRFU's books to begin with. He also took over O'Sullivan's coaching job in Galwegians. The very nature of that little bit of business meant that they weren't off to a great start. In the interim, O'Sullivan had gone to work with the US Eagles, and was assistant coach there when they were in Ireland's World Cup pool in 1999.

Eddie O'Sullivan had ambition written in broad capitals across his forehead. Once he was put on the national ticket one of two things would happen: he would succeed Gatland at some stage, or in time he would move on in search of fulfilment. They weren't going to grow old together.

Straight away there was unease. O'Sullivan was hired on a three year contract, while Gatland was still being strung along as if on probation. His first deal had been for the remainder of the Five Nations in 1998, and the second was up to the end of the Six Nations in 2000. And O'Sullivan walked in on a three year deal to start?

"That was always the frustrating thing," says Gatland. "And that always made it difficult. You always felt as if you were looking over your back." The irony was that O'Sullivan had been cut by Connacht in 1996 because he had been looking for a longer-term contract. There was no way he would settle for less the second time around. Meanwhile, the man who succeeded him—Gatland—soon came to understand these problems as well.

The Connacht business wouldn't go away. Gatland's friends from there were O'Sullivan's enemies. "At the time I was told that when Philip Danaher had gone (after Lens) that the decision to employ someone else was completely my own, and would I meet him (O'Sullivan)," Gatland says. "And I did. I sat down and met Eddie. And I spoke to a few people (in Connacht) I knew, and they advised me against taking him as an assistant coach, but you know . . ."

He maintains—unconvincingly—that he had no problem with O'Sullivan's arrival, even though he had to be prodded into picking up the phone to call his new assistant.

"No, I didn't have a problem with Eddie coming on board. Absolutely. For me it was always about getting the right person in the job. But I knew there was a bit of baggage."

Their first game together was against England in Twickenham in 2000. They were blitzed, 50-18. Ireland defended like they were in a stupor. The pair had disagreed on what system they should operate, and subsequently Gatland said they went the O'Sullivan route, which had been a dead end. After the game things only got worse.

That night—much later that night—a handful of players arrived into the crowded bar of Jury's Hotel in Kensington. The only circumstances in which an appearance like that could make any sense would be on the back of a stirring victory. Before long Frankie Sheahan, who had been on the bench that day, was confronted by some halfwit who ran off at the mouth about the shortcomings of the national team. Sheahan head-butted him. It got a lot of coverage in the media. Manager Donal Lenihan, who was doing the job part-time, was beginning to wonder if this gig had any upside to it.

"I had an interview for the Lions on the Monday or Tuesday after that England game," he says. "And I got a call from Syd Millar to say I'd been appointed as manager—on a tea break from the disciplinary committee for Frankie. So what should have been a very proud individual moment I had to put to the back of my head and say absolutely nothing. So then we picked a team (to play Scotland) where we made nine changes. I'm sitting in my room on the Thursday morning and Shane Horgan comes to me, at 10 to eight, I'll always remember him knocking at the door—tears rolling down his face saying: 'Look there's a story coming out tonight that I did something to a bouncer in Galway.' And I'm thinking: 'Fuck, this can't get any worse.' The one thing I pride myself on is that in terms of a crisis we were able to keep going. I remember being raging with the Leinster Branch—they knew this thing was on the back burner and nobody told us. I had great time for Shane and I said: 'Look, do your parents know about this?'

"And he said 'No.'

"'Well the first thing you do is go and tell them because they don't want to pick up the *Herald* and read it.'"

The story did appear in the *Herald* and a few other papers as well. Some months earlier, on the night of a Leinster game against Connacht, Horgan had been in an altercation with a bouncer outside a nightclub in Galway. What next?

The Twickenham setback inspired a classic IRFU reaction, albeit a delayed one. Some months later they came up with a mechanism to monitor performance: The Match Review. It had a great capacity to infuriate, making the coach justify himself on an ongoing basis.

"The frustrating thing about those match reviews was you'd have Brian O'Brien (who replaced Donal Lenihan as manager), Eddie and myself—and Eddie didn't often say a lot in those reviews; he kept very, very quiet," says Gatland. "And there was Wigglesworth, Coleman, Noel Murphy and Syd Millar. It would be up to Dublin on a Wednesday night and by the time you'd have done all your work, all your analysis, all your reviews, you had all your information and you're sitting there discussing the game with guys who didn't have the information. I found that frustrating. Then they'd go: 'In my day when we played against Wales in the '60s and blah blah blah, and this is what we used to do.' I found it incredibly frustrating sitting there talking to a group of guys who didn't understand the modern game. Obviously they were good players in their own day but the reviews weren't on specifics; it was just on general performance really. And if we won it was fine and it was well done; and if you lost, the questions were not questions from people with a specific knowledge of the game.

"The other thing too is that we used to meet with Wigglesworth on the morning (of a game) and he'd say: 'What are you planning?' I can remember one day he asked me what we were planning to do. 'Will you play a rucking game or a continuity game?' That's a question from somebody who thinks he knows what he's talking about . . . And I'm sitting there trying to say the right things and talking to people who don't understand the modern game. To me that was frustrating."

The other side of these question and answer sessions was that in order to evaluate how the coach was performing, the union needed to know what he had planned in the first place. And that the time to ask these questions was not a week out from the game—for fear of being blamed for leaking information if things went wrong—but in the immediate run-up. Wigglesworth would have serious issues with Gatland's portrayal of him as being tactically challenged, while Coleman, Murphy and Millar would all maintain they were well clued in to the modern game.

If the coach was patently frustrated, then on the union side of the fence there was an increasing disenchantment with their taciturn Kiwi. If he could avoid talking to them he would. They had this impression of him brooding in his house in Galway while they were in Lansdowne Road, stewing over a sequence of crises. He had never been slow either to suggest how they might sharpen up the organisation. He was only eight months into the job when I interviewed him in the *Sunday Independent* and he said: "I think maybe it's time we looked at the structure at the top. I'd like us to take a lead from New Zealand, South Africa and Australia where there's a CEO and a board of management, and the committee can run the AIL and the professionals can run the top team."

It was good copy. Moreover it made absolute sense. The dodgy bit was using a Sunday newspaper to make the point to a group of people who gave orders better than they took suggestions. That habit of negotiating through the media would come back to haunt him. In the meantime, however, in the union there was this deepening perception of him as somebody who had to be woken up to the fact that they were ready and willing to invest in the team.

"After 1999 the rugby committee under Stan Waldron was very much driving the issue of increased investment in the national team to take us on," says an IRFU source. "And there was this continuous reticence from Warren in terms of the structural issues that didn't seem to be addressed."

This isn't how Gatland remembers it. Lenihan too reckons the shift in attitude from on high came after he left, which was April 2000.

"I wish that had been conveyed to me," Gatland says. "I was often told about the finances and how John Lyons was going to be the first treasurer in the IRFU to lose money, and how important that was, and we had to look at cutting back on the hotels we stayed in and the expenses."

The best way to measure the IRFU's relationship with him was in the contract. They may have been catching on to the idea of working from one World Cup to the next, but they didn't extend that vision to their coach. Rather, they had punted for safety—short of the full cycle. And his future wasn't looking too good after the Twickenham setback. All changed when Scotland came to Lansdowne Road on 19 February. And before you knew it, things took off in the other direction.

THE TURNAROUND, FEBRUARY 2000

Ireland hadn't beaten the Scots since 1988. They had become a painful reminder of how bad things had become here. History united the pair on a few fronts: the social profile of the game in each country was almost identical, as were the structures and resources, and the traditional lack of success. Yet in that period of Scottish supremacy they had picked up a Grand Slam—an item not even up for discussion in Ireland—and won a Championship. They had also finished above Ireland in every one of those seasons, bar one.

If you ran a line from Lens in 1999 through Twickenham in 2000 to the opening quarter at Lansdowne Road on the fateful day in February, at which point Scotland were 10-0 in front and playing really well, its natural conclusion would be at 5 p.m. with Gatland's resignation. He had brought in five new caps, three of them from Munster, and along with a recall for Mick Galwey it was a reflection of their form in Europe. For the coach there was nowhere else to go.

"That was the day where if we'd lost I would have resigned. I think I would have been under a lot of pressure and they might have pushed me anyway. It would have been time to go and give somebody else a crack at it because to me, being in a position like that, you really need to have the support of the people behind you, the committee, and the people in the job, and if we had lost that day that support would have been almost zero. I'd made the decision beforehand that if we'd lost that day I would have resigned."

The match swung on a decision by referee Joel Dumé to forget about an advantage he was playing for Scotland. Ireland had managed to overcome the 10 point start to lead 13-10 at the break, but still they looked fragile, and about to concede again. Scotland were on the attack. We expected Dumé to give them a scrum as the move broke down on their advantage play. Next thing you knew, the ball was hacked half the length of the field and Shane Horgan crowned his debut with a try. Ireland raced away to win 44-22. Gatland was still in a job. It would get better.

They hammered Italy 60-13 in the next game, and with Gatland's contract deadline approaching I got a line from a senior union source that they would give him another year. The stated rationale was that they wanted to see how the relationship developed with O'Sullivan. I rang Gatland with that news before it went to print, and he wasn't overly impressed. It was an extension, but it was no endorsement. The following Saturday Ireland were playing France in Paris, where they hadn't won since 1972. It didn't look like an opportunity to strengthen his hand with his employer.

Brian O'Driscoll was one of the new breed. When the committee men were digging their heels in to resist professionalism, they wouldn't have thought it possible that rugby could ever accommodate a creature like O'Driscoll. Nor would they have liked the thought, even if they believed it. He went from school in Blackrock to UCD's new rugby academy, and from there to a full-time contract with Ireland. If he had ever worn a suit it had a designer label on it, and it wasn't for going to work. Work was rugby, and he was brilliant at it. One of the weaknesses of the Irish system was its slowness to complete the cycle from spotting talent to getting it onto the tv screen. O'Driscoll's feet touched the ground, but only in spots. From the moment he made his debut, as a 20 year old on the 1999 tour to Australia, he looked special. In Paris on a warm afternoon in March 2000 he became a sensation.

He scored three tries that day, which was the equivalent of Ireland's total from the previous 10 games in that city. A week later he showed up at a Schools final in Lansdowne Road, and there was a stampede of kids looking for a piece of him. If Keith Wood had been the first Irish player to understand the pro game, then O'Driscoll was its first stellar creation. Overnight he became a celebrity. People who didn't know a rugby ball from a sack of spuds knew Brian O'Driscoll. And his emergence would open a new chapter in the relationship between the IRFU and the professional game. There were wages, and then there were the wages of a young man who could command enough wedge to spin past presidents out of their graves.

In the euphoria of that 27-25 win, Gatland skipped out of the Stade de France knowing that a one year deal needed to be doubled at least. The union stretched it to the conclusion of the 2002 Six Nations. It wasn't his ticket to the 2003 World Cup, but at least the pressure was off. When it came back on it would be his own doing.

The coach's contract extension had obvious implications for his assistant. The back line had looked a whole lot better for O'Sullivan's input, and on the face of it the two men worked well enough on the training field. Yet O'Sullivan was in a dilemma. If things continued on an upward trend then he would be kept on as assistant, short of where he wanted to be; if they went disastrously wrong then he could get washed down the pan with the coach. If O'Sullivan was to further his career then he had to keep his end up, protect his position, and hope that it would be enough to keep him afloat if and when Gatland sank.

A fortnight after that win in France, Ireland lost at home to Wales. It didn't matter, for they had secured a third place finish, their best in the Championship since 1987.

Of more importance was the departure of Donal Lenihan as manager. He had been appointed to lead the Lions to Australia the next summer, and stepped back to devote himself to that. Brian O'Brien came in to fill the gap.

It dramatically altered the make up of the management trio, and indeed the role of the manager from that point onwards. Lenihan was a front of house man: he led the press conferences and made the decisions. Moreover he had protected Gatland when the mud started flying after Lens. Gatland has no doubt he wouldn't have survived as long as he did if Lenihan hadn't been in his corner. O'Brien was more a facilitator than a leader, and that's the way he viewed the job. The coach was the boss and he was there to support the coach. It suited the union and it appeared to suit Gatland. He got on well with O'Brien, but the Munster man was no buffer between him and the IRFU. That left Gatland more exposed: he was clearly the number one, but with no secure future, and an ambitious assistant he didn't trust, it wasn't exactly an all powerful position. Moreover, on Lenihan's watch it was more likely that the differences between Gatland and O'Sullivan would be driven underground. After the win over Scotland earlier that season, for example, O'Sullivan was picking up a lot of the kudos for the turn-around in fortune. Lenihan launched into him one day, accusing him of covertly promoting his case in the media. O'Sullivan knocked it back, but the manager was highly sensitive to the optics of the situation. Did the coach not feel a chill wind blowing when Lenihan opened the door to leave?

"I didn't feel that way at the time because the team were going pretty well and there was support for the team and support for myself. I wasn't thinking politically at the time. I wasn't thinking: who was going to try and win points and who's backing me, who's supporting me? It was only when I left and looked back on all those things . . . For me the most important thing wasn't about that. It was about Irish rugby and the team and doing what I felt was best for Irish rugby. I wasn't dealing with the political things and making phone calls and ringing the president and ringing Syd Millar and ringing Eddie Coleman and getting them onside, and ringing certain people in the press."

It is ludicrous to suggest that Gatland didn't use the media himself. He had an especially close relationship with Gerry Thornley in *The Irish Times*, which would be his prime medium for making his case with the IRFU. That it backfired badly was nothing to do with O'Sullivan, whose media operation was less energetic than Gatland presumed.

When the Six Nations rolled around again in 2001 the progress of the previous campaign had stalled. In the summer they had blown a winning position against Argentina in Buenos Aires—Gatland was steaming after that one—and then ran South Africa close in the autumn. In between there was a mix of the mediocre and the meaningless against USA, Canada and Japan. A good start to the Championship was a must.

Italy were first up. Ireland had lost on their only previous visits— 1995 and 1997—so there was baggage, and it weighed them down in an awful first half before they won 41-22. They had an especially hard time at the scrum. Rather than call in specialist help, however, Gatland ploughed on. In fairness, he was an All Black front rower, but in any case there was an issue with him bringing in outsiders. In 1998 he had used Des Fitzgerald briefly, but he was inclined more towards insularity. By nature he was a loyalist, and wanted to surround himself with people he knew and could trust. This always sat uncomfortably with his claims that it was he who brought in O'Sullivan when he neither liked nor trusted him.

The scrummaging problems persisted, but they were partially buried in the delight at beating France two weeks later in Lansdowne Road. It was the first back to back wins over this opposition in 29 years. Who knew where this could end? Then it broke off, just like that. Not unlike 1972 when Ireland's promising start was undone by the weakness of Wales and Scotland who wouldn't travel, this time nobody wanted them. An outbreak of Foot and Mouth closed everything down. When life restarted in the autumn, things had shifted dramatically again.

SINK OR SWIM
It would be inappropriate to go into detail. There is a review in November, a long-standing arrangement in essence at Warren's request. As Warren told the media, we will sit down and discuss the progress we are hopefully making.—Philip Browne, October 2001

There was enough in those few lines from the IRFU chief executive to suggest that all was not well. Gatland's strategy was to get to the World Cup in 2003 with an experienced squad, one that could atone for the disaster of 1999. Ireland needed it and he needed it. Badly. One of his tactics was to mention in interviews that he was trying to plan for something without having the security of knowing if he would be there to witness it. He hoped it would prod the union into positive action when it should have been apparent to him that it was counter-productive. In his campaign for security of tenure he was handed what was effectively another probationary period. Browne agreed to review his status when the rescheduled Six Nations games and the autumn internationals concluded in November, five months ahead of the scheduled contract date. There were only two possible outcomes: success, or the sack. There could be no kicking to touch.

"I wasn't upset about that," Gatland says. "They had a chance to see: is this team really progressing, is it going forward? And we don't have to make up our mind until after the next series of games, and I was reasonably happy with that. It could have been sorted out beforehand. The other thing too—from an IRFU point of view—is that if they're not going to keep you on, for me as a coach you've got to start thinking about what you're doing in the future. You talk about me in that position and I got criticised for it (agitating ahead of time) but Eddie did it effectively through whatever means."

The set of six got off to a good start when the Canada game was cancelled—interestingly, over a row where the players backed their sacked coach Dave Clark and refused to travel. So the schedule would be one game shorter, and Gatland's future would be sorted straight after the New Zealand test on 17 November. A positive opening against Scotland then and Team Ireland would be back in business. Buoyed by the two wins back in February, Gatland and O'Sullivan went for a raft of changes that were designed to push the team on another step. They were disastrous. Of the new selections, Guy Easterby, Jeremy Davidson and Kieron Dawson suffered most. It rivalled any of the awful days Ireland had endured in Murrayfield. Mostly it reflected the inconsistency that plagued the Ireland team. Win a couple, lose a few, what had changed? To senior members in the IRFU it supported their view that Gatland was hit or miss. "Anything could happen in the planning process and that used to piss people off big time," says one who was closely involved in the process. "And when Eddie came in it used to drive him bananas."

There was a scene in the bar that night that didn't do much for Gatland's relationship with the blazers. Brian O'Brien realised what was unfolding and moved to intervene.

"I saw it happening," he says. "I said: 'Come on Gatty, fuck it, get out of here.' Into the lift and upstairs and put him into the bed. I said:

'Thanks be to God.' And went away with myself. He went back down. And there was hassle." The committee men had arrived back from the function and were having more top ups, extending the post mortem. Not a great time for rational conversation.

"And they'd have been feeling the pain: 'Here we are over here, and we've gone down again.' There's a lot of negativity emanates from guys who should know better," says O'Brien.

A few weeks later Gatland was back in another hotel bar after an Ireland game. This time it was in Cardiff; Ireland had won 36-6 against a Welsh team destroyed by injury, and significantly the only few blazers who were celebrating with him were from Connacht. He was out on a limb.

England was the last of the postponed games. They came to Lansdowne Road in search of the Grand Slam, having been denied that title in the final game of the previous two campaigns. Keith Wood looked at the opposition line-up and told his colleagues that, without Martin Johnson, England was a different animal, and nothing like as formidable. Ireland went for them from the off, and applied a Munster-like stranglehold on the game. Wood got a storming try to set the scene, peeling round the back of a lineout. They had to hang on in the end but it was a tumultuous day. Surely Warren was safe now?

There was one game to clear out of the road before the All Blacks in November. Samoa fetched up and were routed with 27 points to spare. As a journalist it was hard to stay focused because the following Saturday there were so many angles to cover: it was Gatland's first game in charge against his native country; coincidentally it was the first time in charge of any game for his old mate John Mitchell, who had been appointed New Zealand coach the previous month. Like Gatland, Mitchell—a former team-mate in Waikato—had been an All Black but was never capped. This was the opening argument in Mitchell's case to take New Zealand to the World Cup in 2003.

On the day, it didn't look like even getting off to a winning start. After a blistering first half, at the end of which Ireland led 16-7, your attention shifted to the first few minutes after the break, to see if the backlash would be immediate, and what damage it might wreak. It wasn't and it didn't. And then Denis Hickie scored. Ireland were leading New Zealand by 21-7 early in the second half, and all around Lansdowne Road there were fans wondering if they were about to witness the first ever Irish win in this fixture. Three tries in 12 minutes restored normality to the scene. New Zealand ran out winners by 40-29, and the nature of the Irish collapse splintered another few planks in Gatland's case for survival.

Defence had long been an issue in the coverage of Ireland's performance that season. There had been many calls for Gatland to bring in a specialist coach in that area. He had used Leinster's Matt Williams for a couple of sessions, and maintains now that it was O'Sullivan who was uncomfortable with the arrangement. "At the time I would have continued to use Matt. But it just did not go down well with Eddie at all. Leinster were doing well at the time and Matt was doing a good job. I'd seen some people do defensive stuff and I felt he was as good as anything I'd seen. Maybe on reflection I should have bitten the bullet and done that and invited him on board."

Or maybe he should have brought in someone else. There was no mention at the time—privately or otherwise—that O'Sullivan was the stumbling block to Ireland getting up to speed on defence. "The problem I had with Mattie was that I didn't think he was a very good defence coach," says O'Sullivan. "I felt we needed a specialist, and that's what I got when I brought Mike Ford in soon after I was appointed."

In any case, the effect of not attending to this critical problem was seen at its worst against the All Blacks. It nearly drove the captain out of the game altogether.

"I nearly retired after the New Zealand game," says Keith Wood. "I remember having a conversation with Eddie when he got the job and he said: 'I want you to play till the World Cup.' And I said: 'I will,' but I was nearly gone. Because that just . . . it killed me. That was my chance to beat New Zealand. I'd never beaten them. We had it not done, but nearly done, and literally it was the harum scarum defensive structure that can work for 60 minutes but can't work for 80 minutes because it's inefficient. I was just so sick of it."

So the sequence had started with humiliation in Edinburgh and ended with frustration in Dublin. In between there had been the euphoria of seeing off England. And there you had it: ups and downs, and the hangovers were getting harder to shake off. If the IRFU were going to throw a few bob at this professional business then they wanted less heartache in return. They believed Gatland would cause them more pain, that he had taken them as far as he could. There was a perception of him as a poor planner, and that plans for training sessions would be written on the back of scraps of paper which were likely to be torn up at the last minute. He denies this.

"I don't sit down and plan a whole week's training," he says. "Some people do that. But I plan every day. And every day I would say to the players: here's the plan for today, this is what we're doing. There would be times in a session when I felt something wasn't going right or whatever that needed change, and I think every good coach should do that anyway, but definitely never, ever would a whole session be shredded by me."

COUNTDOWN

The general impression was that the win over England, the runners-up spot in the Championship, and the thrill of coursing the All Blacks for nearly an hour, would be enough to keep the coach in a job. That wasn't the feeling in 62 Lansdowne Road, however. Or at least among those who were deliberating on Gatland's future. They were given more cause for thought soon after that final test when I got a tip that O'Sullivan was the target of USA rugby who wanted him to take over through to the 2007 World Cup. It struck me as remarkable that this should fall into my lap at such a sensitive time, but I confirmed that the offer was genuine. That was on Sunday 25 November. Instead of the standard match review for the management group, all three—O'Brien, Gatland and O'Sullivan—were to attend individual sessions the next day. A sequence of events had been set in motion.

Monday 26 November, Dublin

The Review: Gatland met with Eddie Coleman (chairman), Syd Millar and Noel Murphy, who were effectively the appointments committee. Coleman was not a fan of Gatland's, while the other pair were lukewarm. Eddie Wigglesworth, the director of rugby development, was also present, and he didn't like Gatland much either. Then there was treasurer John Lyons, who had a fractious relationship with him, and chief executive Philip Browne, who got on well enough with Gatland but who didn't carry much weight on what was more a rugby decision than an administrative one. It was driven largely by Coleman. There was no naked hostility, and Gatland went back to Galway thinking it had all gone fairly well. At the back of his mind was the request made by Browne, in the weeks running-up to that meeting, that he use his time back in New Zealand over the Christmas to do a recce for the Ireland tour there the following June. Not unreasonably, Gatland inferred that Browne believed he would still be the coach by then. Browne hadn't intended it as a ring fence around his job, however. In any case, it wasn't his decision to make. The key figures were Coleman, Millar and Murphy, and Coleman was at the wheel.

Wednesday 28 November, Dublin

Gatland arrives up to the Berkeley Court as arranged, still believing everything is OK. "I thought they were offering me a contract," he says. He went up to the appointed suite where Browne and Coleman were waiting. "I came in and sat down and Eddie Coleman said to me: 'Warren, we want to thank you for everything you've done for Irish rugby. Thanks for that, but we're not going to renew your contract, effective immediately.'"

He was stunned. He mumbled something about being disappointed not to be taking the squad through to the World Cup, but it was a blur. They asked him if he wanted to ring anyone. He rang his wife, Trudy.

"And she was like: 'How's it going?' And I said: 'They're not going to renew my contract. They're going to let me go.'

"She said: 'What?'

"And I said: 'Have you got Billy Glynn's number?'"

Even though Glynn, a solicitor, was on the union committee, there was no objection to him representing Gatland in the severance discussions. "So I rang Billy and said: 'They're not going to renew my contract; they're going to let me go now.' And he went 'What?' He was gobsmacked on the other end of the phone. He didn't speak for a bit. Then he said all right, that he was quite happy to represent me. I went downstairs, and as I was going out the gate Eddie (O'Sullivan) was driving in."

Gatland bumped into union committee man, John Hussey, as he walked around to Jury's Hotel to catch the airport express and fly back to Galway. "All the best with the negotiations," said Hussey, seemingly oblivious to what was going on. At the airport, Gatland bumped into fitness coach Mike McGurn. He made small talk and said nothing. Then he went back to Galway and Glynn took over.

Thursday 29 November, Dublin

Glynn travels up to sort out Gatland's severance package. The IRFU planned to pay him off with €50,000 and six months' notice, as per the terms of the contract. The only problem was that there wasn't six months left on the contract, and so due notice couldn't be served. Glynn said that he could play the country shopkeeper, and put on figures to be taken off, or else he could give them the bottom line. The union's representatives went for the bottom line, but it was more than three hours before it had two signatures on it. It was a handsome, six figure sum.

Friday 30 November

The news breaks on RTÉ radio, just before the union make an official announcement.

Philip Browne rings Keith Wood in London to give him the news, and warns him to expect an avalanche. Wood is on his way into lunch in the Irish embassy, with the Irish ambassador and President Mary McAleese, and turns his phone off. When he turns it back on it's about to melt. He just has time to ring his brother Gordon in Limerick to collect him at Shannon. Gordon is pretty sluggish. He hmms and haws and eventually reveals he's just had a heart attack.

"What?"

"I've taken a valium. I'm here with the doctors. We're waiting for the ambulance to bring me to the hospital."

"OK, who's with you?"

"Nobody."

"Who knows?"

"Nobody."

"Right I'll call you back."

Keith presses the red button to end the call, and hits the menu to call up family numbers. Before he can access any of them the meltdown starts. It's a journalist looking for a comment about Gatland's sacking.

"Keith, if you have a minute there can you . . ."

"Sorry I can't talk to you . . ."

"But Warren's been fired . . ."

"Well my brother's just had a heart attack . . ."

"Oh . . ."

He had to leave his phone on so family could contact him, except that journalists kept getting in the way. They all rang off fairly quickly. Eventually Wood burst through the door of the cardiac care unit in Limerick Regional Hospital.

"Gordon," he gasped, "you wouldn't believe the shit you got me out of today!"

AFTERMATH

The reaction was immediate and dramatic. What the hell were the IRFU up to now? Talk radio, press reaction, the man in the street—it was virtually unanimous: Ireland had just dumped their most successful coach (49 per cent) since Ronnie Dawson's hit rate of 58 per cent at the beginning of the 1970s. Gatland had coached Ireland through 38 matches, of which they won 18. Their Championship record on his watch was progress on a page: having taken over after the first game of the 1998 campaign from Brian Ashton, the results went from last to fourth to third to second. And then they get rid of him?

Naturally enough the official statement didn't go into any detail, nor should it have, for personal as much as legal reasons. At the Belfast Harlequins dinner on the Saturday night, union president Roy Loughead had to refer to the development in his speech. He told the guests that Warren Gatland had taken the team as far as he could. It was as close to a public explanation as the union would get.

They shafted him because they wanted to get to the next level, and they thought O'Sullivan was the man to take them there. It was a good call. Just as Gatland had been the right man in 1998, O'Sullivan was the best candidate for 2002 and beyond. It might have been different had Gatland not happened across the job when the IRFU didn't know which end was up, but that's how it worked out. It might have been different too if Donal Lenihan took up where he left off as manager after the Lions tour. But he didn't. So Gatland's reluctance to engage with his employers, to bring in specialist help where clearly it was needed, to develop the structure and get Ireland beyond the point where there was a calamitous result around the next corner, went unchecked. This overtook the good he had done. He had put himself wholeheartedly into bonding a disorganised, demoralised group and giving some continuity to their careers. He coaxed more of them back home from abroad, and what they found on their return under Gatland was a great improvement on what they had left.

On the Monday morning news broke of an impending offer for him to go to Wasps. That was the start of the next phase of his career. He took with him what he had learned in Ireland, and later their former fitness coach Craig White, and turned Wasps into a silverware gathering machine. In his three seasons there as head coach they won the European Cup, the Parker Pen (European Challenge) Cup and three Premiership titles. Many presumed that because he went on to be successful at Wasps that it was a mistake to let him go in the first place. Why? Because a footballer scores against his old club does it automatically follow that the decision to transfer him was wrong? Being sacked by Ireland was the best thing that ever happened to Warren Gatland. Or perhaps the second best. Getting the Ireland job in the first place was a fantastic opportunity for someone of his age and experience. He took what he learned from that and applied it in his new life. It was one where he was spared the pain of trial by committee.

Into his place stepped O'Sullivan, who with a straight face managed to say that it was "a pleasant surprise". For the captain evidently it was a relief also. Wood had lost faith in Gatland, and you wonder would he have packed it in if the coach had been kept on?

"Who knows? I hadn't made any decision. I found that game (New Zealand) annoyed me more than I could possibly say. I can't make that call. He was fired and then Eddie was there and he asked me to make a commitment to the World Cup.

"I'd say Warren probably struggled near the end, because the team wasn't that team any more. You had Denis Hickie on fire, Brian O'Driscoll, Rog (Ronan O'Gara), we had lots of ball and lots of things to do, and it needed a new structure, and it needed to be technically astute because the game had moved on and it needed to be very technical. You still had to have all the passion and blah blah blah but it needed a bit more, and it needed more specialist coaches. We badly needed a defensive coach. We needed that for so long and were asking for that for so long."

It was ironic that when Gatland was at Wasps they developed a defensive system that terrorised other teams. And while he had never been close to Keith Wood, he became just that with Lawrence Dallaglio. Everything that had gone wrong in Ireland went right in London. And that wasn't an accident. He had moved on, with more knowledge and with a fresh appetite. And those he left behind were about to move on as well.

Chapter 9 ∿

WAKING THE WEST

The Assault on Connacht, 2002

Before you could shut down the laptop and sign off for the season, there was always one hurdle waiting right at the end. The agm: that crusty session in the ballroom of the Berkeley Court where the IRFU council would gather, and over the course of a few hours tick all the boxes on the season just gone, and elect many of the same faces for the new term ahead. Like most meetings of its kind, it was hard going. We would sit at the back of the room, scribbling down the bits and pieces that mattered, like how much money the union had managed to stash, and who would be elected to sit around the committee table for the next season. Sometimes there would be an item to break the monotony, but largely the operation would chug along predictably to its conclusion, whereupon all the blazers would adjourn for dinner.

There were two aspects of this get together that used to intrigue me. The first was about the colour of money. When the treasurer would give his report, it seemed a singular honour to be recorded as one of the pair who proposed and seconded its acceptance. In that little rigmarole there would be kind words for the splendid job done in bringing in such good figures, just as in the delivery of the report itself there would have been notes of caution about the future. The IRFU always seemed to have loads of money, and keeping it that way was a very big deal to them. It was as if the accumulation of wealth was a more satisfying business than the pursuit of silverware.

The other thing it took me a while to catch on to was Connacht. On a summer's evening in 1991, Tony Browne made his acceptance speech as the incoming IRFU president, with a nice little poem written for him by his daughter. Describing the journey of her dad to this high office, it ended with the lines:

What a long, long way to go
From the bogs below Belmullet
In the county of Mayo

Browne was only the sixth Connacht representative to be president. And there was something almost poignant about the scene, because you knew that he was there only because the big boys allowed it. There was a hierarchy, and nothing illustrated it better than the voting system. Every year, the four provincial branches would each nominate two names to go forward uncontested to the union committee. Then, at the agm, another six would be voted in from the floor. That six would be split evenly between Ulster, Munster and Leinster. Always. There would be nominations for Connacht men to have their names in the hat, and they would always be left there when the other names were fished out. It was pathetic. I asked a seasoned observer what the story was, how it had come to be fixed like this. "That's just the way it's always been," he said.

It reflected their fortunes on the field. They had never won the inter-provincial championship. If they beat any of the other provinces it was a cause for great celebration. They had fewer players and fewer clubs than the big three—just less of everything. In Ciaran Fitzgerald, who in the space of 10 years captained Ireland to two Triple Crowns and coached them in a World Cup, Connacht had not just their most famous son but their only son to operate at that rarified level. In his time, Tony Browne had gone forward for interview for the Ireland coaching job. When asked what he would bring to the party, Browne replied that he thought the team was in for some lean times, and coming from Connacht he knew a thing or two about lean times. It was a good line, but he didn't get the job.

These things popped up on the screen in November 2002 when it became clear that Connacht, the poor relation, was in grave danger of being chopped off the family tree. In a macabre way it was fitting that this was happening in one of the rare seasons when a Connacht man, Don Crowley, was in the president's chair. The way it was presented, this was a simple accounting procedure. The IRFU were looking at losses for the next two seasons, and they would sooner cut off a limb than see that situation continue.

In fairness, it wasn't as if Connacht had been the business model for professional rugby. In their own document—*Development Plan 1995–2000*—they had identified a poor support base and weak marketing structure as two serious issues. They had even gone as far as painting a picture which didn't feature themselves. It would have involved splitting the clubs along geographical lines and merging them with Ulster, Leinster or Munster. Under the heading: "Disband—An Easy Option?"—it was included, as the title suggested, more as a simplistic response to an ongoing problem than an ideal solution. By the end of that five year plan, however, the appalling vista was taking shape.

It was shortly before Christmas 1999 that a delegation from the Connacht branch was summoned to a meeting in the airport hotel in Dublin. There it was made clear to them that they were in a perilous position, that they were a drain on resources. It was Team Ireland who were generating the revenue that ran everything, and Connacht weren't exactly propping up the national squad. That was where the idea of Connacht as a development province was born: if they were going to fulfil a function, then let it be by exposing to competitive rugby young players who weren't front line choices in the big three. It was survival, so Connacht were happy enough.

It had its attractions. For a start, it would cost less, and a year later they would have their budget capped at €1.2m, less than half that of the other provinces. Moreover, it gave some comfort to the others that there was no chance of Connacht usurping them as they had been doing under Warren Gatland in 1997. It would have been interesting to see just how well they could have done had the plan been implemented as outlined. It wasn't. Perhaps it was a cultural issue that kept Ulster out of the party, but they would sooner have sent someone to the moon than to Galway. And as it was, they had enough problems trying to stop the flow of young talent to universities in Scotland and northern England. Leinster and Munster however had issues on neither front. They just suited themselves, and weakening their squads in any way didn't appeal to them. When the Celtic League expanded into a home and away format, in 2003/04, that would kill off the idea of sharing altogether.

Connacht soldiered on. In the background they were making real headway.

Since the game went professional they began making big inroads with the success of their under-age teams. Between 1994 and 1997 their under 21s lost 10 out of 10 matches. In the period 2001 to 2003 they won nine and lost three. Their Schools team had gone from losing every time they ran out, to breaking even against the second strings of the other provinces. Connacht contributed 17 players to the Irish Youths from 2001 to 2003. In the three years leading up the game going open that figure was five. They had grown impressively the number of Schools and the number of underage club players, and it was impossible to divorce this sales job from the fact that there was a shop window, which was the Connacht professional squad.

None of this impressed the accountants a great deal. They were transfixed by different figures. The forecast deficits for 2002/03 and 2003/04 were €4m and €6.9m respectively. The Foot and Mouth shutdown in 2001 had been a disaster; the revenues from television money were under pressure; the 2003 World Cup would cost them not just in preparation and travel, but also in its timing because the October/November scheduling in Australia killed off the usual autumn series in Ireland. That would be three paydays down the drain. And all this in a climate where the price of the professional game was frightening. From 2000 to 2002 the costs of national players and coaches went up by 40 per cent, from €4m to €6m. You wondered how poor John Lyons, the IRFU treasurer, would cope with this at the agm. He wasn't a happy man.

Philip Browne didn't sound too chipper either. He got to trot out a lot of figures to illustrate the grim picture. And his bottom line was this: "One of the major issues we have to face is the number of professional players that, one, we can afford to pay, and, secondly, the number that we have in the country," he said at the time. Naturally he didn't go into the historical reasons for why Ireland were struggling with numbers.

In 2002 there were 120 players on the books. The union talked about getting that figure down to 90, but more likely their vision was of 100 spread across three provinces. And they would be competing in a compact Celtic League of 10 teams: four from Wales—who were forging ahead with their cuts—and three each from Ireland and Scotland. Connacht didn't feature.

KICK-OFF

It got going in earnest in the week leading up to Connacht's Celtic League quarter-final against Munster in November 2002. The coverage about impending doom had broken the previous weekend, and on the

Tuesday their team manager, John Fallon, was interviewed on NewsTalk radio. Fallon was a local journalist who had taken a year out to do the Connacht job. From a personal point of view it was an especially interesting career break. And it proved useful for Connacht as well to have a journalist in a frontline position when the public battle started. Before going on air, his boss Gerry Kelly, the Connacht Chief Executive, had been reminded by head office that essentially Fallon was a union employee. He went ahead with the interview and called it as he saw it. He did even better in a subsequent interview with BBC Radio Ulster, suggesting to the presenter that if the culture of cuts took hold, Ulster could be next. "And I said: 'Well it's not going to solve the problem, it (cutting Connacht) won't even get rid of 50 per cent of the IRFU debt, so they will need then to go for the next weakest, and that's Ulster.' And the next minute he threw this back at me: 'How dare you say that!' He launched into it and got totally defensive."

Two days after his spin on NewsTalk, a union delegation comprising Philip Browne, Eddie Wigglesworth, John Lyons and accountant Conor O'Brien landed in Galway for what would be a stormy session with the local branch. Fallon was able to give them a printout from the union's own website which had added to the consternation in the Connacht camp.

Pat Geraghty was the Munster PR man but he was also editing the site, and in his preview of the game he had written:

". . . on Friday night Connacht players could very well be fighting for their livelihood and the existence of Club Connacht. Reports of union cost cutting don't automatically mean that the professional game in Connacht will be ditched, but there is always the chance that they just might be right."

Browne wasn't best pleased and subsequently wrote to Geraghty: "We are having difficulty enough in dealing with serious financial issues facing Irish rugby without our own website correspondent posting what at best could be called highly insensitive articles."

Postman Pat got it in the neck from the Connacht crew on the Friday night as well. Munster won 33-3 and went through to the semifinals. In a perfect metaphor, the lights at Musgrave Park had failed for a period early in the game. Connacht never quite recovered on the night, and strangely they were slow to get going off the field as well.

There was no more momentum to their PR campaign, no updates on how they were going to avoid the axe or what they had planned. Meanwhile the union were getting their four horsemen of the Apocalypse around to all the provinces as part of their review on costs. Optically this was good, and fitted in with their mantra that no decisions had been taken about anything and they would look at all the options, and not just Connacht. In fact they had three possibilities on the table: take the pain of a couple of budget deficits and look for other ways of generating revenue; make cuts across the four provinces; or simply scrap the professional team in Connacht.

With a view to staving off the third item on that list, Connacht exercised their right to demand an emergency general meeting of the union, and forked out the €13,000 that would cost. The meeting was scheduled for February, but the cheque was cashed as soon as it landed. They knew that it would be a rehash of the stitch up that passes for the agm, but this wasn't about a vote, it was about raising the temperature, about forcing the IRFU into the open where they were least comfortable. Early in the New Year the union found themselves in the eye of a very public storm.

BATTLE STATIONS

On Thursday 9 January, Gerry Kelly was driving into work in the Sportsground when an explosive item about Connacht came on RTÉ's Morning Ireland. According to the report, which was quoting from an article in that morning's *Irish Independent*, Kelly would be as well off turning the car around and going home. This was virtual confirmation that it was all over before it had started. There was an IRFU committee meeting scheduled for later that day, and according to Tony Ward, who had written the story, that was when the axe would fall. Kelly nearly crashed the car.

Not far away, Eric Elwood was getting a call from his wife Tara, who had just got a call from her mother. If Ciaran Fitzgerald was Connacht's most famous son, then Elwood was its most loyal. Over the years he had knocked back many offers to go abroad. Regularly during the 1990s he had been their sole international representative. He was their ambassador, and a very good one. By this point he was on the last lap, on one year deals because of his age, but it hadn't affected the way he felt about the place.

"Tara rang me and she said: 'What's this in the paper, what's going on?'" he recalls.

"I dunno Tara, I'm only after finding out myself. I'll ring you during the morning."

"What does that mean?"

"It means that after this year, this contract . . . I don't know, maybe I'm back on the road selling drink."

Elwood had been a rep with Irish Distillers. The advent of full-time professional squads meant that he could return to Galway from Lansdowne and play for his hometown team. He had taken some pride in the results they had carved out of hard days, and the players they had brought through: Johnny O'Connor, Gavin Duffy, Damian Browne. What were these guys going to do now?

The next phone conversation he had was with Tony Ward.

"And he went: 'Oh don't shoot the messenger, I was just given the story.'

'Jesus Tony I've been hit for six here, I'm after coming into work and I've no job now.'

"We were all distraught, and me being one of the senior players my phone was hopping with various people from the players to people around Galway. We just went upstairs to the Cawley room in the branch here and it was just: 'Fucking hell, what's going on?'"

Players were swapping notes, asking each other how long remained on their contracts. Then it would pop into someone's head that his girl-friend had just moved in and got set up in Galway. What next? A move to Ulster, Leinster, Munster . . . nothing?

"We were getting some clarification from Steph Nel (the Connacht coach) and Gerry, and they were saying not to worry that it was all speculation and we were asking: 'Where did Wardy get the story? It must have come from a reliable source. We need answers. Please help!'"

Help was coming. If Connacht had taken their foot off the gas in the wake of the story first breaking back in November, now it was full throttle stuff. Galway East TD Frank Fahey was one of the first politicians out of the traps, and soon there would be a pack close behind him, yelping away. This was the last thing the union wanted—outsiders telling them how to run their business. And how the outsiders had been invited in became a hot topic at the union meeting that afternoon.

It was significant that the story had been planted in the *Irish Independent* and not *The Irish Times*, which was the traditional rugby paper in Ireland, with a history of support for the IRFU. Eddie

Wigglesworth, the planter, knew that there was zero chance of a positive spin from Gerry Thornley in the *Times*. Over the years Thornley
had developed a close affinity with the West, but Ward was more likely
to present it as a fait accompli. The actual planting process began one
day over the Christmas when Ward was out shopping in Dún Laoghaire
and bumped into Wigglesworth. They chatted a bit about Connacht's
predicament, and the union man suggested the former international
outhalf might drop into the IRFU office and he could run through the
figures. On Tuesday 7 January Ward dropped in as invited. Two days
later he ran the story. The only things you could infer from the piece
were that Connacht were already dead, and all that remained was
the official burial; and that Ward had been briefed by somebody a lot
higher up the food chain than the nice man who runs the carpark.

> The cold financial facts of modern day professional rugby dictates
> an end to the traditional nurturing of the four-province system . . . .
> It hardly takes rocket science to deduce that some form of remedial
> action is urgently needed and it's understood the process of change
> will begin almost immediately.

Not only did Ward say that Connacht were done for, but he presented
it as an unpalatable task which the union were obliged to carry out. If
Wigglesworth had written it himself he couldn't have done a better job.
But if the director of development had hoped to remain under cover he
was disabused of the notion soon after the union committee convened
next. He had to admit to his colleagues that he had spoken to Ward, but
said that the Indo's man had added two and two and got five. Ward
remains absolutely adamant that his maths were on the mark. What
happened next supports his contention.

In order to pursue Wigglesworth's defence, Connacht representative
Billy Glynn suggested the IRFU write to the editor of the *Irish
Independent*. Given the degree to which the union's position had been—
allegedly—misrepresented, it seemed a natural course of action. The
motion was defeated by 14 votes to four. Instead it was decided that
Philip Browne should issue a statement to clarify the situation. If in
doubt, put a statement out. They also opted to bounce any cost-cutting
decisions back until their next meeting, a fortnight later. This was done
after Glynn had pointed out that any decision taken ahead of the egm

could risk a High Court injunction. The safe thing to do was kick to touch. And in that gap Connacht mobilised like there was no tomorrow.

There were two things they needed to achieve: to be seen to be coming up with credible alternatives for the union to save cash; and to further infest the political water so that the union couldn't risk dipping back into it. And the fear was they would, that they would bide their time and come back after dark when the heat had burned off and the story was no longer on the media's menu. For the first, they would come up with a good document which was respectful in tone but damning in content. In effect they said that the IRFU should have had L plates on the door of 62 Lansdowne Road, for if you opened the same door you wouldn't be able to find the office of the commercial manager. There wasn't one.

They produced figures from three cross channel clubs—London Irish, Harlequins and Pontypridd—which made the Irish operation look like a jumble sale. By that stage Ponty were already on the slippery slope—they would be gone by the end of the next season—yet their total corporate revenue exceeded the combined figure from Ireland's four provinces. How could that be?

Merchandising was another area where the Irish market was asleep. Between them, Harlequins and London Irish had generated nearly €1.4 from product sales.

Bear in mind, Irish provinces had contested three of the four previous European Cup finals. There were other things that seemed like common sense when you read them on a page, and mystifying when you realised they weren't already in place. The 2003 World Cup in Australia was a classic example. The IRFU used the tournament as an example of how preparing for it only drained their coffers. Connacht suggested it was a fantastic opportunity to turn a few bucks, to build events around the tournament that might cash in on the huge Irish population Down Under.

They also suggested that the union might like to get up to speed on the value of its property portfolio. Conveniently, these figures hadn't been revised in the previous three years, and so it facilitated the policy of woe and foreboding. Three years in the property game represented a whole lot of appreciation. If you knew the figure, it might leave you less inclined towards shutting down one of your four production plants. The irony in all of this was that if Connacht themselves had initiated some of what they were suggesting for head office, they might not have been in the predicament in the first place. Nonetheless, that didn't invalidate the points they were making.

Then there was the political campaign. At the lower end was IRUPA, the fledgling players' association which had been formed in October 2001. At the top end were the people who go in to Leinster House for a living, and know a bandwagon when they see one. IRUPA were in an awkward spot. They were dependent on the IRFU for their existence so when it was reported in the media that they were all hot for strike action it was a slight exaggeration. In fact they had never been balloted, but there was real support among their ranks for the threat to their colleagues in the West, and every report of that did no harm. They weren't always on the same political page as Connacht however. For example, at one point IRUPA suggested the egm be put back, which would have only relieved the pressure on the IRFU. Billy Glynn nearly lost his mind with Liam Toland, IRUPA's chairman, and bawled him out of it down the phone.

Occupying the middle ground in the political process was the public. They turned out in record numbers at Athlone for the first leg of Connacht's European Challenge Cup quarter-final with Pontypridd. Beforehand, Connacht Branch honorary secretary John Power was interviewed on RTÉ television and got across a powerful message of the good work that was being done west of the Shannon in building the rugby stars of the future. Ponty had demolished Connacht by 40 points earlier in the season in the Celtic League, but after a pulsating contest in Athlone they had only a five point lead to take with them into the return leg.

The memory of that day stands out for Dan McFarland, Connacht's players' representative. He had been under some strain from the start, not least because he came to Galway from Richmond, having seen that club become a casualty of the professional game. At the end of a typical day toing and froing between Steph Nel and the players, he would sit down at the kitchen table with his wife and wonder if the new life they had made for themselves was about to go down the pan. Again. It wasn't all stress though.

"That day was very emotional because all the walls were covered with faxes of support," he says. "You almost felt like you were Munster preparing for a final and you could imagine all the people from Limerick and Cork sending in faxes of support. You could imagine that all the time for Munster, but that wouldn't be normal for Connacht. I remember reading them all and it was absolutely fantastic. And then the crowd in Athlone were fantastic. The noise when we came out onto the pitch was something in Connacht we don't normally experience."

Four nights after that game a public meeting was organised for the Radisson Hotel in Galway. This was going to be an interesting test of the temperature. Poor crowds had always been an issue for Connacht, and team manager John Fallon went along that evening expecting the meeting to gather in a backstage bar, and hoping there would be a quorum. Instead hotel manager Mike de Haast, who was one of Connacht's sponsors, opened the door to the hotel's nightclub which was packed with rows and rows of seats. Fallon started to sweat. By the time it kicked off the place was packed with 600 people. The keynote speaker was former Galway hurler Joe Connolly.

In 1980 Connolly had made the acceptance speech from the Hogan Stand after the county had won their first All Ireland in 57 years. That scene has a special place in GAA lore. In the Radisson that night he spoke about the power of sense of place, and how, with the demise of GAA's Railway Cup series, Connacht rugby had become the sole representative of the province. Many in the audience were GAA players. This was an issue that went beyond rugby's clubhouses. It was oratory of a high order, and by its end the decision had been taken to march on Lansdowne Road. The backdrop to the meeting was a message on the video screen which read: "The IRFU have problems—The problem is not Connacht."

CLIMBDOWN

Hard on the heels of that decision to take to the streets came an IRFU statement that the union meeting of 23 January—the one where a decision had to be taken—would be postponed pending submissions from IRUPA and Connacht on a way forward. One way you could interpret it was as a move to allow the team some breathing space ahead of their second leg Challenge Cup tie with Pontypridd. Another would be that the union were trying desperately to defuse the situation. On the morning of that game in Wales however there was another incendiary device planted on the scene.

The squad were in their base in the Vale of Glamorgan when supporters, coming from the airport, arrived into the hotel waving copies of *The Irish Times.* "It was like *Playboy* arriving into first year in secondary school," recalls Fallon. "Everybody just pored over this." The article in question was a front page piece exposing the junket which the union committee and their wives were about to embark on in Rome, for the Ireland game against Italy. Juxtaposed with the public comments of Philip Browne about the need to cut costs and tighten belts, it was mortifying stuff.

Gerry Thornley wrote: "Although the Irish team will also be staying there, the cost of the trip, excluding the playing squad and management, is likely to be in excess of €100,000 and possibly as much as €140,000. The hotel has confirmed that even group rates would not dip below €325 for a double room or €270 for a single room. The Westin Excelsior is a luxurious five-star hotel and is described accordingly in the *DK Eyewitness Travel Guide to Rome*: 'Exotically sculptured balconies supported by statues set the tone for this extravagant hotel, which houses boutiques, saunas, a restaurant and a famous piano bar.'" There were differing accounts of whether or not the partners would be paid for. There was no argument about the scale of the exercise however: the booking was for 88 rooms for 3 nights.

Connacht lost that afternoon, 12-9, but the next week brought a powerful boost to their campaign. On the Wednesday, a series of meetings were held with TDs in Buswell's Hotel, opposite Leinster House. Over the course of a few hours, 28 representatives from across the parties dropped in. They were briefed on the catastrophe that would be the disbandment of Connacht's professional team. On the one hand you had a region of the country with a history of being dumped on; on the other you had a powerful sporting organisation with a reputation for secrecy. If you were in the business of garnering votes, there was only one side to this story. That whole exercise was powerful, and a further endorsement of the fact that this was an issue that would be dealt with very publicly.

The next day the march on IRFU headquarters took place. With only a week and a half to organise it, the newly formed Friends of Connacht rallied support from around the country. An estimated 2,000 travelled to Dublin and marched from St Stephen's Green down Baggot Street to the union's office at 62 Lansdowne Road. It made all the news bulletins. By that point it had become a *cause célèbre*, and clubs outside Connacht were keen to be seen on board, baling out water to keep the ship afloat.

Even though the union had postponed D Day until February, it was crucial for Connacht that they keep the story alive. It worked.

The only blot on their copy book was the clown who carried the placard with the legend: "IRFU Scum". Predictably the union were going ballistic over that one, but while across the board relations between HQ and Connacht were seriously strained, the respective chief executives Philip Browne and Gerry Kelly never lost touch. A week later all the contact came to a head in a series of phone calls made around simultaneous management meetings of the IRFU in Dublin and the Connacht Branch in Galway. In the end they agreed to keep on going, that Connacht would withdraw their request for the egm, and that the union would plough ahead with four pro teams. A statement to that effect was issued that night, 30 January.

In the end it came down to politics: in the climate of resistance created by Connacht, the union's bottom line would have to give way. They didn't like it, but that's the way it was. There were a few things in the background contributing to this. The day before the union's climbdown, sports minister John O'Donoghue spoke in the Seanad on the debate on the IRFU and the Connacht Professional Squad. That union business was being discussed at state level didn't sit with the IRFU way of doing things. O'Donoghue banged on about the great job the union had done, and how well Connacht had developed, and how he knew the union would come to the right decision. Of course he said that it was inappropriate for Government funding of the IRFU to be withdrawn, either through the annual Sports Council grant of over €3.75m which had come on stream in 2002, or through capital funding from his own department. But the fact that he had to touch on these issues at all was disconcerting for the union. What the minister didn't point out was that it might be a different story in a year's time if the union came looking for cash, and one of their four proud provinces had been ditched. Throughout, the IRFU's position was that the amateur game in Connacht was safe, as if it was unrelated to the professional side of the operation. It was a ludicrous position.

In March 2003, Philip Browne would address a Dáil joint committee on sport and tell the deputies that in the wake of Lens, the IRFU had woken up to the realities of professional rugby. "That (defeat) demonstrated that we had not really embraced professionalism the way we should have done, particularly in respect of support personnel," he said. "One cannot just pay players to do what they did when they were amateurs. One has to put all the support structures in place to allow them reach their full potential."

It escaped the IRFU that when you inverted that premise, it exposed their assault on Connacht as plain crazy. Why would you invest in support structures for developing players in the West when they had nothing to graduate to? John Fallon remembers one day when he requested from head office some promotional material to hand out at a Schools gig. Sure enough, a van pulled up outside the branch office, packed with posters. They were of Mick Galwey—in his Munster shirt.

There was another figure in the background: Mike de Haast, the general manager of the Radisson in Galway and a rugby nut from South Africa. His sponsorship of Connacht had got him interested in how the operation was run, and how it might be saved. When the crisis developed, he emerged from the background with a proposal. "When they wanted to cut Connacht off I thought there was a business opportunity there because bureaucrats don't run businesses," he says. "There was an opportunity I felt to take Connacht and commercialise it and there were three or four backers there to come in and we mooted the idea. It didn't get past a couple of phone calls, and it was put to us that even if they did disband Connacht there was no way they were selling the franchise, so they were prepared to bury it rather than make some money out of it and keep the province alive."

It's impossible to know to what degree de Haast's interest encouraged the union to stick with Connacht, but for sure the notion of selling, renting or leasing any part of the family silver left them cold. Remarkably, the union were prepared to give him a seat on their marketing committee. Unremarkably, he chose not to take it.

"You needed to market it (Connacht) and commercialise it in a way that didn't look at it from a cost point of view, but looked at it from a revenue point of view," he says. "They were looking at it as: 'We'll cut costs here and we'll cut costs there and we'll survive.' That's not the answer to saving the franchise. The answer to that was in increasing revenue, changing the profile of the players, putting the franchise on an even keel as everyone else and building a brand around it. That was the key to it. They still haven't seen that. And in fact they're only now seeing what the brand can do in Munster. They're only scratching the surface."

AFTERMATH

There was a price to be paid. Naturally enough, in the climate created by the IRFU, Connacht's young players had started to look elsewhere. Within two months of the reprieve, coach Steph Nel was going to England and 11 of the squad were also making tracks. On Good Friday, Gerry Kelly and John Fallon found themselves in Dublin's Montrose Hotel for a meeting with Eddie Wigglesworth. "If you think about it, one of the guys who had a serious amount of bricks and shit thrown at him was Wigglesworth, and once the decision was made he worked very hard for us, I remember, to his credit," Fallon says. "And if I was in his shoes I wouldn't have been half as accommodating. I was impressed by him. The decision was taken and he moved on. He knew I was responsible for a lot of the media stuff, and it just wasn't an issue for him. We went up there looking for help and we needed him to break into a sweat. It would have been the easiest thing in the world for him to busy himself with something else."

Connacht kept going. Michael Bradley came in as coach, the Sportsground was revamped successfully and by 2006 the long awaited floodlights had arrived. The development of Friday night rugby would help with building the brand, and how it needed to be built. It never made sense, as the IRFU were fond of doing, to compare Connacht's poor attendances with those from bigger catchment areas. But that didn't mean that a city the size of Galway, never mind the other towns in the province, had given all they had to give. Indeed the picture on crowd generation was clarified in 2004. On the day Munster were packing out Lansdowne Road against Wasps in the Heineken Cup semi-final, Connacht were filling the Sportsground for their Challenge Cup semi-final with Harlequins. People responded to success. And earlier that season, the place was thronged to witness the comeback game of England's World Cup hero, Jonny Wilkinson, when he lined out for Newcastle. So evidently people would respond to big names as well. Connacht didn't have much track record in either department.

The union never did lose as much money as they had forecast. For 2002/03 the deficit was €3.5m, and for 2003/04 it was €6.3m. This was achieved, according to treasurer John Lyons, thanks to savings made "where possible" and by events on the field. Between the varying successes of Ireland, Munster and Leinster, the intake had gone up. The most significant statistic though is from 2005/06, where there was a surplus of €800,000. Quite a turnaround. It has borne out the contention at the height of the Connacht crisis that putting them to sleep wasn't going to solve any financial problems. And had the needle been administered, there was no way you could wake them up again. It was a close call. The experience did nothing to suggest that—three years after the great wake-up call in Lens—either the IRFU or Connacht were alive to what professional rugby was all about.

Chapter 10 ↪

COACH AND CAPTAIN

O'Sullivan and Wood, 2003

Monday morning press conferences are never big with Sunday journalists. This one, we were assured, would be worth the trip. So on 22 September 2003, we made our way up to the Donnelly Suite in Dublin's Berkeley Court Hotel. It was an appropriate venue. My first time in that room had been nine years earlier when we were preparing for the last of the great amateur tours—Australia, 1994. The purpose of this assembly was indicative of how much things had changed in the interim.

Without much delay, union chief executive Philip Browne got to the point. The man on his left had a training session to get to, so the preamble was brief. And the punchline made an impression. "We're delighted to announce that Eddie O'Sullivan's contract has been extended by four years," he said. By the time Browne had got to the end of his spiel, your mind was focusing on the impact of the decision. It went beyond the simple fact that the IRFU were happy that they had the right man, and were moving early to hang onto him. It went as far as the assistant coach, Declan Kidney, and then up to the union's appointments committee, which had made the decision. It was a lot to take in.

By that stage, Kidney had been assistant to O'Sullivan for nearly two years. He had been put on the ticket when O'Sullivan succeeded Warren Gatland in November 2001. It seemed reasonable to infer at the time that he was being groomed to succeed O'Sullivan—five seasons as Munster coach; another few as Ireland assistant; next stop the top job. It was never stated to be the case, but if the union were getting into the business of logical progression, this seemed to be the start. Then, after two years wearing the bridesmaid's dress, they appeared to be telling Kidney that the best case scenario was to model it for another four years. That's a long time to be admiring the bride. Except that it was worse than that. When Browne's statement was teased out a bit, it emerged that O'Sullivan was not just head coach for four more years, he would have the ultimate say in hiring and firing his support staff. At that moment you couldn't see Kidney surviving in the job, even if he wanted to. In the grand tradition of Irish rugby management, they didn't get on.

Immediately questions were asked about the wisdom of making the announcement less than a week before the Ireland squad left for the World Cup in Australia. Why announce *de facto* that you were taking excess baggage with you, with the potential for disharmony in the camp? Why not simply wait until after the tournament and make the announcement then? Indeed, why invest four more years in O'Sullivan before a ball had been kicked Down Under?

In fact, the questions started back in 2001 when O'Sullivan and Kidney had been teamed in the first place. As Warren Gatland was stumbling from the scene, Eddie O'Sullivan was being fitted for the green jacket. Eddie Coleman, the chairman of the appointments committee, put a little drama into the question, as he addressed him across the table.

"Would you coach Ireland if you were asked to coach Ireland?" he asked.

"I would," said O'Sullivan.

"Would you have a problem working with Declan Kidney?"

"No."

"Well, you're now the Irish coach."

It's likely that had O'Sullivan been offered George W. Bush as his wingman he would have accepted, so close was he to realising his ambition of coaching Ireland. According to Coleman, Kidney's presence on the ticket was a joint decision by himself, Syd Millar and Noel Murphy, the other members of the appointments committee. The common perception at the time was that it was Murphy who produced Kidney's name. But Coleman maintains that it was a simple enough conclusion to arrive at because a) Kidney had the most experience of any of the provincial coaches at the time, and b) he was Irish. Nationality was a key factor, for there was a strong feeling throughout the game that we needed to develop from within. This fed the inference that Kidney was on a journey that would conclude with the top job.

"Well I don't know about that," says Coleman. "That wasn't part of it." So what about their compatibility as head coach and assistant?

"Our problem was that we'd have to ask both of them did they think they could work with each other," Coleman says. "I think the overall situation in relation to that was that, whether they could or not, they wanted the job. And they could work out whatever situation they had between them afterwards. But their immediate reaction was positive, and we didn't have to ask again."

This "executive selection" process gives you an idea of how the IRFU works. Effectively they had teamed two ambitious head coaches and given one of them top billing. This left the other one—Kidney—needing to excel in an area where he is not actually that good: technical coaching on the training field. His expertise is in overseeing an operation, charting its course and tuning its detail. All of which O'Sullivan was doing. It also made it harder for Kidney to do the brain bending with players, which he enjoys. Even before you got into whether or not the two coaches could be pals, the union had created a structure that militated against them succeeding.

Straight away there were columns of comment that this was an ill conceived partnership. But by the time they had racked up 18 wins from 24 games together, the issue of how much they liked each other had receded into the background. O'Sullivan's contract extension brought it back to centre stage. He was more than happy with the input of Niall O'Donovan as forwards' coach and Mike Ford who ran the defence. Both of them had been brought in at his request, soon after his appointment. Kidney, on the other hand, had been foisted on him. O'Sullivan was satisfied that he could pick up his deputy's workload with the backs and make a better job of it himself. By now the IRFU recognised that maybe it hadn't been a great match in the first place, so they would sit back and let O'Sullivan clean up the mess for them. Naturally enough, they didn't tell Kidney any of this. The first he knew of the new arrangement was when O'Sullivan announced to the coaching staff at breakfast, on the morning of the press conference, that he had signed a new contract.

"I think Declan was a bit stunned by it in the sense that he had gone in with Eddie," recalls Niall O'Donovan. "The two of them were appointed together by the IRFU; he felt that the IRFU should have spoken to him as well. He was taken by surprise and probably could see the writing on the wall."

For O'Sullivan, Kidney's removal had the added attraction of taking with it any threat to his own position. There had never been a bust up between the pair, but not long after their appointment there was an incident which O'Sullivan interpreted as a power play by Kidney. It occurred between the first and second tests on Ireland's tour of New Zealand in 2002, when at a management meeting the coach reckoned he was being railroaded by his assistant. Opinions from others who were there vary from the assistant trying to undermine the coach, to Kidney just being Kidney, and O'Sullivan taking it up the wrong way. Regardless, the only perception that mattered was O'Sullivan's. If they hadn't been close up to that point, thereafter the gap only grew wider. The first chance to put real distance between them came with O'Sullivan's change of status from head coach to kingmaker.

The issue of Eddie O'Sullivan's contract was first raised after Ireland had been blitzed by England in the Grand Slam decider, in March 2003. Both Syd Millar, who had succeeded Coleman as chairman of the appointments committee, and Philip Browne had suggested talking about the future, after the World Cup was over. It was O'Sullivan's agent, John Baker, who came up with the idea of securing a deal ahead of the tournament in Australia. Not only did he nail that down, but where the IRFU were talking about a two year extension, Baker got it doubled, all the way to the Six Nations in 2008. And best of all, he secured executive powers for his client. It was an extraordinary hat trick. Back in the early 1990s, when "Whither Irish rugby?" was a pop- ular enough fireside game, inspired by increasingly awful results, pun- ters used to look at Jack Charlton's success in taking the Ireland foot- ball team to successive World Cups, and conclude that, most of all, rugby needed a supremo. Well, they had one now. His coronation was the final seal on a campaign that had started in unlikely circumstances.

COACH

It was in late August 1996 that O'Sullivan walked into the office of solicitor Billy Glynn in Galway, and told him he was resigning from his position as Connacht coach. Glynn was the chairman of selectors— effectively the team manager back then—and he was taken aback, not least because the squad were due to convene in Dublin the next day and fly out for a pre-season tour to Sweden. For the previous few days O'Sullivan had been considering his position. Already he had sat down with Connacht officials and—he thought—sorted a deal for a three year contract at £25,000 a year. Then he got a call telling him the only thing on the table was one year at the same price.

Connacht's rationale was that the provincial season was only 13 weeks long, and they weren't about to commit to three years at that price. O'Sullivan's position was that he had already knocked back an offer to coach Ulster, and that it deserved some recognition. And he wasn't about to pass up a 40 year contract as a teacher for a one year arrangement with Connacht. He had been on leave of absence from the Holy Rosary Convent, Mount Bellew, since 1988, when he took up a job as a regional development officer with the IRFU. From there he had been seconded to Connacht. That IRFU job was now gone. It was time to choose: teaching or full-time rugby. He gambled on Connacht blinking, either in time for him to join the trip to Sweden, or perhaps when they came back after a painful few days without their coach. He lost on both counts.

Glynn left his office and was half way down the street when he bumped into fellow Galwegians clubman, Joe Healy. He explained what had just happened with O'Sullivan. "What the hell are we going to do now?" he asked Healy. The two of them thought about it for a minute and then Healy had a brainwave. "What about Gatty?"

In the blink of an eye, Warren Gatland was on his way from Hamilton NZ to Stockholm to hook up with the squad. Connacht had their new coach. There was worse to come for O'Sullivan. He had been combining the Galwegians coaching job with his Connacht duties. He thought the club arrangement was a stand-alone affair. Then he got a call from Galwegians telling him that job was gone too. They gave it to Gatland. "I was bitter at the time because I felt I had turned down Ulster and been genuinely up front with them (Connacht)," says O'Sullivan. "I hadn't asked for ridiculous money, just security of tenure and I couldn't see the problem. They were always talking long term and if it was a long-term job what was the big deal about?" He went back into school on the Monday morning, believing that the only way his two coaching jobs could have been filled so fast was with pre-planning. It was an understandable conclusion to reach, but it was wrong. O'Sullivan had a while to stew on what had happened. In that period he realised that he couldn't hack teaching any more, but he had to expand what was left of his rugby involvement. Where a week earlier he had enjoyed a busy portfolio that comprised Connacht, Galwegians and the Ireland under 21s, now there were just the youngsters. That episode had a profound impact on O'Sullivan. It defined his subsequent credo: you are what you negotiate. It hardened him; focused him on his ambition to go far beyond the level from which he had just been dropped like a stone.

Eddie O'Sullivan grew up in Youghal, the eldest of six children: three boys, three girls. His father was the chief electrician in a local co-operative, his mother was the homemaker. The two brothers followed the trade of their father. Eddie had other plans. He had played rugby from a young age in the local club, following the path of his uncles, and it developed his interest in sport. He started off as a hooker, opposing his brother Kieran with predictable consequences. His mother asked the coach that they be separated. That was the start of Eddie's career as an outhalf.

His first brush with a real career came during his first year in the local CBS. The Christian Brothers were on a recruiting tour for the order, and the young O'Sullivan signed on for a move to Ignatius Rice College in Dún Laoghaire. It was a moulding process for future brothers. After two years, and a good intermediate certificate, he went back home. There were more interesting things in life than becoming a Christian Brother. What he took back with him however was a basic grounding in studying and passing exams.

"It was a very strict regime obviously, and it was tough. Tough leaving home. Mass early in the mornings. Lots of prayers, lots of study, and after a couple of years of it I decided: 'This is not for me.' I just told my mother when I went home: 'I'm not going back.' It was no big issue. Lots of guys dropped out."

His next lesson in career guidance came one day in his last year in the CBS, back in Youghal. He tipped out the cardboard box which contained the leaflets about jobs. Architecture and PE fell face up. In the late 1970s, there was a queue down the street of people trying to get into Thomond College to study physical education. So they could afford to set the bar high. He worked hard to get over it, then harder still to stay up there when he got in. It was a heavy schedule and the attrition rate was high. Around him there were casualties occurring all the time, but it never entered his head that he wouldn't come out the far end in one piece. He had it figured. Maths was a problem, though. He wasn't a natural mathematician, so he had to put in the hours getting to grips with it. That was fine, because he didn't mind the work, and sleep was something he could wrap in a small parcel.

When he was a teenager, O'Sullivan would have passed a few summers keeping anti-social hours and getting by on minimum rest. It didn't involve late nights running with a fast crowd. There was a fishing tradition on his mother's side of the family—the same uncles who would have brought him down to the local rugby club—and he followed along without asking too many questions. The uncles had licences to fish salmon, and two open 14ft boats, each with a half mile of nets, for the task. In summer the salmon ran, and you could chase them between 6 a.m. on a Monday and 6 a.m. on a Saturday. "You got paid for what you caught," he says. "If you caught nothing you got paid nothing. It was 14 hours a day in an open boat and you'd fish at night: out at midnight and in at three in the day. Eat, go to bed, get up. It was like Groundhog Day.

"Funny enough I nearly had my lemon salad a couple of times out there. It was miserable. And it would freeze the balls off you. And you didn't wear a buoyancy aid. You were paying out net, and if you got caught you were gone with it. At the time you could make a reasonable summer's living out of it but it's died out now. My grandmother used to call it the famine season, not the salmon season. It was no big deal— you got a spot in the boat and off you went. And some nights the weather was shite and you'd be scared stiff out there. You didn't think about it at the time. But it was precarious, physically and financially."

Tony Ward was a colleague of O'Sullivan's in Thomond College, and it was he who dragged him out to Garryowen. With Ward at outhalf, wing seemed a better place to station himself. He was a good player; he weight trained hard and made the most of himself. It led to a regular spot on the Munster team with whom he picked up nine provincial caps over three seasons. But he was never mentioned in the 'best wings never to play for Ireland' category. Coaching would take him a lot further than playing.

That part of his life started a few years later when he was teaching in Mount Bellew. One evening Padraig McGann—one of the most inspirational figures in Irish rugby—called to his door and inveigled him into helping out with the kids in Monivea. It's a rugby dot on a GAA map in Galway, but McGann had contrived a military operation to get kids playing the game. At the appointed hour, O'Sullivan was there for his first session, standing in the field, having been given a fertiliser bag full of balls and a few two by four planks, for whatever. The place was deserted. From nowhere, two buses appeared. "And the Barbarian hordes descended," he recalls. "All looking for the Coke and crisps." There was no going back.

By the time his career stalled in Connacht in 1996, he had a reasonable CV that included club coaching in Galwegians and Blackrock—the first was a failure, the second a success—and plenty of experience in Connacht both as assistant and head coach. Plus the Ireland under 21s. Now he was stuck. Then, over the Christmas, he got a call from his friend George Hook. Things were looking up.

Their relationship has soured now, which is a pity, because there was a time when Hook and O'Sullivan made a very good team. Hook believes his old friend has paid scant regard to the role he played in the development of O'Sullivan's career. O'Sullivan thinks he has it about right.

It was a little and large combination where their polarised personalities seemed to attract. Hook was driven by the desire to please people; O'Sullivan by the need to succeed. Hook was Connacht coach when he borrowed O'Sullivan from the IRFU. He was in the background too when O'Sullivan had succeeded him in Connacht, and again when his successor was trying to negotiate a more secure contract in the West. It was Hook also who turned to his friend for help in structuring and running coaching courses in the United States. This time, when Hook rang, there was more work in America, and also the possibility of linking up with Jack Clark, coach to the US Eagles. Soon enough, O'Sullivan was breaking the news to his wife Noreen that from April to September 1997, he would be criss-crossing America, coaching coaches with George Hook and coaching Eagles with Jack Clark.

Things got better again when the Buccaneers came looking for a coach. They needed someone to help them into the first division of the All Ireland League, and O'Sullivan needed a winter job. They won promotion with him in his first season, and it put his face back in the frame in Ireland. In fairness to Eddie Coleman in the IRFU, he had put the odd call into George Hook to see how O'Sullivan was getting on in the us. He was doing very well thanks. So well that Clark had offered him an improved package that would have involved moving lock, stock and barrel to California. "It was a good salary and the scope to develop my own programme," O'Sullivan says. "I would have had to move Noreen and the two kids out to Berkeley, and they would have found us a nice place to live in the Bay area. I was thinking: 'Why not? You've taken one step in that direction, why not two?' And then the IRFU came in and offered me the assistant's job after Lens. And I thought: 'They're not going to ask me a second time.'"

CAPTAIN

It started with a bang in the neck in the first game of the season 2002/03 for Harlequins. Nothing significant, but enough to register as a problem. Then circumstances conspired to make it worse. Which was nothing compared to what would unfold off the field. It was the start of the World Cup season, and Keith Wood was full of enthusiasm. He was happy as captain of his country; he had a great relationship with the coach, Eddie O'Sullivan; and Ireland had a decent squad. This might well be his final fling. If so, he planned on signing off with magnum force. Wood didn't know it then, but his route to Australia would be an endurance test of the mind and body, of the head and the heart.

In the first week of September, Ireland were preparing to play Romania in Thomond Park. It was a warm-up game for later in the month when the squad would go to Siberia to play Russia in a World Cup qualifier, a burden passed down from the defeat in Lens in 1999. By failing to make the last eight in that World Cup, they had to qualify for the next. In the run-up, Wood wasn't too bothered about his sore neck. He was training away, with half a mind on Romania and the other half on his wife, Nicola, who was due to give birth to their first child back in London. The match had an extra dimension to it because Wood was to lead out the team with his nephew, David, as mascot. There was a web tying these characters together. David is the son of Gordon Wood, Keith's brother. As it happened, Gordon was seeing Siobhan, daughter of team manager Brian O'Brien. They planned to marry. Two days before the test, O'Brien pulled Wood aside as he was on his way into a team meeting. He told him that Gordon had just suffered a fatal heart attack. He was 41 years of age.

It was extraordinarily difficult for lots of reasons. Wood's mother, Pauline, had been in poor health for some time, and having to bury her son was a trauma none of the family had bargained on. Keith is the youngest of seven—three boys and four girls—and though his brother John is closer to him in age than Gordon, when it came to talking about the game it was invariably Pauline and Gordon who were the sounding boards. As soon as the funeral was over, Keith had to think about getting back to his wife. The earliest flight to London was out of Dublin, so his brother-in-law drove him from Clare in the middle of the night to make the connection. The moment he landed in Heathrow he called his wife's sister.

"She wouldn't tell me because she wanted me to have a surprise," he says. "But I was in such a bloody mess I was thinking: 'Is this a good thing or a bad thing?' It was quite unusual because Gordon dying had left me incredibly numb. Everything was really all over the place when I got into the car. I got in to the hospital after Alexander was born. And I watched and I saw the baby and it was brilliant and fantastic, but I didn't . . . I was happy but I was almost sad in equal measure. It was an incredibly strange feeling. And it was very strange for about three weeks."

He played a club game the next weekend, with a view to getting back on track. He is eternally grateful to Harlequins coach Mark Evans for letting him stay on the field, for his form was brutal. In his head he was miles away. And he had to get it sorted for the trip to Siberia. For the rest of us it promised something different: a detour from the well beaten track of rugby destinations. Getting there was an end in itself. For the media, the only feasible option was to take up seats on the IRFU charter, which was flying from Dublin to Moscow to Krasnoyarsk. They charged top dollar for the privilege. Unfortunately, the aircraft was from the bargain basement. A marathon journey across seven time zones concluded at last in a Siberian airport at 3 a.m. It was a horrible trip, and the sight of the players struggling with the economy seats reminded you of a previous era when the committee flew up the front. There was nothing like business class on this one.

The game was never one Ireland would lose, but against a massive and very physical home team, and fatigued from the journey, it was as uncomfortable as had been feared. Ireland won 35-3, and the captain got on the scoresheet—his 14th try for his country. He looked utterly exhausted as he took questions, still in his gear, under the dodgy looking stand in Stadium Centralny. Like Wood, it looked like it could collapse at any moment. On the journey home he was in a bad way, and his hand was numb. It turned out he had a burst disc in his neck. For a front row forward, this is as bad as it gets. He was told to forget about the second World Cup qualifier, against Georgia, and the autumn series as well. At that stage the medics would take another look.

Unusually for a professional athlete it was a good time to be injured. It gave him the time to do two things: bond with his son; and present the same boy to his grandmother. The first bit unfolded beautifully on a long day watching the Ryder Cup. Wood had passed up the offer of tickets for the Belfry, and followed it from a distance instead. "I sat on the bean bag in front of the telly with Alexander on my chest. And I remember watching (Paul) McGinley—and I'd played with him a few times—and I was looking at him thinking: 'God McGinley, you're playing great; I don't think you're going to win but you're playing great.' And then ultimately he sank the putt to win it at the end and he went ballistic. And I bonded with my son at that time. It was the first time my head had nothing really going on in it. I mentioned it to McGinley and he gave me the shoes he was wearing that day, which was very cool. We didn't move from that bean bag all day, apart from when Alexander was being fed."

The second bit—bringing his son home to Killaloe—was a happy trip. It was perfectly timed. The autumn series was a significant period for him to miss, starting with Ireland's first win over Australia since 1979. Beating a southern hemisphere nation was a huge step. Fiji were wiped the next week, and then Argentina arrived into town for the concluding game of the series. Ireland had lost the previous two tests against the Pumas, and were due to face them again in the World Cup pool nearly a year later. There was a lot riding on it. For this one, the plan was for Siobhan's son Alan to be mascot. Then Pauline Wood died at home in Killaloe on the morning of the game. Wood got from London to Clare in record time. He stayed a while.

"I needed to get over it," he said soon afterwards. "I needed to get over it in Killaloe. If you go away you just distance yourself from it a bit. It was very, very hard. The three weeks I spent there were invaluable. Then I went back again for a week at Christmas. In a lot of ways being injured helped me on the grieving side of things. Mark Evans at

Harlequins was fantastic and Eddie was fantastic. Brian O'Brien was out at the house a lot and it was hard for him."

The in-between week was his all clear to come back for Harlequins—22 December. He got a run as a replacement in the second half against Leeds. Things were going grand, and then he tackled the rampaging Zac Feaunati, a tricky business at the best of times. Wood's recent history suggested these weren't the best of times. Within minutes of cooling down afterwards his arm wasn't working too well. He contacted his surgeon, Ian Bayley.

Wood was able to refer to him as 'his surgeon' because they had a long relationship. It was Bayley who fixed him after the shoulder dislocation in the 1995 World Cup. By then the hooker had undergone major surgery for the same problem in Ireland two years earlier. Now, combined with the neck injury which had cost him the autumn, here was more trouble. For sure he was going to miss the start of the Six Nations in February 2004. At that point, the odds lengthened on him getting as far as the World Cup in Australia. Bayley scoped the shoulder, tidied up a couple of things, but was happy there was no structural damage. Ireland forged ahead without him, with hooker Shane Byrne making the most of a late arrival to test rugby. The next point in the plan was the France game in early March. He missed it. The rest of the Six Nations was written off. And increasingly, so were his chances of ever coming back.

Luckily, Ireland were doing well without him. In a perfect finale to the championship, Ireland and England were unbeaten coming to their meeting on the last weekend in March. A Grand Slam finish. Meanwhile, in the gym at Harlequins, Wood was becoming increasingly confident about his own situation. He turned to the physio in the week of the game and said: "You know what, if Frankie Sheahan or Shane Byrne got injured I'd be ready. I could say to Eddie: 'Come on, slot me on the bench, I'll do a job. I don't care if I wreck my shoulder, this is a chance of a Grand Slam. I'd be on for that baby!'" Then he went outside for some light running, picked up a ball and stopped after a few throws. Revise that opinion. More trouble. Back to Ian Bayley. He prayed that the surgeon would find something simple that could be fixed. Mercifully, he did. And within a week the joint was moving freely again. The World Cup was now six months away, and there would be warm-up games where he needed to show he could still function. Wood moved back to Ireland to cover the last few miles of the journey from there. He felt good. For the first time in a long time, he felt good.

PARTNERSHIP

As soon as he had cleared the protocol after succeeding Warren Gatland, Eddie O'Sullivan hopped into the car and drove to Killaloe. And there he spent the day, listening to what Wood wanted. As the captain pointed out something that needed to be changed, O'Sullivan ticked the box on the sheet in front of him. They were on the same wavelength. They wanted a better plan of attack, a coherent form of defence, better analysis of themselves and the opposition. They wanted more information for the players about what was happening and when. And they wanted to change Wood's role: he needed to have more influence on direction, and he needed to share the load of leadership.

It was significant that Wood had taken over the captaincy in the most turbulent period of Irish rugby history, yet had so few opinions on what was going on around him. The departure of Murray Kidd; the arrival and departure of Brian Ashton; the Pa Whelan controversy—all these things happened around him, yet it was if he was the last man who could tell you what the hell was going on. He was only the captain. He was also the captain who did all the talking in the dressing-room and on the training field and on the pitch. If he was getting tired listening to himself, what was it like for the rest of the team? So the load would be shared with old hands such as Mick Galwey and Peter Clohessy—both of whom commanded huge respect in the squad, and both of whom were coming to the end of their careers—and Anthony Foley, who had plenty of time ahead of him and was also a natural leader.

"I wanted more input at that stage because I didn't want to be responsible for the team without having an input," Wood says. "I wanted us to win. I was opinionated. I wanted my opinion heard. It didn't matter to me that I didn't get my way, it mattered that I had a say and an input and that that might have an influence. It was very hard to get to that stage previously because there was a whole host of coaches beforehand, and people were uncomfortable in doing it. Now you had a situation where there were more guys to rely on and they gave a different perspective."

Wood and O'Sullivan got on from the start. There was a mutual respect that each knew what he was about, and it was enhanced by a friendship that developed when O'Sullivan was assistant to Gatland. Before one game in that era, Gordon Wood had suffered a heart attack in the US, and O'Sullivan mobilised his American connections to get Siobhan out there at the drop of a hat, and to have Gordon looked after. The longer they worked together, the better they got on. It did, however, cause Wood to fear that their friendship was putting O'Sullivan in an awkward position. True, it was the coach who had presented the World Cup as a target for the captain to aim at, but with the injuries mounting, it changed the complexion of things.

"I'd said to him at one stage: 'You don't have to worry about picking me or picking me as captain, it's not something you need to be thinking about because we're good friends.' I wanted to make certain that he was looking at it totally logically and I said: 'Look, you don't have to worry about that, I'll respect you anyway so it doesn't really matter.' And he said:

'Will you play in the World Cup?'

'I will.'

'Will you play well?'

'I will.'

'Well you're captain so.'"

AUSTRALIA

To his credit, Declan Kidney swallowed the bitter pill and didn't complain about the taste. At least, not within earshot of anybody. He wasn't exactly at the heart of the operation, but he was absolutely professional in going about his work. And it was hard for him. There were press conferences almost daily, and he would sit alongside O'Sullivan—just the pair of them—with only a fraction of the traffic flowing in his direction. One day in Terrigal, where the squad was based to begin with, I asked him a question about something or other, just to break the monotony. He seemed startled. I don't know who was more embarrassed, him or me.

It was an entirely different set-up to the same gig four years previously. Now, in beautiful sunshine and with the Pacific Ocean as a magnificent backdrop, Ireland looked every inch the professional outfit they aspired to be. The measure of that would come in their penultimate pool game, against Argentina. Defeat by the Pumas in 1999 had redefined the way the IRFU approached professional rugby. The infrastructure around the national side since then had been transformed. Now there was real autonomy for the man charged with running the show—O'Sullivan—and by extension to his commander in chief—Wood. Losing to Argentina again could rob the union of its appetite for the new order. It was unthinkable.

Ireland's programme read: Romania, Namibia, Argentina, Australia. The consensus was that the hosts would top the pool, leaving Ireland and Argentina in a dogfight to qualify for the quarter-finals as runners up. They would meet in Adelaide. The expectation was that Ireland would get there easily enough, but that the Pumas would lose in the opening game of the tournament to Australia. It all went according to plan. Ireland took care of Romania and Namibia; Argentina lost to Australia before beating Namibia and Romania. We arrived into Adelaide from Terrigal on Monday 20 October. It would be a long week in perhaps Australia's dullest city. Lots of time to think about the magnitude of Sunday.

Everything about this game induced tension. O'Sullivan's selection reflected the tenor of the battle. He passed over Keith Gleeson at open side and Anthony Foley at number eight, and opted instead for a massive back row combination of Simon Easterby, Alan Quinlan and Victor Costello. No leashes, no muzzles, just a dog fight for the biggest canines around. The days leading up to the game were dominated by flashbacks to Lens. Even the meeting between the teams in November 2002, which Ireland had won on a foul day in Lansdowne Road, had ended in a welter of bad blood and accusations by the Irish over incidents of eye gouging.

Twenty four hours before the game, also at the Adelaide Oval, the stage was set by a meeting so lopsided that it served to emphasise what was coming. Australia beat Namibia 142-0, scoring 22 tries. After five minutes of that one, people were willing Ireland and Argentina to get it on.

I've never felt such a sick feeling as that day, the worst I've ever felt either playing myself or being involved with the national team. The players I'd say were worse because I remember the meeting room we were in and it was like we were being sentenced to death. It had been a hard week, and more so I suppose psychologically. But that meeting had a sick sort of atmosphere. It wasn't like anybody was looking forward to the game. I'll never forget it.

Mervyn Murphy is the video analyst. It wasn't as if he had to play, yet the tension he felt was replicated to varying degrees by everybody with more than a casual interest in the outcome. Only the punters downstairs in the lobby of the team hotel seemed oblivious to the burden. The players trooped out and onto the team bus looking like they might never be back. The atmosphere at the ground was strange. Tea time on a Sunday didn't help. The Adelaide Oval is a picturesque setting, with stands like pagodas, and at one end of the ground there is a magnificent scoreboard defining the scene. But the distance between the crowd and the rock hard pitch left you wondering were you really there at all. And that's a bit like how Ireland played in the first half. They appeared to be having an out of body experience. A painful one at that.

There was a passage midway through the half that summed it up. Malcolm O'Kelly stole a Puma throw, only for Wood to miss Alan Quinlan at the tail just as Ireland looked like generating some momentum on the next throw. From that possession, Gonzalo Quesada sliced the ball out on the full. And Ireland promptly lost the lineout again. When Quesada kicked it down to Girvan Dempsey, the full back put that one out on the full. And when Denis Hickie kicked a ball on the next play, he sliced it straight into the arms of an opponent.

The Pumas had started as nervously as Ireland, but all the possession they got in that half calmed them down a bit. Were it not for Quinlan's intervention, Ireland would have turned over at the break in arrears, despite having had the wind. He scored a cracking try after a great break by Wood, but dislocated his shoulder hitting the ground as he bounced over the line, tackled by Ignacio Corleto. At the half time whistle, Eddie O'Sullivan turned to Niall O'Donovan as the coaches made their way towards the tunnel. Ireland were 10-9 in front but the lead meant nothing. "We have to get them refocused," he said. "We have to get a grip on the game. This is going down to the wire."

The interval was devoted to bracing themselves for the endgame, to get there in one piece without doing anything stupid. In the second half things got a bit better, but not much. Quinlan's departure didn't help their lineout. At least Federico Mendez was in the horrors with his throwing, so it could have been worse. Then disaster struck. O'Sullivan sprung Ronan O'Gara from the bench in an attempt to get some authority into the outhalf slot where David Humphreys was having no positive effect. O'Gara was on the pitch a minute when he got a pass under pressure from Wood, in his own 22. He scrambled the clearance kick and left it short. It was fielded by Diego Albanese, the try-scoring hero from Lens. He passed infield to Corleto. The previous November, it was Corleto's spillage of an O'Gara kick that cost Argentina the game. He took one look at the posts, and from about 50 metres dropped a magnificent goal. Argentina were in front. It was happening again. High in the stand, Eddie O'Sullivan's life replayed on fast forward.

"If we'd lost that game you could sum up my tenure as a complete 'gone nowhere' situation. So we'd lost in Lens, and even with forewarning we'd lost again in 2003. Now you could argue the toss but it would be very hard. It was the most stressful match I'd ever sat through, where your whole life was flashing before you. Like, everything that happened was going to impact on your life. If we'd lost that, people would have said we'd actually gone nowhere in the past two and a half years. The bottom line would be that we failed to get to the quarter-finals of the World Cup."

The O'Gara substitution paid out, however. He came off the bench determined to have a go, and not sit back, and he did that. His two penalties gave Ireland enough breathing space to withstand another three points from Quesada. When the final whistle went in the 83rd minute, Ireland were 16-15 in front. They had just about enough energy to celebrate the long shrill blast. It had been a monumentally bruising battle. Both Reggie Corrigan and Wood had been gouged, which would cost the perpetrators, Mauricio Reggiardo and Roberto Grau. That was for another day and another court. For now, the decision that mattered had gone in Ireland's favour. It was the first full game Wood had completed in a year.

"Jesus that was so hard," he says. "I had a meltdown immediately after it. I'd a guy who caught me to do a flash interview while I'm standing on the pitch. I said: 'No, I'm going into the changing room first; I'll come out then.' He said: 'You're contractually obliged.' 'Fuck off,' I said, and he followed me all the way down the tunnel pulling at me. And I said: 'Pull me once more and I'll bust you with whatever energy I have.' He was waiting outside for me when I came out and I said: 'Sorry, now can I do anything else for you?' I did the flash and came in and sat down and got full-blown shakes. I was retching inside there. I had nothing left after that. I've a photograph of me covered in ice: under my arm, over my arm, my elbow."

END OF THE ROAD

Of course the load carried into that fixture was unreal. It didn't make sense that everything that had happened post Lens would be invalidated if it had been Ireland on the end of a one point defeat instead of Argentina, but that was the atmosphere of the time. And in that mood you didn't know how the union might have reacted if it had gone wrong. So it was a good night for the committee men as much as the players who looked towards the Australia game the next weekend like it was the first day of the rest of their lives. If the team meeting before the Pumas game had been deathly, then this was at the other end of the scale. And they played accordingly. The performance that night in Melbourne was the best since O'Sullivan and Wood had taken over. In a thrilling contest, they lost 17-16. This time it was David Humphreys who came on for O'Gara, and he had a drop goal to win it which drifted inches wide. Seconds after the final whistle, I came across Tim Horan, who had been next door to us commentating for Australian television. He looked as relieved as any of the Irish had a week earlier. "Aw mate, you should have won it," he said. "You had your chance." He was right.

And the prize for winning was fantastic. Victory would have brought Ireland north to Brisbane for a quarter-final with Scotland. After a generation of heartache against them, Ireland didn't know how to lose to the Scots. They had won the previous three meetings with ease. It was a ticket to the World Cup semi-final. A ticket which the Wallabies picked up without breaking sweat. Instead, Ireland stayed in Melbourne for another week, at the end of which there was France. And wouldn't you know it, after cruising out of their pool, the French were about to hit their peak.

Keith Wood had a theory about them. It was the 20 minute test. After that period, he reckoned, you knew if you were in with a chance or already dead in the water. The opening quarter in Melbourne was the best 20 minutes France put together that season. Ireland were floating, face down. It finished 43-21.

"We'd worked so hard at defending against (Olivier) Magne in the wide channel," recalls Mervyn Murphy. "And to see it fall apart for the first try in front of our eyes—everything we'd practised in training—after that it was all downhill. I remember walking home across the bridge that night with Fordy and Mike McGurn and we were distraught. It was a dreadful feeling. I really felt against France that we could do a bit of damage."

During the week, Wood came across France's captain Fabien Galthie at an official gig. They knew each other reasonably well at that stage, and shared a few words about the impact of what was around the corner. One of them would be going home for the last time; the other would get to play another day. Retirement wasn't a subject Wood had spoken about. Given the way it had all ended, there was little doubt about what would happen next. Ireland's greatest player of the professional era was wrapping up. Eddie O'Sullivan stood back in admiration.

"He went through hell and high water, and all the way through the two us kept saying: 'It's just another setback—the World Cup, the World Cup. We kept thinking towards the World Cup. And he got there, and the great thing was that he had a great tournament. A lesser man would have packed up his tent and said this isn't going to happen. And then when he got there he didn't just say: 'I'm here now isn't it great?' He actually delivered. He was outstanding, a great captain and great around the lads. So all that emotion was bottled up. It's not something you'd talk about. It sounds dramatic, but to witness up close the end of one of the greatest Irish rugby careers of all time . . . It's hard to argue: who is a better ambassador or player? He ticked all the boxes. He was the man. And suddenly you're going into Melbourne's Telstra Dome to play a test match against France at 8.30 p.m., and at 10.30 p.m. the best career in world rugby—as I saw it—is over. Just like that."

Chapter 11 ⌒

CLUBS

The Never Ending Story, 2004

To understand where the clubs were at in 2004, you have to go back a bit—to the time when the results round-up on a Saturday afternoon was broadcast to a captive audience in the middle of winter. When you look at what they once had, at the position they enjoyed in Ireland's rugby hierarchy, you begin to appreciate their predicament years later when the professional game took off, leaving them trailing behind. Their pain was especially hard to bear because they had been in Sleepy Hollow before, and had no wish to go back. They had hauled themselves clear and into the heady new world of the All Ireland League. In the early 1990s it was a vibrant scene. Thomond Park on 25 January 1992 captured it perfectly.

From the double doors into the function room at one end, to the wall at the other, measures 30 metres. It wouldn't seem like that if you're moving in great big strides, and Brent Anderson is eating up the ground. He is 6'5", over 17 stone, and dressed in crisp white shorts, sky blue socks and sky blue Garryowen jersey with the star of the sea on one side, and the Audi logo on the other. His bullet head is defined by the tight white headband. His eyes are on fire. Outside, the ground is packed with somewhere between 10,000 and 15,000 people. Estimates vary. Either way, the numbers inside there on this day is new territory for a competition that has taken Irish club rugby by storm. Shannon are playing Garryowen in this make or break round of the All Ireland League.

Shannon are leading their opponents at the top of the table by a point. There are three games to go after this, but whoever wins today will get a turbo boost towards the title. The focus is on Limerick, and which of that city's clubs will be the first to lift the trophy.

Underneath the stand it's as if Anderson is in a world of his own. It's best to flatten yourself against the wall as he storms past. Of course there have to be people coming and going at that time, for the match is only minutes away. Nobody gets in his way. This is what his team-mates in Waikato used to call The Polar Bear Walk. Back in the dressing shed—as they would call it—in Hamilton, Anderson had a similar track. At one end there was a steel beam; at the other a wash basin. He would stomp back and forth between the two, looking like a father prowling the streets for the boy who had kept his daughter out late.

"I'd walk up and down, and lo and behold anyone who got in my road. I was just thinking about what we were going to do; what was I going to do; how was I going to react to certain situations that occurred. The last thing I needed to be doing was running up and down on the spot, pulling the chains high, pulling the chains low and hitting myself and all the other stuff that used to go on. I often thought about it afterwards, that I'd seen Irish teams coming out and playing like men possessed, like there was something inside them to make them go nuts. I always remember Willie Anderson leading the charge into Buck* and that sort of thing. And having been in the Garryowen dressing shed beforehand I could see how that sort of thing happens, and sometimes because of that players would run out of emotional energy. They'd burned everything up. I sort of moved away from that. I was probably a bit like that when I was younger, and as I aged—I was 31 when I came over to Ireland—I'd worked out what worked for me, and that was a sort of up and down pacing and really trying to focus and concentrate on different events that were going to occur in the game and how was I going to deal with them."

For Garryowen it seemed to be all going wrong. They had lost out-half Nicky Barry in the run-up. In the game itself winger Gary Quilligan was carried off early, and before half time flanker Paul Hogan had followed him. And yet they won a thrilling contest, 20-9. They were irrepressible that season, and the player who epitomised it was their hooker, Keith Wood. Anderson reckons that day against Shannon was when the hooker came into his own. Certainly he was the player of the league that season, and by the time they got to Temple Hill for the penultimate game, against Cork Constitution, Wood and his team-mates were within touching distance of the title. At the same time, back

* Wayne Shelford, former New Zealand captain

in Limerick, Shannon were at home to Ballymena and needed to win to keep the campaign alive going into the final week. Down in Cork, Garryowen kept their end of the bargain and were deserving winners over Con. There were a few minutes to spare before the Shannon game ended. The Garryowen fans gathered outside the dressing-room. It is etched on Anderson's mind.

"My undying memory was that somebody had a cell phone—and we're talking 1992 here—so you can imagine what the cell phones were like. It was a brick. And they were listening to the radio commentary down a phone line from Limerick. So all the Garryowen supporters were gathered around because if the Shannon/Ballymena game finished in a draw we won with a game to spare. I was looking out the window at all these supporters gathered around and then they exploded into the air, and at that moment we knew we'd won the All Ireland League. So our last game was against the Cookies (Young Munster). So they had the trophy there, and the Cookies clapped us onto the field and then kicked the bloody shite out of us during the course of the game. And I was pleased we beat them because it was a hard thing to do mentally to get up for it when you know you've won the thing. And if I remember rightly we had a rather large party for about four weeks, and had to play Shannon in the first round of the cup and got our butts kicked from one end of Thomond Park to the other. I had a shocker."

It's a measure of what the AIL offered back then that Anderson considers it a highlight of his career. This is someone who had 20 good years of competitive rugby, playing in one test and two other games for the All Blacks. He was a Ranfurly Shield winner, and played on the Waikato team that beat the Lions in 1993. Four of that Waikato pack had played some club rugby over the previous few years in Ireland's league: Warren Gatland (Galwegians), Graham Purvis (Highfield), Anderson and John Mitchell (both Garryowen). It was Mitchell who got Anderson involved. He had just returned to New Zealand having played in the opening season of the AIL and told Anderson they were looking for someone to take his place. Mitchell explained that it was a dogfight every week, carried out by players high on passion, and driven on by supporters who dreaded the prospect of defeat and having to face their rivals in the street. At least that's how it was in Limerick. And in fairness to the other teams that kicked off the first few years of the new order, everybody was wading in. Anderson was up for it.

"My experience in Limerick was helped by the fact that I did the business. I came over here and delivered and played well, and tried to lift the standards of my team-mates through application and that sort of thing. And I'm not sure that's always been the case with Kiwis coming over here, and they probably let themselves and us down if they took that attitude. I was determined that the Brent Anderson that arrived as a player in Limerick was the same model that played NPC rugby in New Zealand."

The AIL was a bloody hard competition to win in those days, and the measure of its difficulty was that the top quality Kiwis, like the Waikato crew, were put under pressure to keep their end up on the field, even though they were playing in a competition with a much lower skill base than the provincial scene in New Zealand. The intensity of it was captivating to supporters and media who before that had been muddling along watching provincial competitions of varying quality. This was a new lease of life. Whatever about the conception though, its delivery was painful.

Ireland was the last of the four home unions to get up to speed on a national competition. The closest we had come was the Bateman Cup, which wasn't continued after the Second World War, and in any case was a play-off of provincial cup winners, not a cross border competition run on a league basis. The staple diet of the season was friendly fixtures, especially in Leinster. Everyone would have a few regulars they would play in other provinces, and after those games the speeches would focus on the length of relationship between the clubs and the value of the contact. Tradition. You couldn't beat it.

There were glimpses of what it might be like to get away from the dull diet when Blackrock and Garryowen ran one-off tournaments to celebrate their centenaries in 1982 and 1984 respectively. I remember arriving out to the Blackrock event, run off in the school, and all but five of the senior clubs in Ireland partook in the blitz. At the time it was almost exotic. And it was also risk-free. When the day was over, you went back to your club and got on with your life—one conducted as a senior outfit. In Irish rugby, senior status was everything. In fact, the less successful you were on the field the more enamoured you became of your status.

Preserving your place was one of the main fear factors when the IRFU got the debate up and running in the mid 1980s. Initially, when canvassed in 1985/86, the clubs were marginally in favour of a national competition, but the IRFU backed off given the closeness of the margin. Some clubs were excited by the prospect and were keen to get on with it. Others were desperate not to get left behind, and voted for self preservation, even if it meant preserving a life that was hardly worth living. There was in Ulster though a wariness about any cross border competition with a name like 'All Ireland' on it. Moreover, unlike Munster, Leinster or Connacht, their provincial side had developed a club ethos all of its own. Up north there was more respect for the position held by the representative side. This was manifest in the submission made by Jimmy Davidson to the IRFU's game development committee when they were exploring the possibility of going national.

Davidson had been an opponent of it from the start. For his troubles he was dismissed as a basket case. The notion of Davidson as a header had taken hold soon after he succeeded Mick Doyle as coach of Ireland after the 1987 World Cup. Whereas Doyle was full of bluster and ego, Davidson wanted Ireland to adopt a scientific approach to preparation, as Ulster had done under him. He might as well have asked the lads to parade buck naked around Lansdowne Road. His relationship with the media soured quickly as well, and it was easier to dismiss him rather than make the changes he was asking. So when he told us the league concept was a crock, you know the rest.

Davidson wanted progress through the provinces, which he recognised as being better able to provide the platform to launch into international rugby. He advocated developing contact between the provinces and clubs/districts across the water, as well as the provincial sides in Australia, New Zealand and South Africa. Logistically this wasn't as straightforward as it sounded, though there was no appetite in the IRFU to push the boat out to see if the concept could float. And this fuelled Davidson's suspicions.

Part of the problem with his proposal was that the Irish interprovincial series had lost much of its appeal, certainly south of the border. The rest of the country was fed up with Ulster's domination. They wanted to switch the focus to the clubs. Davidson interpreted the AIL concept not as a union moving to provide an appropriate building block for the Ireland team, but something else entirely.

As recently as May 2006 he wrote in his *Belfast Telegraph* column:

"(David) Irwin's team laid the foundation for a decade in which

Ulster dominated the Irish provincial championship but jealous, and politically powerful elements, in the IRFU sought to castrate the provinces in favour of developing the Irish Clubs. Legislation was even introduced to prevent the provinces holding training sessions at certain times of the year. Disillusioned by the political machinations of the ruling body, and ashamed of the sham-amateurism that pervaded Irish Club rugby I, along with the entire population of the island, suffered the humiliation of seeing the National team prop up the bottom of the Five Nations championship throughout the 1990s." (Ireland were bottom in five seasons in the 1990s).

One of the sales platforms for the AIL was that it would concentrate the best players in the first division, with an immediate dividend for the quality of the product and a delayed one for Ireland. Once the size of that top flight became fluid, it scuppered the notion of cream rising to the top. And in any case, it was hard to see how Ireland being successful was the top priority back then. Ahead of the 1989 test against Buck Shelford's All Blacks, Davidson sought a weekend session with his squad. Oliver Twist got a more sympathetic hearing from Mr Bumble. He kept a note of the experience on his office wall in Stranmillis College. It read:

"It took three approaches, and two appeals, to get one session for the All Blacks match. Only then did they grant permission but with two stipulations. 1. The Sunday session must finish at midday. 2. There was to be no physical contact. It is f——ing madness!!!"

Davidson was informed of the restriction by IRFU committee member Niall Brophy, who came down to Lansdowne Road one day to convey the news, thinking the coach would be pleased. To his eternal regret, Davidson lost his temper and manhandled Brophy into the fence around the pitch. The rationale was that Leinster would be playing the All Blacks in midweek, so it was deemed appropriate to wrap up the Ireland session at midday so their players could train with the provincial side in the afternoon. If you were preparing Leinster you would have thought it reasonable. If you were coaching Ireland it was quite the opposite. Davidson ignored the directive and ploughed ahead. And in turn, the union ignored his views on the AIL. After any amount of debate and meeting at club and branch level, in the end the IRFU grew tired of its own democracy and imposed the new competition for the 1990/91 season. The results of the four provincial leagues over the previous two seasons determined who would be in the two divisions of the league: nine in the first and 10 in the second. Those with the best results over that period were invited on board. Nobody was forced to take part, and of course they all jumped at the chance. Soon after it kicked off in October 1990, the rest were gagging to join.

The arrival of the AIL played a significant role in the development of the profile of rugby in Ireland. Press, radio and television cleared acres of space and time to devote to it. We turned up to every game, and, not unlike our colleagues in the southern hemisphere when the Super 12 took off, lavished unqualified praise on the concept.

Yet for all the passion of the derbies, soon enough there were question marks about its benefits. I remember Gerry Murphy, when he was Ireland coach, complaining that the win at all costs policy of AIL teams had in fact a negative impact higher up the ladder. What would win a derby game for Shannon was not what would win a test match for Ireland. And in the atmosphere of that derby game there was no chance of developing skills by taking risks. The competition was only up and running a couple of seasons when an outside view was sought. Former All Black captain Andy Leslie was invited over to Ireland for a three month stint in October 1992, to have a look at the Irish game from top to bottom. He got around a lot of places in that time and spoke to a lot of people. His report concluded, among other things, that for all its attractions, the AIL was not a final staging post for test rugby, and that the model of country/province/club was best suited to us, as indeed it was in his own country. His report was shelved. Maybe the timing of its delivery wasn't ideal.

"I can remember I had the pleasure of speaking to them prior to a Six Nations (sic) game in Scotland I think it was," Leslie says. "And people weren't used to getting up at eight o'clock in the morning to listen to a report. It wasn't a great time to be addressing a board. People weren't exactly sharp."

It was the dawn of professionalism, two years later, that would prove Davidson, Murphy and Leslie right. In the time it took Ireland to catch on after 1995, the league was on borrowed time as the shop window of the domestic game. Shannon's four consecutive years as champions marked the decline of the great days out, and the beginning of the second phase of the competition. And that would be one where the stars shone in a different firmament. It became increasingly infrequent that the professional players would feature in the AIL. The provinces took over.

Managing that change has been traumatic. There was a period in the post Paris 1995 vacuum when some clubs had notions about elevating themselves to a whole new status. The issue of them—instead of the provinces—representing Ireland in the European Cup bounced around for a year without ever having a real chance of taking off. Establishing that competition in the first place, and keeping Ireland on board in the second, had occupied the mind of the irascible Tom Kiernan. Neither he nor the union were about to risk it all by sending forth the clubs when their eggs were already in the provinces' basket. By Christmas 1996, whatever momentum was behind the clubs was spent. Without control of player contracts it was never a runner for Irish clubs to operate at that level, to corral the provinces into a lower field. And while the union were slow out of the traps in setting up full-time squads in the provinces, at least they had enough players on some sort of contract to be able to dictate to them who and where they played. Well, the ones who were still left in the country.

The European Cup continued from strength to strength, and every surge in its power robbed the club game of more energy. They became increasingly disenchanted at providing players for the professional game while their own competition slipped further away from centre stage. Worse still, the escalating costs of running the professional game resulted in belt tightening below decks, and soon it was the clubs who were struggling for air as the IRFU cut back on their grants.

There were changes along the way in the competition structure. The first division started with nine clubs, and by the time we got to 1993/94 the jamboree had gone nationwide with three divisions of 11 clubs each and one of 13. In the 1997/98 season a play off system was introduced with the finals being run-off in Lansdowne Road. If you compared the atmosphere generated by the 17,000 who saw Young Munster beat St Mary's in what was a de facto final in 1993, none of the actual knock-out finishes came close.

By the time 2004/05 came round, the league's first division comprised 14 clubs, which was a good indicator of how far removed it had become from the original concept of concentrating the talent in one tight group. It was far too big. It was becoming increasingly clear that some sort of halfway house was needed between the purely amateur and the totally

professional games in Ireland. And a fat first division wasn't it. The
IRFU could have streamlined it, but instead flew their flag of democracy
and let the clubs vote each other into a standstill. They could always
have employed a mechanism similar to the one used to establish the
competition in the first place: results over a set period of time, followed
by inviting clubs to take part in the restructured divisions. But if the
clubs sounded like turkeys getting close to Christmas, then their representatives on the union committee were making similar noises.

LOSING THE PLOT

It was there in black and white in the *IRFU Strategic Plan*, launched in
March 2004. On page 34 were the chilling words: "Accordingly we have
decided to realign the AIL. A new competition model will be introduced
in September 2005. The Domestic Game Standing Committee will
oversee the introduction of the new competition model." The 'realign-
ment' had started a year earlier with the publication of *Taking Irish
Rugby Forward—Consultative Document*. There, the union's strategic
planning group outlined the AIL models that they would take on the
road for the consultative process. Option one was to retain the status
quo of 14 clubs in the first division and 17 each in the second and third.
Option two was to have a premier division of 14 clubs, and two other
divisions split on a north south basis. And option three was the crock:
everybody would revert to their original status—i.e. simply as senior
clubs—before getting into regional leagues at the start of the season,
qualifying for All Ireland divisions some time later. Then the whole
process would start again the next season. It's fair to say that very
few people took this seriously when it appeared in the consultative
document. Personally I thought it was there as a device to direct people
towards options one or two. Not so.

The next step was to get around the country, talking to the clubs and
branches, and to take all those views on board before presenting the
final solution. Having completed their travels, the union line was that
the clubs were begging the IRFU to be saved from themselves. Costs had
gotten out of control, and the by-product of paying people who used
to work for free was that volunteerism was under attack; give us back
our local derbies and let's all get back to the way we were; give us back
our clubs where the spirit was about the collective and not just the
senior team who were picking up a wedge the club couldn't afford to pay.

Certainly the pain felt in the club game could be diagnosed as having come from some of those evils. You had to remember that the advent of the AIL facilitated a competitive urge that had previously no other outlet. Clubs went crazy with the cheque books. They bought players from overseas like they were fumbling in the dark. If they were playing outside the parish then an overnight stop it would be. When the reality dawned that this couldn't continue, the Celtic Tiger and professionalism had combined to make a double whammy. If the second one stole the best players, the first one took away many of the others— to longer working hours, or alternative forms of exercise that didn't involve getting soaked on a Tuesday and Thursday night.

All these issues influenced how the union came up with their grand plan to recalibrate the club game. What they left out, however, was the group of clubs that felt they had come through those tough times, and were ready to push on and play a higher quality of rugby in an environment that had some relevance to the professional game. And it was only when the awfulness of the grand plan was explained that the rest of the clubs realised what they were also about to receive. It spawned a unique development in the history of Irish rugby: clubs united.

You looked at it and went away, and came back to it and re-read it to make sure it was for real. And in those moments when the madness of it couldn't be interpreted any other way, you simply despaired. In February 2004 the IRFU committee agreed the following structure for the AIL: there would be four provincial leagues running up to Christmas, and from that backwater teams would qualify for an all Ireland set-up, across three divisions, playing from the New Year through to the end of the season. The whole process would start fresh each year. So you might win the AIL title one year, and not even qualify for the first division the next. Of course that would be an unlikely scenario, but it told you something about how the reverse process might work: one season you could be scratching around at the bottom of the third division, the next you could be enjoying the heady heights, challenging for All Ireland glory. At a stroke it opened the door for clubs to bypass years of effort in getting their internal structures right. Why not get out the cheque book for a quick blast of success? The rationale behind the new structure was that it would address several key issues, from discouraging clubs to spending money they didn't have, to raising the standard across the board, to promoting the local derbies that had been lost in the national context. None of them made any sense.

The vote that passed this lunacy into IRFU legislation had only five names in opposition. And that was an interesting little group. It comprised IRFU legends Noel Murphy and Syd Millar, the then president John Quilligan, Pa Whelan, and Shannon's Bob McConkey. At the vote, Quilligan made a plea for the other committee members to take into account the advice of Murphy and Millar, who could see the craziness of the new proposal. As one of those who voted in favour of the plan told me at the time, there was a certain appeal in sticking it to that pair who had enjoyed so much power over the years, and who had been less than sensitive in how it was wielded.

Hard on the heels of the announcement that the union had agreed the way forward, the Strategic Plan was launched. At the gig to introduce that document, a union man was busy telling me beforehand that I had it all wrong about the first division clubs being ill at the prospect of the new order. "They're in favour of this," he said. No, they weren't. In an effort to paint a picture of sweetness and light, statements had been issued by the Leinster and Ulster branches welcoming the union announcement. This was political spin inspired by Lansdowne Road. And it told you something about how far removed both the branches and the union committee had become from what their own clubs wanted. Over the next few months, that gap would widen.

It didn't dawn on everybody at the same time that the plan was a crock. It was more of a gradual realisation. The punchline came in the small print of the union plan.

It read:

"The structures of the provincial leagues will be determined by the branch committees over the coming weeks."

This told you two things straight off the bat: the plan hadn't been thought through in detail; and the implications of each branch figuring out how the clubs would qualify for the national stage of the league, post Christmas, were frightening. Suddenly the prospect emerged of local derbies being done for by a branch who decided to split their little league into two sections of clubs who would never meet. And what if the sections were arranged on a merit basis? So the weak section would be a corral of the useless playing the hopeless. This had the

potential to take us back 20 years to the days when the IRFU were starting the debate on a national competition. It was that appalling vista
which did most to galvanise the resistance.

Given the history of distrust between the clubs of the first division,
and those below them, it needed something on that scale of awfulness
to do the trick. You wouldn't have thought it possible for the First
Division Clubs Association, and the Association of Second and Third
Division Clubs, to cosy up together without tearing each other's eyes
out, for prior to this they had nothing in common. But the romance
started at a meeting in the Great Southern Hotel, Dublin Airport, on 11
March 2004. Representatives of the two bodies walked away that night
with hope that this could be the start of something uniquely positive.
Over the next three months they achieved two things: a brand new
alliance, and a coherent alternative to the union plan for the AIL.

The first goal was to draw the three strands together into one group
representing all. The All Ireland Senior Rugby Clubs Association
(AISRCA)—good idea, awful title—was a 14 man executive body drawn
from two associations. There were six from the first division, and four
each from the other two which gave them the comfort of being able to
outvote the first division reps. They quickly set up sub-committees on
league structure, finance, and promotions and marketing.

It was this group which produced an alternative plan for the AIL.
Instead of the killing fields that would have been the provincial leagues,
the clubs proposed a national competition over three divisions, each
split into conferences of eight. The only reason the conference
element—which would never have worked—was added, was to render
the proposal different to the status quo which the union were so
adamant to ditch. And for good measure they threw in a proposal for
an All Ireland Cup. Set alongside the lunacy of the IRFU model it was a
rock of sense. The fact that all the clubs were on board with this gave it
an immediate momentum that put the IRFU in the slow lane.

The emergence of AISRCA was bad news for the union. The IRFU's
structure is a federal system, built on four provincial branches where
the clubs send forward representatives to the branch and, in time, some
of them are called to serve at the top table—the IRFU committee.
Ostensibly this is the very essence of democracy, but in reality it allowed
for wholesale manipulation and control of which individuals made

progress and how far and how fast. Under this system there were no bolts from the blue onto the union committee. They had an unimpeded view of the hinterland, and that's how they liked it. So the arrival overnight of an executive body representing all the senior clubs in the country, one with all sorts of ideas on how the union should run its business, was alarming. Pretty soon they would be going through the IRFU accounts and asking awkward questions. The last thing the union wanted to do was open the door and sit down with these people. But they had to do something. That something was to resurrect the All Ireland League Clubs Working Party. This forum had been on snooze control for the previous two seasons, but in July 2004 it was about to be woken up and dusted down.

The union wouldn't go so far as to formally recognise the existence of AISRCA. It followed then that their sponsors couldn't hop into bed with them either. So when subsequently the clubs approached AIB directly, proposing to discuss a range of issues regarding their sponsorship of the league, the bank wrote back, thanking them for their communication, but that their deal was with the IRFU. Down at 62 Lansdowne Road they would sooner have handled a rattlesnake. To them, dealing directly with AISRCA would have undermined their own federal system. It would have further insulted the branch committees about whom AISRCA had a clear idea: 'It's a national competition, stick to your provincial leagues and we'll represent ourselves.' So when the union rolled out the old Working Party, it included the four branch honorary secretaries as part of the group. From the very first communication between the association and the union, it was clear that this was a game the union would play on their terms. This whole approach to business maddened elements on the clubs' side of the fence. Already they were enraged by union cuts in club funds, and the situation had been compounded by the IRFU diverting 700 international tickets from the clubs into their own commercial programme to deal with union debt. Nevertheless, despite the protocol, and the union's attempts to effect asphyxiation by red tape, there was progress. It was helped by the fact that the reaction among ordinary club folk to the union plan was so virulent. The IRFU realised they would have to change course.

REVERSE

In some respects you could say that the first meeting of the Working Party got off to a flyer. On behalf of the union, chairman Der Healy said that he would be going back to the full committee with a recommendation that the wishes of the clubs should be respected, and the crock thrown out. Moreover, the idea of an All Ireland Cup was fine, though it might take a while to organise. On the highest profile issue, the clubs' association had been rewarded quicker than they could have hoped. When it came to the other stuff, they were pushing up a steeper hill.

It was in the spring of 2005 that AISRCA's model was modified to what was the virtual status quo. The impetus for this actually came from a nudge and a wink from the IRFU, who wanted the old order back but couldn't say so. Instead of 15 teams in the first division, and 17 in the second and third, as was the case in 2004, there would be 16 in each of the three divisions, playing a full programme as before. Out went the pre-Christmas Mickey Mouse, Make It Up As You Go Along Leagues, followed in the New Year by the excuse for an All Ireland League. It was virtually as you were, which was the very position the union had said was unacceptable. You could interpret this as wonderful democracy at work. Alternatively you could marvel at the neck of those who sold the plan in the first place, to pick up the new product and flog it like it was about to change everybody's life.

They dug in on most of the other issues put to them by AISRCA. Perhaps the union looked at its own longevity and wondered who these guys thought they were? Or more importantly, how long they would be around? It was a valid question. The arrival of the new association was a significant landmark in the development of the club game in Ireland. The speed with which they organised themselves, and then tried to address issues which affected them, highlighted how inappropriate the IRFU structures are to running the game. Yet just when they seemed on the brink of forcing radical change, the old suspicions which had always divided them rose to the surface.

NEUTRAL

The league is due to be reviewed at the end of the season 2006/07, and in May 2006 the clubs started preparing their submission. The compromise model had done its job, but nobody ever regarded it as a permanent structure. At the top end of the game there was panic over the widening gap between it and the provincial tier above. The problem was, the province wasn't immediately above them any more—a new layer had been inserted to Ireland's structure.

In 2004/05 the IRFU had decentralised its national academy into four provincial units. As long as the increase in numbers didn't dilute the quality of the experience, this made perfect sense. It began to look somewhat different, however, when it was combined with the introduction of another tier of games at provincial level. These 'A' games used academy players and back-up players from the senior provincial squads and it squeezed the clubs even further out of the picture. You can't, for example, run an A game between Ulster and Leinster on a Tuesday using players who will be needed by their clubs in the AIL first division the following Saturday and claim it won't impact negatively on the club game. Nor can you increase the frequency of these fixtures and suggest, with a straight face, that you're not tearing the backside out of the domestic league. This move was based on the misconception that the only way to develop young professionals is to have them playing against other young professionals. Worse still, it has the potential to be as damaging to the professional game as to the club game, providing a false environment for the first and withdrawing players from the second.

AISRCA met several times over the summer of 2006 and on 24 August decided unanimously to recommend a new format that would reduce the first division from 16 to 10 clubs, supported by a second and third division with 16 clubs each. Nobody had ever thought this point could be reached so fast. It had the potential to revolutionise the top end of the club game, making it a meaningful halfway house to the professional tier. A Top 10 competition played mostly in the Saturday afternoon slot vacated by the Magners League (as the Celtic League has become), or Friday night slots when the local provincial team was away from home, would have real potential to draw punters and press alike. It would be a competition where the professional players who didn't get a run with the province could get important action with their clubs. It was an opportunity to breed home-grown players and coaches in a competition that had the heat of club rivalry and the quality of professional input. Sixteen years after it all started, here, finally, was a chance to give back to the league some of the momentum that had driven it in the first place.

Then the bubble burst. There was a one-month gap between AISRCA announcing their proposals and all 48 clubs actually sitting down and voting on them. Within a fortnight, the idea that the union would be forced into action by an overwhelmingly positive majority of the clubs had been rubbished. First, the IRFU wrote to all the clubs reassuring them that they were still the third tier in the Irish system and they would be loved and cherished for evermore. Second, the clubs in the lower divisions started to panic about being left behind by an elitist breakaway group that would skip planning permission and erect a fence around themselves in jig-time. Faced with the prospect of internal strife, AISRCA thought better of putting it to a vote. If their initial proposal had been dramatic—delivered unanimously by 14 men across the three divisions—then so too was the row back. It was ironic that AISRCA considered the branches of the IRFU to be out of touch with the clubs when they themselves had not read the warning signs from their own members.

In the space of a few days the momentum dissipated, and the season unfolded into another of Ireland's grand consultative processes. These are classics: opinions are sought from every dog in every side-street in the land, but when it comes time to take out the leash and start walking, the handlers go missing. Unfortunately, the summit of union leadership on the issue was back in 1990/91 when the All Ireland League was first started. Thereafter it has all been downhill, or sideways. Without a willingness to vote for the future instead of the present, the recovery of the Irish club game won't even get underway. We will never see it again at a level where a five figure crowd is ready and waiting for the Brent Andersons to take the field, but it is not beyond help.

CONCLUSION

The stadium clock shows 73 minutes, but Ronan O'Gara doesn't know whether to believe it or not. He never trusts those things. Is it real time or game time? Is it going to run on past 80 minutes or does 73 minutes mean that there are actually seven minutes left? It doesn't make that much difference because he's already made the decision to kick for goal. It is the European Cup final, and the scores are 20-19 in Munster's favour.

Referee Chris White has just awarded them a penalty within 40 metres of the Biarritz posts. As soon as he raises his arm to indicate the award, the Munster crowd are on their feet in celebration. Even the casuals among the estimated 60,000 Munster fans understand the implications of this: if O'Gara is successful, Biarritz will probably have to score a try to win. Unlike O'Gara, most of them know that 73 minutes means 73 minutes, and the chances are remote of conceding two kickable penalties in the period remaining. There is no decision to be made. He nods towards the posts and prepares to go through his routine.

It is only right that it has come down to something like this. It is not quite the black ball finish that he faced in Twickenham in the 2000 final against Northampton, but it's not far off it. His goal-kicking has been the backbone of this campaign. In the two knock-out games in 2006, against Perpignan in the quarter-final and Leinster in the semi-final, he has succeeded with 11 from 12 attempts. Now, in Cardiff, he is four from four when all of Ireland is praying he can put a bit of daylight between Munster and the Basques. He didn't just stumble across these kinds of stats.

It was less than a year after that Twickenham final that O'Gara began the transformation. He had been selected to tour Australia with the Lions, and on his initiative sponsors Adidas arranged for him to get together with Dave Alred, England's kicking coach. They both flew to Dublin and met up at Wanderers' ground on Merrion Road. That was the start of a process that would see O'Gara's kicking action deconstructed and rebuilt. When the tour got underway, things moved on. That's when he came into direct contact with Jonny Wilkinson.

"At that time you could learn an awful lot from watching other people and someone like Jonny was fascinating because that's what he was best at—goal kicking," says O'Gara. "Even back then I would have had the talent to match him out of hand, but off the ground he was just so consistent. I was fascinated by the fact that it seemed all he had to do was place the ball on the tee correctly, and after that it was an automatic conclusion. That intrigued me for years and I always wanted to get to that level. And I think unless you've expert coaching you won't get to that level, you have to trust your natural ability. What I've done is combined what I've learned from Mark Tainton in Ireland with what I've learned from other fellas on the Lions and from Dave Alred. And with a little bit from myself, through trial and error and bloody hard work, it's got to a stage where it's 80 per cent plus."

As he progressed he stopped kicking just with his leg and started using his whole body to get through the ball. He developed a mental routine from the time the kick had to be taken. Knowing where to find the sweet spot on the ball was an obvious thing, but the visualisation took more practice. In the bigger stadiums there would be physical aids, like a letter in an advertising hoarding high in the stands behind the posts. And when he was ready to go, the action in his mind was that of pulling a trigger.

"So you can visualise the ball like a bullet, going straight to the target and it's reached that target before wind or anything can deviate it if you get a proper strike. I'd be lying if I said that up to this year goal-kicking didn't occupy 90 per cent of my thoughts going into a game. Fear of failure. Fear of letting the team down. And that's a different pressure. Obviously in the quarters and semi-final and final especially I felt pressure, but I never doubted my technique, whereas in previous years of course I had worries about it. This year, once I've hit the pitch I've clicked into routine mode."

There was another difference from his first final. Back then, the presence of Mick Galwey was hugely important to him. On international days it was more obvious, for during the national anthem the second row was like a protective parent, clutching O'Gara and Stringer under either arm. What you wouldn't see or hear was the roar of approval Galwey would give him when a penalty went over. He would line up behind O'Gara on those kicks, and every success was greeted with loud acclaim. "Gwan O'Gara!" Nobody had filled that role when Galwey

retired in 2003, and O'Gara had come to miss it. Then an unexpected
replacement stepped into the breach that day in Cardiff.

"I saw Hayes as I was running back and he gave me the outstretched
hand, and I'd say that's the first time he's ever done that in his career. It
caught me for five seconds. I was emotionless before that, but it gave
me a few shivers because before it was always Gaillimh. It was a
poignant moment for me, I felt. It put me off slightly for a second. I
hadn't felt any pressure taking that kick—I dunno if it was just confidence that I was going to get it. It was a bloody important kick but I
don't think I appreciated it at the time because I didn't believe the
clock. Hayes was wrecked. He doesn't do any fancy shit. He doesn't ever
put his hand out. That's not John Hayes. I was kinda going: 'Fuck it,
that's cool!'"

Seven minutes later it was bedlam. Twickenham in 2000 was washed
away, along with their second loss in a final, to Leicester in 2002. The
emotion that greeted the final whistle was unprecedented in Irish
rugby. O'Gara's progress as a rugby player, and not just a goal kicker,
was illustrative of how Munster had moved forward. Losing to Wasps
in the European semi-final in 2004 had been a catalyst for further
change. The on-field model of 2006 was hardly a complete rugby
package, but it was very effective nonetheless. It was also a shining
example of how professional preparation could maximise resources. It
reinforced how Irish rugby had been transformed in the new era.

This new state of affairs is as positive with the national team as it is
with the provincial sides. The Irish structure is the envy of many
because, to their credit, the IRFU have invested in looking after their
players. We can bring a fresh squad to the Six Nations each year because
they have not been flogged from the start of the season. And when we
arrive there, we are contenders. It is good luck that the likes of Brian
O'Driscoll and Gordon D'Arcy—the world's best centre combination—
arrived onto the planet within roughly a year of each other. It is good
planning that allows them perform at their best. When O'Driscoll
opted in 2006 to extend his Irish contract up to his likely retirement, it
was an endorsement of what is on offer in this country.

The national team are well coached, and well looked after, mostly by
home-produced staff. For our first three coaches of the professional era
we had to look for imports. In Eddie O'Sullivan we have the perfect
man for the job. His squad will go to the World Cup in France in 2007

as the strongest and best prepared in our history, and with more realistic alternatives in selection than ever before.

This brings us to a critical juncture. As far back as Warren Gatland's early days in the job, he spoke of Ireland one day being top five material, regular challengers to the traditional super powers. Now that we are probationary members of that club, there will need to be some off the field amendments across the board to make us permanent.

You might have wondered, for example, how the cottage industry that is Munster's commercial operation could be equated with winning the European Cup. It tells you something about the IRFU's structure: 11 years after the game had gone professional, their governance was still rooted in the amateur era.

In all that time, their dealings with those who got the drop on them in the early 1990s—namely the Australians—had been constant. And yet the old guard in Ireland were still trying to apply amateur mechanisms to a professional game. In 2005 the Australians took the decision to bring two independent directors onto their board of seven, thus reducing the interests of the major states—Queensland and New South Wales. Prior to that, the board had been exclusively made up of representatives who also sat on the boards of the states.

The impetus for this change started in the late 1990s but only happened recently, and 2006 was the first year of its effect. "If we were going to be as strong on the commercial element as on the rugby side of things then we needed to reflect that and have some independence and objectivity on the board," says Paul McLean, the ARU president. "It's early days but it's been very positive." Incidentally, McLean can contribute to board matters but he doesn't have a vote.

Imagine that happening in Ireland where in 2006 the IRFU committee was the same size as in 1995. True, there had been a shuffle of the deckchairs, and more power has been vested in a smaller management committee, but it is window dressing. The closest they came to independence was inviting the odd outsider onto one of their sub-committees, which was akin to fitting them for a strait jacket. It was wholly inappropriate to a game that was racing ahead of those who ran it.

Naturally enough, this reluctance to embrace change extended below the top table. The European Cup was the vehicle that had carried Irish rugby out of the slow lane, yet the structure of the four provincial branches is hard to fathom. We ask Munster, Leinster, Ulster and

Connacht to compete primarily with the commercially driven clubs of England and France, and then tell them to submit to committee first. These are operations that need to be run as franchises, with board status and independent directors. Instead they are hobbled by structures from another era.

The perversity is that the triple crowns and provincial successes militate against fundamental change, the kind of shift required to put Irish rugby where the IRFU want it to be. It's like in the old days, when some of us dreaded the odd moral victory for the comfort it would induce in Lansdowne Road. Back then, we wondered would we ever get up to speed. The journey has been at times exhilarating, and other times maddening, but now that we've had a close up of the good life it would be unforgivable not to park here long term.

APPENDIXES

DEVELOPMENT SQUAD, 1997

(Chapter 4)

Full Backs

CONOR O'SHEA (London Irish)
Lived up to his status as a senior player and survived the experience well. He was back on the Ireland team for the 1997/98 Five Nations championship and was first choice for the 1999 World Cup, but was dropped after the defeat by England in 2000. A serious ankle injury forced him out of the game in November that year. In 2006 he was appointed director of England's National Academy, having spent three years as managing director of London Irish, where previously he was their director of rugby. He is married, with a new daughter, and lives in Berkshire.

CIARAN CLARKE (Terenure)
Clarke was already an international when he travelled on the original Development trip to Africa in 1993, but was restricted to four A caps between then and the New Zealand experience. He did well enough on the trip, but thereafter only got two more games for Ireland—against Wales and England in 1998. He gave up club rugby at the end of the 1998/99 season, by which point he had 23 AIL tries for Terenure. In 2006 Clarke was married with one child, living in Dublin and working for Pinewood Laboratories.

Wings

MARCUS DILLON (Lansdowne)
Considered one of the big casualties of the tour, Dillon reached the end of his tether long before the finish. He returned to play with Lansdowne in 1997/98 and scored seven tries and a drop-goal in 13 league matches. Along with Brian Glennon he was the club's joint top try scorer in the All Ireland League, scoring 20. He suffered a serious leg injury in 1999 and missed most of that season, after which he drifted away from the club. In 2006 he had no known connection with the game.

NIALL WOODS (London Irish)
Never recovered from a bad start and the tour ultimately set him back. Woods didn't play for Ireland again until the win over Wales in Wembley, in February 1999—an historic victory, but not the restart of his international career. He ruptured his cruciate ligament seven months later and moved to Harlequins, where he saw out the next season before retiring through injury in 2001. He worked for

the players' association in England before taking over as CEO of the Irish Rugby Union Players Association in 2003. In 2006 he still held that position, was married and living in Co. Wicklow.

DAVID COLEMAN (Terenure)
He had a hard time of it: this tour was nothing like the AIL, where he could bounce people out of his way. Typical of his experience, he scored a try that night against King Country, but was responsible for conceding another. The tour killed his chances of ever winning a cap. He returned to club rugby with Terenure and finished his career as their top AIL try-scorer with 29, which record was intact going into 2004/05. He gave up the game at the end of 2000/01. In 2006 Coleman was working in sales for a media company and living in Dublin with his wife and two children.

JUSTIN BISHOP (London Irish)
Bounced back into a good season with London Irish and toured South Africa with the senior Ireland side the next season—scoring a try on his debut in the first test in Bloemfontein. Played in the World Cup in 1999 but was banished after the hammering by England in the first game of the 2000 Championship. His career looked finished until recalled for the tour to New Zealand in 2002. Scored his eighth international try, against Fiji, in November of that year. In 2006 he was still with London Irish and living in Sunbury with his wife and daughter.

Centres

ROB HENDERSON (London Irish)
Henderson was one of the few to benefit immediately from the experience. Dropped after his first cap, against the Samoans in 1996, he was back in for the autumn series in 1997 thanks to his form on tour. Thereafter injury cost him a pile of caps, but he was fit enough to make the Lions tour to Australia in 2001 where he was a big success. He moved to Munster the next season, but injury followed closely behind and his career there never reached fulfilment. In 2006 he was poised to move into coaching with Garryowen, but then opted to take up a playing contract with Toulon, in the south of France. He is married and has one daughter.

ALAN MCGRATH (Shannon)
Travelled with low expectations and wasn't disappointed. Came back to a £7,500 Development contract with Munster and combined it with the practical year of his quantity surveying course. He never got past the Munster Development side and went back to college full-time the following year. McGrath gave up the game in 2001 and despite flirting with the idea of making a comeback, he never got around to it. In 2006 he was working as a quantity surveyor, married with two children and living in Limerick.

MIKE LYNCH (Young Munster)
One of the successes on the trip, but it didn't propel him towards a cap. Came home to a full contract with Munster, for whom he played 27 times over four seasons without nailing down a place. He gave great service to his club, Young Munster, before spending three seasons as player coach with Bruff. He returned to Munsters, where in 2006/07 he was playing and assisting as coach. He is married with two daughters, teaches physical education in St Clement's secondary school and lives in Limerick.

KEVIN MAGGS (Bristol)
This was the start of Maggs's unspectacular but very profitable involvement with Ireland, which would include playing in two World Cups. The steady accumulation of caps—70, with 15 tries—got under way against New Zealand in November 1997 when he made a try-scoring debut alongside fellow tourists David Erskine, Malcolm O'Kelly and Kieron Dawson. Maggs went on to become a pillar of Ireland's defence. He signed for Ulster from Bath in 2004 and was still there two years later. He is married, with one daughter, and lives in Belfast.

Outhalves
DAVID HUMPHREYS (London Irish)
He gave the lie to the old adage that there's never a good time to get injured. He was blessed to escape so soon and get on with what developed into a very successful career. By the end of the 1999 World Cup he had become first-choice outhalf, ahead of Eric Elwood. Ronan O'Gara arrived the next season and their battle for supremacy developed into an interesting sideshow. In 2006 he had just retired from international rugby with 72 caps but was still playing with Ulster, whom he had led to the European Cup in 1999. He is married, has three children and lives in Co. Down.

RICHIE GOVERNEY (Lansdowne)
Worked hardest and, ultimately, got least out of the experience. Governey's suffering should have paid off with a lengthy professional career, but it never happened. Got a full-time contract with Leinster when he came home, but it wasn't renewed. After a season in Oxford University he settled back into club rugby with Terenure. In 2006 he was working on the marketing side of the family business (designing golf courses), was unmarried and had just wrapped up his playing career with Terenure.

Scrumhalves
BRIAN O'MEARA (Cork Constitution)
He won his first cap in the preceding Five Nations, but this tour did little to further his chances despite being first choice of the three scrumhalves. He came on

as a replacement for Conor McGuinness against the All Blacks in November 1997 and started against Scotland in the next Five Nations, but never established himself. Then Peter Stringer arrived to haunt him. O'Meara left Munster for Leinster in 2000 and won a Celtic League medal, beating his old province in the final. In 2005/06 he jointly coached Lansdowne, and was released by Leinster at the end of that season. He returned to Cork, where he got a late call back into the Munster squad. He is single.

STEPHEN MCIVOR (Garryowen)
Made a significant contribution to the tour, even though it would do nothing to add to his three international caps. On the field his battling qualities were undermined by a poor passing technique. Off the field he kept the troops amused with his willingness to wind-up Pa Whelan. He went west to Buccaneers in 1999/2000 for two seasons before taking up coaching with Corinthians. After a season there he moved back to Dublin and coached Blackrock for two seasons. In 2006 he was playing some veterans' rugby and had coached the Ireland women's Sevens side. McIvor has a franchise on a Cartridge World outlet, is single and lives in Dublin.

ANDY MATCHETT (Portadown)
Got married straight after the tour, went on honeymoon to the Far East and forgot all about New Zealand. He went on to win a European Cup medal with Ulster in 1999. Having flirted with Bedford for half a season when the game was opening up, he was happiest back in Ulster where he played for his home club, Portadown, and for Ballymena before moving to Belfast Harlequins. He played for them in the AIL final defeat by Shannon. In 2006 he was playing junior rugby for the club and working as a sales consultant for Clerical Medical Investments Group. Matchett is married with two children and lives in Belfast.

Props
DARREN MOLLOY (Wasps)
He was a good player, but not fit enough to beat off Justin Fitzpatrick for the loosehead spot. Bizarrely, his Irish credentials were effectively wiped out the next season when he played for England A against France A—he had been unaware that the IRB were moving towards the One Union rule, which restricted players to representing one country only. Leinster signed him in 2002/03, but domestic difficulties restricted his availability. He moved back to England and had a season coaching Canterbury RFC before switching to Westcombe Park in England's National 3 South. Married with two children, he lives in Suffolk.

JUSTIN FITZPATRICK (London Irish)
He did well and looked to be immediate international material. He was slotted into the A team for the following Championship and picked for the South African

tour the next summer, where he made his senior debut courtesy of Reggie Corrigan being crocked in the opening game. When Peter Clohessy switched across the scrum it did nothing for Fitzpatrick's prospects. His career highlight was the European Cup medal with Ulster in 1999. In 2006 he was back in Ulster after a two-year spell with Castres. Married with one daughter and living in Bangor.

GAVIN WALSH (Northampton)
He came over to Ireland after the tour and spent a season with Garryowen and Munster and played four out of five games for Ireland A in 1997/98. It ended in a legal dispute over his contract with the IRFU. He left for Scotland in 1998 and signed up with Glasgow Hawks, going on to become their coach when they then morphed into GHA. In 2006 he was in a living in a small village near Lyon with his wife and four children, playing a little rugby and building a new house.

GARY HALPIN (capt.) (London Irish)
Never fit enough to make a fist of the tour in the first place, he got no personal benefit from it: resurrecting his international career wasn't an option. Halpin returned to London Irish and then had a season with Harlequins before coming back to Ireland for two years with Leinster—the last three seasons, he said, were the most enjoyable of his career. In 2006 he was teaching and coaching rugby in the Oratory School in Reading. He is married with three children.

Hookers

BARRY MCCONNELL (Bristol)
The forgotten man of the tour—which says less about his performances and more about those who were running the game. McConnell had real potential. Bad enough that it wasn't realised, but for him to be left to stew in his own misfortune was shameful. After an aborted comeback from knee surgery he gave up altogether when he was just 22 years old. He has no involvement in the game now other than as a spectator. He works in an investment bank, is single and lives in London.

STEPHEN RITCHIE (Ballymena)
He finished up as the number one hooker on the trip—not that big a deal given that Barry McConnell was crocked and Shane Byrne was a last resort for Ashton. It didn't translate into a higher calling because there was always a queue ahead of him. His Ulster career wasn't helped by the return from Northampton of Allen Clarke. Ritchie captained Ballymena in 1997/98 before moving to Instonians, where he finished out his competitive career. In 2006 he signed for Portadown and represented an Irish Legends selection on tour. Married with two daughters, he lives in Co. Down and works in medical sales.

SHANE BYRNE (Blackrock)
When you see how his career turned out it is hard to credit that Byrne could have been this far down the pecking order. Although a late call-up, he arrived in time to take a full role in proceedings, only to be cut adrift. He returned to Blackrock and Leinster where he plugged away until 2001, when he at last won his first cap—off the bench when Keith Wood was away with the Lions and Frankie Sheahan had been selected ahead of him. Byrne never looked back. In 2006/07 he was heading into the second year of a contract with Saracens, had played three Lions tests in 2005 and had 41 Ireland caps. He is married with twin girls and living in London.

Second Rows
MALCOLM O'KELLY (London Irish)
His lunge for the line against Samoa suggested he was capable of great things and his career took off thereafter. He won his first cap a few months after the tour, against New Zealand, and went on to become Ireland's most capped player. The only downside to a highly successful career was an unfulfilled relationship with the Lions: he was an extra on the trip to Australia in 2001, and then invalided out of the New Zealand trip four years later without playing a game. In 2006 he was still on the Irish squad. He is married and lives in Dublin.

BRIAN CUSACK (Bath)
Already an experienced Ireland A player Cusack had a decent tour but never came close to taking the next step. He picked up another four A caps in 1997/98, but that was the end of his Ireland involvement. He moved to Richmond in 1998, but when they wound up the next year he returned to Lansdowne and Leinster, where he got a one-year contract. In 2004 he retired from the game, partly through pressure of work as a sports trader with Paddy Power bookmakers. In 2006 he was married and living in Kildare.

GABRIEL FULCHER (London Irish)
Fulcher had a fine tour and took over the captaincy from Gary Halpin when the prop was struggling to get on the field. He was one of the most experienced players on the trip—with 18 caps since his debut in 1994 on the tour to Australia— and he played that way. His performances suggested a return to the Ireland team, but in the autumn he was back on the A side while Malcolm O'Kelly and Paddy Johns became the preferred partnership. He retired in 2000 after Lansdowne lost the AIB League final to St Mary's, but subsequently moved into coaching the club's under 20s side. In 2006 Fulcher had the franchise on two O'Brien's Sandwich Bars, was married and living in Dublin.

RORY SHERIFF (Shannon)
Less than half an hour in seven games tells its own story; Sheriff wasn't cut out

for this kind of trauma. When he came back he picked up a Leinster contract and switched clubs from Shannon to Terenure. A year later he went back to college and became a part-time player. He captained Terenure for two seasons from 1999 and got another offer from Leinster for 2000/01. It didn't work out. He left Terenure for Carlow in 2001, played two seasons and then packed it in. In 2006 he was married, living in Wexford and working as a Garda, based in Enniskerry.

Back Rows

DAVID WALLACE (Garryowen)

Along with Richie Governey he saw action in every game—which was good going for a 20 year old flanker. Wallace showed up especially well in the biggest games: against the Maori and Samoa. His reward was an Irish contract waiting for him on his return, although it would be three years before he got capped. In 2001 he became the third Wallace brother to play for the Lions when called out to Australia as a replacement. He won Triple Crowns with Ireland in 2004 and 2006, and followed it up with a European Cup medal with Munster. He rounded off the season by touring with Ireland, where he was first-choice open side, before getting married. He lives in Limerick.

KIERON DAWSON (London Irish)

Dawson played a full part in what was an exciting back-row combination along with David Wallace and David Erskine. He was one of five new caps who faced New Zealand five months after the tour, but injury cost him continuity. The emergence of Andy Ward pushed him out of the picture when Warren Gatland took over in 1998, but he went to the 1999 World Cup and was on standby for the 2003 tournament. In 2006 he was married with one son and had just signed for Ulster after ten happy years with London Irish.

DAVID ERSKINE (Sale)

Erskine had impressed Ashton in the English Premiership and went out of his way to make this trip, in spite of a broken nose. He played well and in the autumn was capped against New Zealand, Canada and Italy. When Ashton pulled out in early 1998, Erskine's star declined. He continued playing for Sale until 1999/2000, when a recurring groin injury forced him out of the game. In 2006 Erskine was still living in Cheshire with his wife and son, and working as associate director in an insurance firm.

EDDIE HALVEY (Shannon)

Halvey had buckets of talent, but never got to show much on this trip thanks to a bacterial ulcer that saw him abandon after a week. He had won his first cap two years earlier and had gone to the 1995 World Cup, so he would have been a useful player to have around. He resumed his Ireland contract when he came back and featured in the autumn series against New Zealand and Canada, but drifted there-after. He remained an important part of the Munster squad until retiring from professional rugby in 2004. He continued with Shannon until 2005/06, by which time he had opened a contract cleaning company and was living in Limerick.

ANTHONY FOLEY (Shannon)

Even those who were on the tour forget that Foley was one of the famous five hauled off against Bay of Plenty. Like Shane Byrne, he recovered well from the experience, but it would be almost three years before Munster kick-started his international career, which had begun back in 1995. The European Cup put the province on the map and opened the door for the number eight, who had been a passenger in New Zealand. He became a hugely important player in the Ireland set-up. In 2006 he was still on an Ireland contract, but had been eclipsed by Munster team-mate Denis Leamy. His finest hour came in captaining Munster to European glory in 2006. It was his third final. He is married, has a son and lives in Co. Clare.

DEAN MACARTNEY (Ballymena)

Macartney played twice for Ireland B in 1991/92 and before the New Zealand experience he had spent four seasons in Pau. He wasn't Development material, but his experience was considered an asset. Afterwards he took up a part-time contract with Ulster, but lost a year through a ruptured cruciate ligament. He came back and actually captained Ulster twice in inter-provincial games early in their European Cup winning season, but wasn't close enough to the action when the medals were being handed out. He also gave excellent service to Ballymena, but lost out on an AIL medal in 2003. He retired in 2005. In 2006 he was married with two children, living in Co. Antrim and working in the computer industry.

Appendix II ∾

CHARTS AND STATISTICS

1. IRELAND TOUR TO AUSTRALIA, MAY/JUNE 1994

Touring party: Captain Michael Bradley; Coach Gerry Murphy; Technical Officer/ Asst Coach Willie Anderson; Hon. Manager Frank Sowman; Hon. Asst Manager Locky Butler; Medical Officer Dr Wesley Rainey; Physiotherapist John Martin; IRFU President Michael Cuddy.

Joined tour: Shane Byrne, Ben Cronin, Niall Hogan, Ken O'Connell.

Results

1. Western Australia 8 Ireland 64
2. New South Wales 55 Ireland 18
3. Australian Cap. Territories 22 Ireland 9
4. Queensland 29 Ireland 26

5. Australian XV 57 Ireland 9
6. Australia 33 Ireland 13
7. NSW Country Dists. 18 Ireland 20
8. Australia 32 Ireland 18

Summary

Played—8, Won—2, Drew—0, Lost—6; PF—127pts (17t, 13c, 20p, 2d) PA—254 pts (34t, 15c, 18p, 0d).

Ireland Squad Appearances

Game Player	No.1	No.2	No.3	No.4	No.5	No.6	No.7	No.8	Tour Apps.	Tour Points	Tour Caps	Total Caps
Bell J. (Ballymena) U	-	13	13 r	13	11	13	-	13	5+1r	5	2	2
Bradley M. (Cork Cons) M	9 c	9 c	-	9 c	9 r	9 c	-	9 c	5+1r	-	2	36
Byrne S. (Blackrock) L	-	-	2	-	4 r	-	-	-	1+1r	-	0	0
Clohessy P. (Y. Muns) M	3	-	3	3	-	3	-	3	5	5	2	9
Corkery D. (Cork Cons) M	7	-	7	7	-	7	-	7	5	5	2	2
Costello V. (St Mary's) C	6	-	6 r	-	8	-	4	-	3+1r	5	0	0
Cronin B. (Garryowen) M	-	-	-	-	-	-	8	-	1	-	0	0
Danaher P. (Garryowen) M	-	12	-	12	-	12	-	12	4	-	2	23
Davidson J. (Dungannon) U	5	-	5	-	5	-	5	-	4	5	0	0
Elwood E. (Lansdowne) C	10	10	-	10	-	10	-	10	5	35	2	9
Field M. (Malone) U	13	-	13	-	13	15 r	13	-	4+1r	10(2t)	1	3
Fitzgerald J. (Y. Muns) M	1	-	-	1	-	1	-	1	4	-	2	12

Game / Player	No.1	No.2	No.3	No.4	No.5	No.6	No.7	No.8	Tour Apps.	Tour Points	Tour Caps	Total Caps
Francis N. (Blackrock) L	-	5	-	5	-	5	-	5	4	10(2t)	2	27
Fulcher G. (Cork Cons) M	-	4	-	4	4	-	-	4	4	-	1	1
Galwey M. (Shannon) M	4	8 r	4 c	-	-	4	-	-	3+1r	-	1	19
Geoghegan S. (L. Irish) E	14	14	-	14	-	14	-	14	5	5	2	23
Halpin G. (L. Irish) E	-	3	1	3 r	3	-	3	-	4+1r	-	0	7
Hogan N. (Terenure) L	-	-	-	-	.	-	9	-	1	-	0	0
Hogan P. (Garryowen) M	-	-	6	-	-	-	-	-	1	-	0	1
Johns P. (Dungannon) U	8	-	8	8	-	8	4 r	8	5+1r	10(2t)	2	14
Kingston T. (Dolphin) M	2 r	2	-	-	2 c	-	2 c	-	3+1r	10(2t)	0	17
McBride D. (Malone) U	-	7	-	-	7	4 r	7	-	3+1r	-	1	16
McGowan A. (Blackrock) L	-	-	10	-	10	-	10	-	3	33	0	0
O'Connell K. (S. Well) M	-	-	-	-	6	-	6	-	2	-	0	2
O'Shea C. (Lansdowne) L	15	-	-	15	14 r	15	-	15	4+1r	29 (1t)	2	7
Ridge M. (Blackrock) L	12	-	12	-	12	-	12	-	4	-	0	0
Robinson B. (Ballymena) U	6 r	6	-	6	4 r	6	-	6	4+2r	-	2	25
Rolland A. (Blackrock) L	-	-	9	-	9	-	-	-	2	-	0	1
Staples J. (Harlequins) E	11	15	15	-	15	-	15	-	5	5	0	14
Soden P. (Cork Cons) M	-	1	-	-	1	-	1	-	3	-	0	0
Walsh B. (Cork Cons) M	-	-	14	-	14	-	14	-	3	-	0	0
Wilson R. (Instonians) U	-	8	-	-	-	-	-	-	1	-	0	0
Wood K. (Garryowen) M	2	-	-	2	-	2	-	2	4	5	2	2
Woods N. (Blackrock) L	-	11	11	11	-	11	11	11	6	-	2	2
	17	16	17	16	19	17	16	15				

Munster—14 players, Ulster—8 players, Leinster—8 players, Connacht—2 players, Exiles—2 players

2. IRELAND A/DEVELOPMENT TOUR TO NEW ZEALAND AND WESTERN SAMOA, MAY/JUNE 1997

Touring party: 32 Players (15 backs, 14 forwards); Captain Gary Halpin; Coach Brian Ashton; Asst Coach David Haslett; Hon. Manager Pat Whelan; Medical Officer Dr Donal O'Shaughnessy; Physiotherapist Denise Fanagan; Masseur Willie Bennett; Fitness Coach Andy Clark; Baggage Master Paddy O'Reilly; IRFU President Bobby Deacy.

Not available: Jonny Bell, Jeremy Davidson, Mark Egan, Denis Hickie, Paddy Johns, Ross Nesdale, Paul Wallace.

On 1993 Development tour (7): Clarke C., Cusack B., Fulcher G., Humphreys D., Matchett A., O'Shea C., Woods N.

Results

1. Northland 69 Ireland 16
2. NZ Academy 74 Ireland 15
3. Bay of Plenty 52 Ireland 39
4. Thames Valley 12 Ireland 38

5. King Country 32 Ireland 26
6. NZ Maori 41 Ireland 10
7. Western Samoa 57 Ireland 25

Summary: Played—7, Won—1, Drew—0, Lost—6; PF—169 pts (23t, 12c, 10p, 0d) PA—337 pts (47t, 36c, 10p, 0d)

IRELAND SQUAD APPEARANCES

Game Player	No.1	No.2	No.3	No.4	No.5	No.6	No.7	Tour Apps.	Tour Points	Age on Tour	Date of first Ireland Cap
Bishop J. (L. Irish) E	13	-	13	11	-	14	14	5	-	22y 6m	13.06.1998
Byrne S. (Blackrock) L	-	-	2	-	-	-	-	1	-	25y10m	2.06.2001
Clarke C. (Terenure) L	15	-	-	15	15	-	15 r	3+1r	5	28y 2m	20.06.1993
Coleman D. (Terenure) L	11	-	14	-	14	-	-	3	5	25y 8m	-
Cusack B. (Bath) E	5	-	5	-	5	5	5 r	4+1r	-	24y10m	-
Dawson K. (L. Irish) E	-	7	7	-	7	7	7	5	-	22y 4m	15.11.1997
Dillon M. (Lansdowne) L	-	14	-	-	-	-	-	1	-	25y 1m	-
Erskine D. (Sale) E	-	6	4 r	8 r	8	8	8	4+2r	10(2t)	27y 7m	15.11.1997
Fitzpatrick J. (L. Irish) E	-	1	-	1	-	1	1	4	5	23y 6m	13.06.1998
Foley A. (Shannon) M	8	-	8	8	-	-	-	3	-	23y 7m	21.01.1995
Fulcher G. (L. Irish) M	4	4	-	4 c	4	4 c	4 c	6	10(2t)	27y 6m	5.06.1994
Governey R. (Lansdowne)L	10 r	10	10	10	10 r	10	10	5+2r	41(1t)	21y 5m	-
Halpin G. (L. Irish) E	3 c	-	3 c	3 r	3 c	-	3 r	3+2r	5	30y 3m	20.01.1990
Halvey E. (Shannon) M	6	-	-	-	-	-	-	1	-	24y 9m	4.03.1995
Henderson R. (L. Irish) E	12	12	13 r	-	12	12	12	5+1r	5	24y 7m	12.11.1996
Humphreys D. (L. Irish) U	10	-	-	-	-	-	-	1	11	25y 8m	17.02.1996
Lynch M. (Y. Munster) M	-	14 r	12	12	10	-	13	4+1r	5	26y10m	-
Macartney D. (Ballymena) U	-	8	6	6	8 r	-	-	3+1r	5	28y 0m	-
McConnell B. (Bristol) E	-	2	-	2	-	-	-	2	-	21y10m	-
McGrath A. (Shannon) M	-	-	-	13	13	-	-	2	-	22y 7m	-
McIvor S. (Garryowen) M	-	-	9 r	-	9 r	-	9 r	1+3r	5	28y 3m	23.11.1996

Game Player	No.1	No.2	No.3	No.4	No.5	No.6	No.7	Tour Apps.	Tour Points	Age on Tour	Date of first Ireland Cap
Maggs K. (Bristol) E	-	13	11	-	11	13	11	5	10(2t)	22y11m	15.11.1997
Matchett A. (Portadown) U	-	-	9	-	9	-	-	2	-	28y 0m	-
Molloy D. (Wasps) E	1	-	1	1 r	1	-	8 r	3+2r	-	24y 9m	-
O'Kelly M. (L. Irish) L	-	5	-	5	-	5 r	5	4+1r	5	22y10m	15.11.1997
O'Meara B. (Cork Cons) M	-	9	-	9	-	9	9	4	10(2t)	20y 1m	15.02.1997
O'Shea C. (L. Irish) L	-	15 c	15	-	-	15	15	4	22(3t)	26y 7m	13.11.1993
Ritchie S. (Ballymena) U	2	-	2 r	-	2	2	2	4+1r	5	27y 4m	-
Sherriff R. (Shannon) L	-	-	4	-	-	-	-	1	-	21y 0m	-
Wallace D. (Garryowen) M	7	7 r	8 r	7	6	6	6	5+1r	-	10y10m	3.06.2000
Walsh G. (N'hampton) E	3 r	3	-	3	3 r	3	3	4+2r	-	30y10m	-
Woods N. (L. Irish) E	14	11	-	14	-	11	-	4	5	25y11m	5.06.1994
	17	17	20	18	19	16	20				

Munster—8 players, Ulster—4 players, Leinster—8 players, Connacht—0 players, Exiles—12 players

3. MUNSTER'S HEINEKEN CUP RUN, 1999/2000
t-c-p-d

Results
1. 20.11.1999 (Limerick) Munster 32 (2-2-5-1) Pontypridd 10 (1-1-1-0)
2. 28.11.1999 (Watford) Saracens 34 (3-2-5-0) Munster 35 (4-3-3-0)
3. 11.12.1999 (Toulouse) Colomiers 15 (2-1-1-0) Munster 31 (4-1-3-0)
4. 18.12.1999 (Cork) Munster 23 (3-1-2-0) Colomiers 5 (1-0-0-0)
5. 08.01.2000 (Limerick) Munster 31 (3-2-4-0) Saracens 30 (3-3-3-0)
6. 15.01.2000 (Pontypridd) Pontypridd 38 (4-3-4-0) Munster 36 (3-3-4-1)
7. 15.04.2000 (Limerick) Munster 27 (2-1-5-0) Stade Francais 10 (1-1-1-0)
8. 06.05.2000 (Bordeaux) Toulouse 25 (1-1-6-0) Munster 31 (3-2-4-0)
9. 27.05.2000 (London) Northampton 9 (0-0-3-0) Munster 8 (1-0-0-1)

Summary
Played—9, Won—7, Drew—0, Lost—2; PF—254 pts (25t, 15c, 30p, 3d) PA—176 pts (16t, 12c, 24p, 0d)
Players used: 25 (12 backs, 13 forwards)
Coach: Declan Kidney; Manager Brian O'Brien; Captain Mick Galwey (all games)
Players' club affiliations: Shannon—9, Cork Cons—7, Garryowen—6, Young Munster—2, Midleton—1

MUNSTER PLAYER APPEARANCES

Game / Player	No.1 pool	No.2 pool	No.3 pool	No.4 pool	No.5 pool	No.6 pool	QF	SF	F	H. Cup Apps. 99/2K	H. Cup Points 99/2K	Total H. Cup Apps
Clohessy P. (Y. Munster)	1	1	-	-	1	1	1	1	1	7	-	21
Crotty D. (Garryowen)	-	-	15 r	15 r	15	15	15	15	15	7	10 (2t)	18
Foley A. (Shannon)	8	8	8	8	8	8	8	8	8	9	10 (2t)	27
Galwey M. (Shannon)	4 c	4 c	4 c	4 c	4 c	4 c	4 c	4 c	4 c	9	5	28
Halvey E. (Shannon)	8 r	-	-	-	-	6 r	6	6	6	5	-	19
Hayes J. (Shannon)	3	3	3	3	3	3	3	3	3	9	5	16
Holland J. (Midleton)	-	-	13 d	13	13	13	-	13	13	6	23 (4t)	6
Horan M. (Shannon)	1 r d	-	1	1	3 r	3 r	3 r	3 r	-	7	5	7
Horgan A. (Cork Cons)	11	11	11	11	11	11	11	11	11	9	5	17
Keane K. (Garryowen)	13	13	-	-	-	-	13	-	15 r	4	10 (2t)	18
Kelly J. (Cork Cons)	14	14	14	14	14	14	14	14	14	9	-	18
Langford J. (Shannon)	5 d	5	5	5	5	5	5	5	5	9	-	9
Mahony C. (Cork Cons)	12	-	-	-	-	-	-	-	-	1	-	3
Mullins M. (Y. Munster)	15 d	12	12	12	12	12	12	12	12	9	5	9
Murray I. (Cork Cons)	-	-	3 r	-	-	-	-	-	-	1	-	12
O'Callaghan D.(Cork Cons)	4 r	-	-	5 r	-	-	-	4 r	-	3	-	4
O'Gara R. (Cork Cons)	10	10	10	10	10	10	10	10	10	9	131(1t)	13
O'Neill J.K. (Shannon)	-	-	-	11 r	10 r	-	-	-	-	2	-	3
Quinlan A. (Shannon)	6	6	6	6	6	6	6 r	-	-	7	10 (2t)	18
Sheahan F. (Cork Cons)	-	-	2 r	2 r	-	-	-	2 r	-	3	-	6
Staunton J. (Garryowen)	12r d	15	15	15	-	-	-	-	-	4	5	4
Stringer P. (Shannon)	9	9	9	9	9	9	9	9	9	9	-	14
Tierney T. (Garryowen)	9 r	-	9 r	9 r	9 r	-	-	-	-	4	-	8
Wallace D. (Garryowen)	7	7	7	7	7	7	7	7	7	9	10 (2t)	13
Wood K. (Garryowen)	2 d	2	2	2	2	2	2	2	2	9	20 (4t)	9

d Players (6) who were making their European Heineken Cup debut

4. IRELAND IN THE 1995 RUGBY WORLD CUP

(a) Ireland Results (Pool C, 3 Matches)

			t-c-p-d		t-c-p-d	Referee
Sat. 27.05.1995 7 p.m.	Ellis Park, Jo'burg	New Zealand	43 (5-3-4-0)	Ireland	19 (3-2-0-0)	Wayne Erickson (Aus)
Wed. 31.05.1995 2 p.m.	Bloemfontein	Japan	28 (4-4-0-0)	Ireland	50 (7-6-1-0)	Stef Neethling (SA)
Sun. 04.06.1995 4 p.m.	Ellis Park, Jo'burg	Wales	23 (2-2-2-1)	Ireland	24 (3-3-1-0)	Ian Rogers (SA)

FINAL TABLE POOL C

Nation	Captain	P	W	D	L	F	A	+/-	Tries	Pts
1. New Zealand	Sean Fitzpatrick	3	3	0	0	222	45	+177	29	9
2. Ireland	Terry Kingston	3	2	0	1	93	947	-1	13	7
3. Wales	Mike Hall	3	1	0	2	89	68	+29	9	5
4. Japan	Masahiro Kunda	3	0	0	3	55	252	-197	8	3

(b) Ireland Result (Quarter-final)

			t-c-p-d		t-c-p-d	Referee
Sat. 10.06.1995 noon	King's Park, Durban	France	36 (2-1-8-0)	Ireland	12 (0-0-4-0)	Ed Morrison (Eng)

(c) Ireland Squad Statistics

PLAYER (CLUB) PROVINCE	First Full Cap	Age at 27/05/95	v N. Zealand	v Japan	v Wales	v France	*	**	***
Bell J. (Ballymena) U	06/94	21y3m	12	-	12	12	3	3	8
Bradley M. (Cork Cons) M	11/84	32y6m	9 x	-	-	-	1	5	40
Burke P. (Cork Cons) M	01/95	22y0m	-	10	-	-	1	1	5
Byrne S. * (Blackrock) L	06/01	23y10m	-	-	-	-	0	0	0
Corkery D. (Cork Cons) M	06/94	22y6m	6	6	6	6	4	4	8
Danaher P. * (Garryowen) M	01/88	27y7m	-	-	-	-	0	0	28
Elwood E. (Lansdowne) C	03/93	26y3m	10	-	10	10	3	3	14
Field M. (Malone) U	02/94	31y3m	15 r	12	-	-	2	2	8
Foley A. (Shannon) M	01/95	21y6m	-	4 r	-	-	1	1	6
Francis N. (Old Belvedere) L	06/87	31y2m	4	4	4	4	4	10	33

PLAYER (CLUB) PROVINCE	First Full Cap	Age at 27/05/95	v N. Zealand	v Japan	v Wales	v France	*	**	***
Fulcher G. (Cork Cons) M	06/94	25y6m	5	-	5	5	3	3	10
Geoghegan S. (Bath) E	02/91	26y8m	11	11	11	11	4	7	32
Halpin G. (London Irish) E	01/90	29y3m	3	-	3	3 x	3	4	11
Halvey E. (Shannon) M	03/95	24y10m	-	7	7 r	5 r	3	3	6
Hogan N. (Terenure) L	01/95	24y1m	-	9	9	9	3	3	5
Hurley H. * (Old Wesley) L	11/95	31y4m	-	-	-	-	0	0	0
Johns P. (Dungannon) U	10/90	27y3m	8	8	8	8	4	4	24
Kingston T. (Dolphin) M	05/87	31y8m	2 c	2 r	2 c	2 c	4	8	25
McBride D. (Malone) U	03/88	30y8m	7	-	7	7	3	3	22
Mullin B. (Blackrock) L	11/84	31y6m	13	13	13	13 x	4	11	55
O'Mahony D. (UCD) L	05/95	22y9m	-	-	-	14	1	1	2
O'Shea C. (Lansdowne) L	11/93	24y7m	-	15	15	15	3	3	13
Popplewell N. (Wasps) E	11/89	31y1m	1	1 c	1	1	4	7	33
Staples J. (Harlequins) E	02/91	29y7m	15	-	-	-	1	5	18
Tweed D. (Ballymena) U	03/95	35y6m	-	5 x	-	-	1	1	4
Wallace P. (Blackrock) M	05/95	23y4m	-	3 ∞	-	-	1	1	1
Wallace R. (Garryowen) M	07/91	27y4m	14	14	14	-	3	3	20
Wood K. (Garryowen) M	06/94	23y4m	-	2	-	-	1	1	6

c   captain
*   Ireland caps during RWC—1
r   replacement during game
**   Ireland caps in three World Cups
∞   first Ireland cap (1)
***   Total Ireland caps after RWC—3
x   last Ireland cap (4)
Players used: 26 + 2 (13 backs, 15 forwards)
*   played no game (3)
Munster—11, Leinster—7, Ulster—5, Exiles—4, Connacht—1.

5. IRELAND IN THE 1999 RUGBY WORLD CUP
(a) Ireland Results (Pool E, 3 Matches)

			t-c-p-d		t-c-p-d	Referee
Sat. 02.10.1999 7 p.m.	Lansdowne Road	Ireland	53 (7-6-2-0)	USA	8 (1-0-1-0)	Joel Dumé (Fra)
Sun. 10.10.1999 2 p.m.	Lansdowne Road	Ireland	3 (0-0-1-0)	Australia	23 (2-2-3-0)	Clayton Thomas (Wal)
Fri. 15.10.1999 7 p.m.	Lansdowne Road	Ireland	44 (5-5-2-1)	Romania	14 (1-0-3-0)	Brian Campsall (Eng)

FINAL TABLE POOL C

Nation	Captain	P	W	D	L	F	A	+/-	Tries	Pts
1. Australia	John Eales	3	3	0	0	135	31	+104	19	9
2. Ireland	Dion O'Cuinneagain	3	2	0	1	100	45	+55	12	7
3. Romania	Tidor Constantin	3	1	0	2	50	126	-76	5	5
4. USA	Dan Lyle	3	0	0	3	52	135	-83	5	3

(b) Ireland Result (Play-Off for Quarter-final)

			t-c-p-d		t-c-p-d	Referee
Wed. 20.10.1999 7.30pm	Lens, France	Argentina	28 (1-1-7-0)	Ireland	24 (0-0-7-1)	Stuart Dickinson (Aus)

(c) Ireland Squad Statistics

PLAYER (CLUB) PROVINCE	First Full Cap	Age at 02/10/ 99	v USA	v Aus	v Rom	v Arg	*	**	***
Bell J. (Dungannon) U	06/94	25y9m	12 r	12 r	12	-	3	6	32
Bishop J. (London Irish) M	06/98	24y11m	14	14	-	14	3	3	16
Brennan T. (St Mary's) L	06/99	26y0m	6	6	-	-	2	2	9
Casey B. (Blackrock) L	10/99	21y2m	-	4 r ∞	-	4 r	2	2	2
Clohessy P. (Young Munster) M	02/93	33y6m	1	1 r	-	-	2	2	33
Corrigan R. (Lansdowne) L	11/97	28y10m	-	-	-	1	1	1	10
D'Arcy G. (Lansdowne) L	10/99	19y7m	-	-	15 r ∞	-	1	1	1
Davidson J. (Castres) E	11/95	25y5m	4	-	4 r	4	3	3	26
Dawson K. (London Irish) E	11/97	24y8m	-	-	7	7	2	2	5
Elwood E. (Galwegians) C	03/93	30y7m	10 r	10 r	10 x	-	3	6	35

PLAYER (CLUB) PROVINCE	First Full Cap	Age at 02/10/99	v USA	v Aus	v Rom	v Arg	*	**	***
Fitzpatrick J. (Dungannon) U	06/98	25y10m	1 r	1	1	1 r	4	4	14
Humphreys D. (Dungannon) U	02/96	28y0m	10	10	-	10	3	3	21
Johns P. (Dungannon) U	10/90	31y7m	5	5	5	-	3	7	57
McKeen A. (Lansdowne) L	10/99	29y7m	-	-	3 r ∞	-	1	1	1
Maggs K. (Bath) E	11/97	25y3m	13	13	-	13	3	3	23
Miller E. (Terenure) U	01/97	24y0m	6 r	6 r	-	6 r	3	3	18
Mostyn M. (Galwegians) C	06/99	25y0m	11	11	11	11 X	4	4	6
Mullins M. (Young Munster) M	08/99	28y11m	-	-	13	-	1	1	2
Nesdale R. (Newcastle) E	02/97	30y2m	2 r	-	2 X	-	2	2	13
O'Cuinneagain D. (Ballymena)U	06/98	27y4m	8 c	8 c	8 c	8 c	4	4	17
O'Driscoll B. (Blackrock) L	06/99	20y8m	12	12	10 r	12	4	4	7
O'Kelly M. (St Mary's) L	11/97	25y2m	4 r	4	4	5	4	4	19
O'Meara B. (Cork Cons) M	02/97	23y5m	9 r	-	9 r	-	2	2	6
O'Shea C. (London Irish) E	11/93	28y11m	15	15	15	15	4	7	34
Quinlan A. (Shannon) M	10/99	25y2m	-	-	6 r	-	1	1	1
Tierney T. (Garryowen) M	06/99	23y1m	9	9	9	9	4	4	7
Topping J. (Ballymena) U	11/96	24y10m	-	-	14	-	1	1	6
Wallace P. (Saracens) E	05/95	27y10m	3	3	3	3	4	5	34
Ward A. (Ballynahinch) U	03/98	29y0m	7	7	6	6	4	4	19
Wood K. (Garryowen) M	06/94	27y8m	2	2	8 r	2	4	5	31

c   captain
*   Ireland caps during RWC—1
r   replacement during game
**   Ireland caps in four World Cups
∞   first Ireland cap (3)
***   Total Ireland caps after RWC—4
x   last Ireland cap (3)
Players used: 30 (13 backs, 17 forwards)
    Girvan Dempsey and David Corkery were original selections
Ulster—8, Leinster—7, Exiles—7, Munster—6, Connacht—2.

6. IRELAND IN THE 2003 RUGBY WORLD CUP

(a) Ireland Results (Pool A, 4 Matches)

			t-c-p-d			t-c-p-d	Referee
Sat. 11.10.2003 5 p.m.	Gosford, NSW	Romania	17 (2-2-1-0)	Ireland		45 (5-4-4-0)	Jonathan Kaplan (SA)
Sun. 19.10.2003 8 p.m.	Aussie Stadium, Sydney	Namibia	7 (1-1-0-0)	Ireland		64 (10-7-0-0)	Andrew Cole (AUS)
Sun. 26.10.2003 6 p.m.	Adelaide Oval	Argentina	15 (0-0-3-2)	Ireland		16 (1-1-3-0)	Andre Watson (SA)
Sat. 01.11.2003 8.35 p.m.	Telestra Dome Melbourne	Australia	17 (1-0-3-1)	Ireland		16 (1-1-2-1)	Paddy O'Brien (NZ)

FINAL TABLE POOL A

Nation	Captain	P	W	D	L	BP	F	A	+/-	Tries	BP	BP	Pts
1. Australia	George Gregan	4	4	0	0	0	273	32	+241	38-2	2	2	18
2. Ireland	Keith Wood	4	3	0	1	1	141	56	+85	17-4	2	3	15
3. Argentina	Agustin Pichot	4	2	0	2	1	140	57	+83	18-5	2	3	11
4. Romania	Romeo Gontineac	4	1	0	3	0	65	192	-127	8-26	1	1	5
5. Namibia	Sean Furter	4	0	0	4	0	28	310	-282	4-47	0	0	0

(b) Ireland Result (Quarter-final)

			t-c-p-d			t-c-p-d	Referee
Sun. 09.11.2003 6.30 p.m.	Telestra Dome Melbourne	France	43 (4-4-5-0)	Ireland		21 (3-3-0-0)	Jonathan Kaplan (SA)

(c) Ireland Squad Statistics

PLAYER (CLUB) PROVINCE	First Full Cap	Age at 11/10/03	v Rom	v Nam	v Arg	v Aus	v Fra	*	**	***
Best S. (B. Harlequins) U	06/03	25y8m	-	3 r	-	-	-	1	1	4
Byrne S. (Blackrock) L	06/01	32y2m	2 r	2 r	-	-	-	2	4	24
Corrigan R. (Greystones) L	11/97	32y10m	3	-	1	1	1	4	5	30
Costello V. (St Mary's) L	01/96	32y11m	6	-	8	-	8	3	3	35
Dempsey G. (Terenure) L	11/98	28y0m	15	15	15	15	15	5	5	43
Doak N. (B. Harlequins) U		31y3m	-	-	-	-	-	0	0	0

PLAYER (CLUB) PROVINCE	First Full Cap	Age at 11/10/03	v Rom	v Nam	v Arg	v Aus	v Fra	*	**	***
Easterby G. (Rotherham) E	06/00	32y6m	9 r	9 r	-	-	9 r	3	2	22
Easterby S. (Llanelli) E	02/00	28y2m	-	6	6	6	6	4	4	27
Foley A. (Shannon) M	01/95	29y11m	8	-	-	8	-	2	3	47
Gleeson K. (St Mary's) L	02/02	27y3m	7	-	-	7	7	3	3	19
Hayes J. (Shannon) M	02/00	29y11m	1 r	3	3	3	3	5	5	39
Hickie D. (St Mary's) L	02/97	27y7m	11	11	11	11	-	4	4	44
Horan M. (Shannon) M	06/00	26y1m	1	1	1 r	1 r	1 r	5	5	17
Horgan A. (Cork Cons) M	06/03	26y11m	-	-	-	-	-	0	0	3
Horgan S. (Lansdowne) L	02/00	25y2m	14	14	14	14	14	5	5	24
Howe T. (Dungannon) U	06/00	32y6m	-	-	-	-	-	0	0	10
Humphreys D. (Dungannon) U	02/96	32y1m	10	-	10	10 r	10 r	4	7	60
Kelly J. (Cork Cons) M	03/02	29y5m	13 r	15 r	-	11 r	11 x	4	4	17
Longwell G. (Ballymena) U	11/00	32y2m	-	-	-	-	-	0	0	25
Maggs K. (Bath) E	11/97	29y4m	12	12	12	12	12	5	8	58
Miller E. (Terenure) L	01/97	28y0m	-	8	7 r	8 r	8 r	4	7	39
O'Callaghan D. (Cork Cons) M	03/03	24y6m	7 r	-	-	5 r	-	2	2	7
O'Connell P. (Y. Munster) M	02/02	23y11m	5	5	5	5	5	5	5	15
O'Driscoll B. (Blackrock) L	06/99	24y8m	13	13	13	13	13	5	9	46
O'Gara R. (Cork Cons) M	02/00	26y7m	10 r	10	10 r	10	10	5	5	38
O'Kelly M. (St Mary's) L	11/97	29y2m	4	4	4	4	4	5	9	59
Quinlan A. (Shannon) M	10/99	29y2m	8 r	7	7	-	-	3	4	18
Sheahan F. (Cork Cons) M	06/00	27y1m	-	-	-	-	-	0	0	13
Stringer P. (Shannon) M	02/00	25y9m	9	9	9	9	9	5	5	41
Wallace D. (Garryowen) M	06/00	27y3m	-	-	-	-	-	0	0	17
Wallace P. (Ballymena) U		24y11m	-	-	-	-	-	0	0	0
Wood K. (unattached)	06/94	31y8m	2 c	2 c	2 c	2 c	2 c x	5	10	58

c   captain
*   Ireland caps during RWC—5
r   replacement during game
**   Ireland caps in five World Cups
∞   first Ireland cap (-)
***   Total Ireland caps after RWC—5
x   last Ireland cap (7)
Players used: 32 (14 backs, 18 forwards)
        J. Bell was an original selection
Munster—13, Leinster—10, Ulster—6, Exiles—3, Connacht—0.
Note: Four Ireland players have featured in three RWC Finals tournaments—Neil Francis, Terry Kingston, Brendan Mullin and Keith Wood.

Compiled by Des Daly, Irish Rugby Statistician

INDEX

'A' games proposal, 216
Aboud, Stephen, 106
ACT Brumbies franchise, 121
AISRCA (All Ireland Senior Rugby Clubs Association), 213–15, 216–17
Albanese, Diego, 114, 115, 199
All Ireland Cup proposal, 213, 215
All Ireland League (AIL), 202–17
  established, 205–8
  restructuring and proposals, 93–4, 209–17
Alred, Dave, 218, 219
amateurism of players, xii–xiii, 11, 39, 45–6, 221
  IRFU statement (1995), 25–6
  see also contracts of players
Anderson, Brent, 202–5
Anderson, Willie, 3, 49, 203
  Australia tour (1994), 4, 7, 14, 15, 16, 19, 20, 23–4
  resignation, 27–8
Argentina v Ireland
  1999 World Cup, 100–101, 113–19
  build-up, 101–8
  2002, 193, 197
  2003 World Cup, 197–200
Ashton, Brian, 84–97, 124, 146
  appointed coach, 58–9, 84–7
  background and career, 85
  Five Nations (1997), 87, 89, 90–91
  New Zealand/Samoa tour (1997), 58–65, 71, 80–82, 91–2
    Governey and, 66, 68–9
    McConnell's injury, 77, 78, 81–2
    tactics, 61–2, 68, 69–70, 75, 83
  professional structure of team, 74–5
  resignation, 97
  role as coach, 86
  Whelan relationship deteriorates, 91–6

Australia
  coaching and training, 3–4
  earnings and sponsorship, 10–11
  independent directors, 221
  1991 v Ireland (World Cup), xi, xiii–xiv, 4
  1994 Ireland tour, 1–24
    statistics, 233–4
    v Ireland, 20–23
  1999 Ireland tour, 105–7
  1999 v Ireland (World Cup), 108–11
  2002 v Ireland, 193
  2003 World Cup, 184, 196–201
    v Ireland, 200
  Australian Institute of Sport (AIS), 3–4
  Australian Rugby Union (ARU), 10, 221

Baker, John, 186
Ballymena, 204
Bangor, 48
Barry, Nicky, 203
Bateman Cup, 205
Bath, 85
Bay of Plenty v Ireland (1997), 69–71
Bayley, Ian, 194
Bedford, 54–5
Bell, Jonathan, 6, 16, 19, 27, 37, 60, 76, 88
Berryman, Norm, 62, 63
Best, Dick, 49–50
Bevan, John, 74, 79, 124–5
Biarritz v Munster (2006), 218
Bishop, Justin, 49, 58, 63, 70, 71, 73, 78, 115
  career profile, 226
Blackrock, 190, 205
Blyth, Andy, 143
Bolger, Patrick, 96
Bordeaux, 120, 139–40
Boreham, Colin, 29
Bourgoin, 132
Bradley, Michael, 16, 22, 31, 34, 36, 42–3, 181

Brain, Errol, 78
Brennan, Trevor, 110, 112, 118
Brewer, Mike, 87, 88–9, 90–91, 122
Bristol, 76
  David Corkery at, 50
Brophy, Niall, 207
Browne, Damian, 173
Browne, Philip, 31–2, 56, 93, 178
  Connacht disbandment and, 170, 171, 174, 179–80
  Gatland and, 157, 158, 161–2, 163
  O'Sullivan appointment, 183, 184, 186
Browne, Tony, 167–8
Buccaneers, 190
Buenos Aires, 116–17
Bunce, Frank, 36
Burke, Paul, 30, 37, 38, 50, 51
Butler, Locky, 4
Byrne, Shane, 15, 60, 69, 70, 73, 194
  career profile, 230

Cabannes, Laurent, 42
Califano, Christian, 139
Camardon, Gonzalo, 115
Campbell, Ollie, 10
Campese, David, 13
Canada v Ireland (1997), 92
Carrington, Matt, 64
Casey, Bob, 73, 112, 113, 118
Castaignede, Thomas, 91
Castres, 132
Celtic League, 169, 170, 171
Christian Brothers, 188
Chuter, George, 133
Clark, Dave, 4, 158
Clark, Jack, 190
Clarke, Ciaran, 74
  career profile, 225
Clohessy, Ger, 133
Clohessy, Peter, 8, 26, 27, 60, 195
  Australia tour (1994), 15, 21, 23, 27
  character, 133–4
  at Munster, 126, 128, 132, 133–4
Clongowes, 67
Clontarf, 5
Code of Conduct (1992), 46

Coleman, David, 60
  career profile, 226
Coleman, Eddie, 59, 75, 151, 152, 156
  Gatland sacking, 161–2
  O'Sullivan appointment, 149, 184–5, 190–91
Colomiers, 120, 128, 132
Commercial Scheme (1991), xii–xiii
Connacht, 168–82
  exodus of players, 181
  Gatland coaches, 115, 148–9, 150, 187
  O'Sullivan coaches, 149, 150, 190
  O'Sullivan resigns, 186–7
  threat of disbandment, 168–82
  under-age teams, 169–70
  v Munster (2002), 170, 171
  v Pontypridd (2003), 176–7
Connolly, Joe, 177
contracts of players, 46–8, 56–7, 93, 97
  Keith Wood stand-off, 103–4
Cooper, Ross, 60
Cork, 124
Corkery, David, 6–7, 16, 19, 23, 34, 36, 126, 143
  move to Bristol, 50–52
Corleto, Ignacio, 198, 199
Corrigan, Reggie, 199
Corry, Martin, 51
Coste, Georges, 30
Costello, Victor, 6, 7, 197
Creamer, Tommy, 146
Cronin, Ben, 30
Crotty, Dominic, 126, 133, 138–9, 141, 142
Crowley, Dan, 18, 110
Crowley, Don, 168
Cuddy, Mick, 1
Cullen, Leo, 73
Cunningham, Jarrod, 73, 78
Curti, Franco Properzi, 31
Cusack, Brian, 60, 80
  career profile, 230
Cuttitta, Massimo, 31

Dallaglio, Lawrence, 165
Danaher, Philip, 8, 14–15, 21, 26–7, 46, 106, 150

D'Arcy, Gordon, 220
Davidson, Jeremy, 6–7, 17, 76, 111, 113, 158
Davidson, Jimmy, 29, 127
  All Ireland League and, 206–7
Davies, Alan, 51
Dawson, Kieron, 114, 158
  career profile, 231
  move to London Irish, 48–50
Dawson, Ronnie, 164
Deacy, Bobby, 56–7, 79
Deges, Frankie, 117–18
de Haast, Mike, 177, 180
de la Rúa, Fernando, 116–17
Dempsey, Girvan, 198
Denney, Mark, 51
Development Tour (1997), 58–83
  match statistics, 234–6
  squad profiles, 225–32
Deylaud, Christophe, 42
Dickinson, Stuart, 113
Dillon, Marcus, 64, 65, 73–4, 82
  career profile, 225
Diprose, Tony, 137
Dominguez, Diego, 31
Dominici, Christophe, 139
Dowd, Craig, 147
Doyle, Mick, 206
drinking by players, 6–9, 31–2, 82
Drohan, Tim, 84, 94–5, 96, 97
drugs fiasco (1998), 103
Duffy, Gavin, 173
Dumé, Joel, 13, 21, 23, 154
Dwyer, Bob, 9, 11, 22, 133

Eales, John, 3, 16
Easterby, Guy, 158
Easterby, Simon, 197
Egan, Mark, 60
Ellis, Doug, 53
Elwood, Eric, 5, 57, 113
  Australia tour (1994), 12, 16, 20, 21–2, 23
  Connacht and, 172–3
  World Cup (1995), 39–40, 43
  England v Ireland
    1994, 5
    1996, 47

    1997, 89
    2000, 150
    2003, 186
English, Tom, 80, 94
  assaulted by Whelan, 98
Erskine, David, 71, 74, 78, 80
  career profile, 231
European Cup, 47, 209
  1996–1997, 56
  1998–1999, 107
  1999–2000, 129–45
    statistics, 236–7
  2001–2002, 66, 220
  2003–2004, 220
  2005–2006, 218, 220
Evans, Mark, 137, 192, 193
exodus of players, 47–56
  from Connacht, 181
  "Operation Repatriate", 93

Fahey, Frank, 173
Fallon, John, 171, 177, 178, 180, 181
Feaunati, Zac, 194
Feeney, Blair, 64
Ferguson, Bruce, 38
Ferrier, Ian, 10
Field, Maurice, 15, 21–2, 88
Fiji v Ireland (2002), 193
Filemu, Joe, 81
fitness and training, 29, 32, 57, 104–5
Fitzgerald, Ciaran, 4–5, 168
Fitzgerald, Des, xi, xiii, xiv–v, 157
Fitzgerald, Garrett, 26, 121
Fitzgerald, John "Paco", 8, 15, 21, 37
Fitzpatrick, Justin, 228–9
Fitzpatrick, Sean, 36, 37, 147
Five Nations Championship, 2
  1994, 5
  1995, 29–30
  1996, 47, 59
  1997, 87–91
  1999, 104
Flatman, David, 131
Fleming, Jim, 110
Flynn, Frankie, 131–2
Foley, Anthony, 30, 70, 130–31, 139, 195, 197

career profile, 232
Ford, Mike, 160, 185, 201
foreign players and coaches, 146–7
Foundation for under 19s, 3
France, 100–101, 111–12, 120, 131–2
France v Ireland
  1995 World Cup, 42–3
  1997, 87, 91
  2000, 154–5
  2001, 157
  2003 World Cup, 200–201
Francis, Neil, 8–9, 13–14, 16, 22, 23, 31, 33,
  103
Fulcher, Gabriel, 6, 16, 23, 70, 74, 75, 80,
  81–2
  career profile, 230

Gallagher, John, 147
Galthie, Fabien, 201
Galwegians
  Gatland coaches, 147–8, 149
  O'Sullivan coaches, 187–8, 190
Galwey, Mick, 8, 15, 16, 21, 154, 195, 219–20
  at Munster, 126, 128, 130, 133, 134–5, 142,
    144
  at Shannon, 131–2
Garryowen, 85, 202–4, 205
  v Shannon (1992), 202–3
Gatland, Warren, 146–66, 221
  appointed Ireland coach, 97, 98, 146
  Australia tour (1999), 105, 106, 107
  background, 146–7, 204
  Connacht coach, 115, 148–9, 150, 187
  Galwegians coach, 147–8, 149
  IRFU relationship, 103, 108, 151–3, 156,
    157–9, 161–2, 164
  media and, 153, 156–7
  sacked as Ireland coach, 161–6
  scrum machine purchase, 108
  Six Nations (2000), 153–5
  style of coaching, 101–2, 103, 106, 111,
    115–16, 148, 157–8
  Wasps coach, 165
  World Cup (1999), 101, 108–9, 111, 112,
    115–16, 118
Gavin, Tim, 21

Geoghegan, Simon, 9, 22, 23, 27, 31, 34
Geraghty, Pat, 171
Gibbs, Scott, 88
Gleeson, Keith, 197
Glennon, Jim, 56
Glynn, Billy, 148, 162, 163, 174, 176, 186–7
Godson, Rory, 98
Governey, Richie, 64, 66–9, 71, 78, 80, 81
  career profile, 227
Grau, Roberto, 130, 131, 199
Grayson, Paul, 144
Gregan, George, 15
Grewcock, Danny, 135
Griffiths, Clive, 74–5
Growden, Greg, 13
Guazzini, Max, 136

Hall, John, 85
Halpin, Gary, 15, 19, 36, 37, 59, 60, 62, 69,
  75, 91
  career profile, 229
Halvey, Eddie, 30, 37, 40, 42, 64, 144
  career and character, 137–8
  career profile, 231–2
Hamilton, Gordon, xiii–xiv, 109
Harlequins, 122–3, 175, 194
Harrison, Justin, 121
Hartill, Mark, 12
Haslett, Davy, 82, 83
Hayes, John, 141, 220
Healy, Der, 215
Healy, Joe, 187
Heaslip, Michael, 147
Heffernan, Sandy, 47
Heineken Cup see European Cup
Henderson, Rob, 71
  career profile, 226
Hennessy, Ray, 48
Herbert, Daniel, 23
Hewitt, Norm, 78
Hickie, Denis, 60, 159, 165, 198
Hill, Richard, 54, 136, 137
Hogan, Niall, 30, 31, 34, 39, 42–3
Hogan, Paul, 15, 132, 203
Holland, Jason, 122, 133, 141, 142, 144
Holland, Jerry, 56, 127

Hook, George, 190–91
Horan, Marcus, 132
Horan, Tim, 9, 200
Horgan, Anthony, 138, 139
Horgan, Shane, 151, 154
Howard, Pat, 16
Humphreys, David, 48, 50, 63–4, 68, 113, 114, 115, 199, 200
   career profile, 227
Hurley, Henry, 37, 53, 54
Hussey, John, 162

Imhoff, Jose Luis, 117
imports of foreign players and coaches, 146–7
IRB (International Rugby Board), xi, 11
   Paris meeting (1995), 45
   Working Party on Amateurism, 25
IRFU (Irish Rugby Football Union)
   agm format, 167–8
   AISRCA and, 213–15, 216–17
   All Ireland League and, 93–4, 205–17
   amateurism and, xii–xiii, 25–6, 39, 45–6, 221
   appointments committee, 149, 161, 184, 186
   blaming culture, 101
   committees, Ashton criticises, 91–2
   Connacht disbandment issue, 168–82
   contracts of players, 46–8, 56–7, 93, 97, 103–4
   drugs fiasco (1998), 103
   exodus of players, 56–7
   finances, 167, 170, 171, 172, 175, 179, 181–2
      Rome junket, 178
      scrum machine, 108
   Foundation for under 19s, 3
   Gatland relationship, 103, 151–3, 156, 157–9, 161–2, 164
   lack of investment, 24
   Match Review, 151–2
   O'Sullivan and Kidney appointments, 183–6
   payment to players (1995 World Cup), 44
   professional era, 58, 74–5, 155, 179–80

reluctance to change, xiv–xv, 2–3, 24, 25–6, 221–2
selection committee, 86, 89–90
Strategic Plan (2004), 210, 212–13
strike threatened by players, xi–xiii
Taking Irish Rugby Forward, 210
traditionalism, xii, 2–3, 25–6, 88, 167–8
IRUPA (Irish Rugby Union Players' Association), 176
Irwin, David, 206
Italy v Ireland
   1995, 30–32
   1997, 84, 92
   2000, 154
   2001, 157
Izama, Ko, 38

Jackman, Bernard, 148
Japan v Ireland
   1991, xiii
   1995, 37–9
Johns, Paddy, 21, 60, 104, 111, 112
Johnson, Martin, 159
Jones, Derwyn, 40
Jones, Mark, 34
Jones, Robert, 51

Keane, Killian, 67, 124, 127, 128, 129, 130, 133
Kearns, Phil, 13, 21, 109–10
Kefu, Toutai, 110
Kelly, Diarmuid, 121
Kelly, Gerry, 171, 172, 179, 181
Kelly, John, 127
Kidd, Murray, 57, 59, 84–5, 94
Kidney, Declan
   background and career, 125
   coaching style, 128–9, 136–7, 139
   Ireland assistant coach, 183–6, 196
   Munster coach, 108, 122, 124, 125–6, 127
Kiernan, Tommy, 33–4, 47, 209
Kilkenny, 32, 33
King Country v Ireland (1997), 75–6
Kingston, Terry, 8, 40, 123

Lacroix, Thierry, 43, 130, 131, 135
Lam, Pat, 144

Langford, John, 121–2, 126–7, 128, 130, 131, 135, 136, 139
Lassissi, Ismaella, 134
Latu, Sinali, 38
Lavery, Billy, 25, 46
Leavasa, Potu, 81
Ledesma, Mario, 114
Leicester
  2002 v Leinster, 66
  2002 v Munster, 220
Leinster
  1995 European Cup, 47
  1999 European Cup, 108
  2002 European Cup v Leicester, 66
Lenihan, Donal, 86, 89–90, 92, 94–5, 96, 98, 151, 153
  Australia tour (1999), 106
  manager role, 102–3, 104, 105, 108, 155–6
  World Cup (1999), 109, 110, 111, 114, 118
Lens, 111–12
Leslie, Andy, 79, 92, 208
Lewsey, Josh, 51
Lille, 100–101, 111–12
Limerick, 124
Little, Jason, 9
Lomu, Jonah, 35, 36
London Irish, 8–9, 47, 59, 175
  Kieron Dawson at, 48–50
Lord, David, xi
Loughead, Roy, 164
Lynagh, Michael, xiii, 10, 16, 21, 22, 109
Lynch, Mike, 64, 74, 75–6, 80, 83
  career profile, 227
Lyons, John, 108, 153, 161, 170, 171, 181

McBride, Denis, 16, 17, 36, 40, 42, 46
McCall, Mark, 48, 50
McCall, Rupert, 20
Macartney, Dean, 60
  career profile, 232
McConkey, Bob, 212
McConnell, Barry, 76–8, 81–2
  career profile, 229
McDermott, Mark, 123
McFarland, Dan, 176–7
McGann, Padraig, 189–90

McGinley, Paul, 193
McGowan, Alan, 15, 22
McGrath, Alan, 64, 69–70, 74, 77, 78
  career profile, 226
McGurn, Mike, 162, 201
McIvor, Steve, 71
  career profile, 228
McLean, Paul, 10–11, 221
McLoughlin, Ginger, 125, 131
Macqueen, Rod, 18
Maggs, Kevin, 51, 58, 60, 80, 113
  career profile, 227
Magne, Olivier, 200
Mains, Laurie, 34, 35
Malone, Dom, 144
Maoris v Ireland (1997), 77–8
Mapletoft, Mark, 134–5, 136
Martin, Marcel, 47
Match Review, 151–2
Matchett, Andy, 64, 69, 70, 71, 74
  career profile, 228
Matthews, Philip, xi, xiii, xiv
Maxwell, Norm, 62
Meates, Roly, xi, xiii, xiv
Mendez, Federico, 144, 198
Mendez, Hector, 107
Menem, Carlos, 116–17
Merrick, Steve, 105
Methody, 6
Miles, Joey, 86, 89
Millar, Syd, 45, 47, 88, 212
  appointments committee, 75, 161, 184, 186
  Gatland and, 151, 152, 156, 161
Miranda, Nicolas Fernandez, 107
"Mission Repeat", 10
Mitchell, John, 159, 204
Molloy, Darren, 228
Morgan, Garrick, 3–4, 23
Morgan, Huw, 122–3
Moseley, 52–4
Mostyn, Matt, 107
Mount Isa, 16–18
Mullin, Brendan, 27, 29–30, 36, 42
  players' representative, xi, xiii, 46
Mullins, Mike, 107, 122, 130, 133, 141, 154

Munster, 107, 120–45, 221
  anthem, 127, 128
  building of team, 121–7
  rivalry within, 123–4
  supporters club, 121
  1999 European Cup, 108, 129–45
    statistics, 236–7
    v Colomiers, 132
    v Northampton, 142–5
    v Saracens, 129–31, 133, 134–6
    v Stade Francais, 136–7, 138–9
    v Toulouse, 139–42
  2002 Celtic League v Connacht, 170, 171
  2002 European Cup v Leicester, 220
  2004 European Cup v Wasps, 220
  2006 European Cup v Biarritz, 218, 220
Murdoch, Alistair, 18
Murdoch, Rupert, 45
Murphy, Gerry, 4–5, 27, 32, 72–3, 208
  Australia tour (1994), 4–6, 7, 11, 12, 13, 16, 20, 23–4
  background and character, 4–5
  New Zealand tour (1992), 3, 4
  World Cup (1995), 33–4, 42
Murphy, Mervyn, 197–8, 200–201
Murphy, Noel, xiv, 4, 31–2, 212
  appointments committee, 75, 98, 161, 184
  Code of Conduct (1992) signatures, 46
  Gatland and, 151, 152, 161
  New Zealand tour (1992), 2
  World Cup (1995), 27, 28, 33, 34, 37, 42, 43–4
Murray, Pat, 131

Namibia
  1991 tour, 24, 149
  1993 tour, 59–60
National Coach and Training Centre (NCTC), 29
Nel, Steph, 173, 176, 181
Nesdale, Ross, 60, 104
New Zealand
  1989 All Blacks tour, 147
  1992 Ireland tour of, 1–2, 3, 12, 149
  1995 v Ireland, 34–7
  1997 Ireland tour of, 58–83
    match statistics, 234–6
    squad statistics, 225–32
  1997 v Ireland, 92
  2001 v Ireland, 159–60
  2002 Ireland tour of, 186
New Zealand Rugby Academy v Ireland (1997), 64–5
Northampton v Munster (2000), 142–5
Northland v Ireland (1997), 62–4
Ntamack, Emile, 42, 141

O'Brien, Brian, 128, 144, 151, 155–6, 158–9, 161, 191, 194
  background and character, 127
O'Brien, Conor, 171
O'Connell, Declan, 120–21, 129, 145
O'Connell, Ken, 18, 142–3
O'Connor, Johnny, 173
O'Connor, Matthew, 15, 21
O'Cuinneagain, Dion, 110, 115
O'Donoghue, John, 179
O'Donovan, Niall, 124–5, 134, 138, 139, 185, 198
O'Driscoll, Brian, 106, 112, 114, 115, 137, 165, 220
  career and character, 154–5
Ofahengaue, Willie, 16, 18
O'Gara, Ronan, 122, 165
  European Cup (2000), 130, 131, 134, 135–6, 138, 141
    final, 120, 143, 145
  European Cup (2006), 218, 220
  kicking improvement, 218–20
  World Cup (2003), 199
O'Kelly, Malcolm, 48, 73, 74, 77, 80, 81, 111, 122, 198
  career profile, 230
O'Mahony, Darragh, 52–5
O'Mahony, David, 31
O'Meara, Brian, 74, 122
  career profile, 227–8
"Operation Repatriate", 93
O'Reilly, Paddy ("Rala"), 90, 101
Orlandi, Carlo, 31

O'Shea, Conor, 16, 21, 22, 40, 71, 78, 81, 114, 115, 116
  career profile, 225
  at London Irish, 49, 50
O'Sullivan, Eddie, 183–91
  background and career, 149–50, 186–91
  compatibility with Kidney, 183–6
  Connacht coach, 148, 149, 150, 186–7, 190
  Galwegians coach, 187–8, 190
  Gatland sacking and, 161, 162, 163
  Ireland assistant coach, 149, 151, 154, 155, 156, 157, 158, 160
  Ireland coach, 183–6, 195–6, 197, 220–21
    appointed, 165, 184
  Wood relationship, 191, 194, 195–6, 197, 201
  World Cup (2003), 196, 197, 198–9
O'Sullivan, Kieran, 188
Ougier, Stephane, 139

Padova, 129
Pagel, Gary, 144
Paramore, Junior, 81
Participation Agreement (1991), xii, xiii, 46
Paul, Henry, 51
Paul, Jeremy, 110
Pichot, Agustin, 107, 113, 114
Pienaar, Francois, 130, 131, 133, 136
Players' Association, 176
Pontypridd, 129, 136, 175
  v Connacht (2003), 176–8
Popplewell, Nick, 5, 34, 37, 40, 88
Pountney, Budge, 143–4, 145
Power, John, 176
Pres Cork, 125
professional era, 58, 74–5, 155, 179–80
provincial coaches, 93, 124–5
Pugh, Vernon, 47
Purvis, Graham, 204

Quesada, Gonzalo, 113, 114, 115, 116, 198
Quilligan, Gary, 203
Quilligan, John, 212
Quinlan, Alan, 130, 137, 197, 198

Ralph, Caleb, 70
Regan, Mark, 51
Reggiardo, Mauricio, 115, 199
Reid, Ken, xiii, xiv, 30, 33, 39, 47
Ridge, Martin "Trigger", 52–3, 54
Ritchie, Stephen, 74
  career profile, 229
Robinson, Andy, 51
Robinson, Brett, 18
Robinson, Brian, 20–21
Rodber, Tim, 144
Roff, Joe, 14–15, 16
Rogers, Ian, 40
Rolland, Alain, 15, 17, 18–19, 53
Romania v Ireland (2002), 191
Ropati, Remi, 64
Ross, Glenn, 122
Rowell, Jack, 85, 89
Ruddock, Mike, 67, 74, 97
Russ, Tony, 56
Russia v Ireland (2002), 192–3

Samoa
  1996 v Ireland, 47
  1997 tour, 61, 79–82, 234–6
Saracens, 53, 54–5, 137
  v Munster (European Cup), 129–31, 133, 134–6
Scotland v Ireland
  1991, xiii
  1993, xv
  1994, 5
  1997, 67, 90–91
  1998, 96
  2000, 153–4
  2001, 158
scrum machine, 108
selection committee, 86
  reduced, 89–90
Shannon, 131, 137, 202–4, 208
  v Garryowen (1992), 202–3
Shaw, Simon, 51
Sheahan, Frankie, 123, 140–41, 151
Shelford, Wayne "Buck", 147, 203
Sheriff, Rory, 69, 70, 72–3
  career profile, 230–31

Sherwin, Jim, 116
Six Nations Championship
  2000, 150, 153–5
  2001, 156–7, 158–9
Smith, Damian, 21
Soden, Philip, 11, 12, 19–20
South Africa
  1993 tour, 59–60
  1995 World Cup, 25–9, 32–42
  1998 tour, 101, 102, 104
Southam, Ray, 33, 34
Sowman, Frank
  Australia tour (1994), 1, 4, 5, 9–10, 13, 16,
    17, 23–4
  selection committee, 86, 89
Spicer, Kevin, 48
Spooner, Nathan, 66
Spotswood, George, 45
Spreadbury, Tony, 31
Stade Francais v Munster, 136–7, 138–9
Staples, Jim, 9, 37, 40, 88, 91, 111
Staunton, Jeremy, 126, 131
Stensness, Lee, 141
Stickland, Billy, 133–4
Stokes, Geoff, 15
Stokes, Jim, 33, 34
Stolz, Conrad, 138
Strategic Plan (2004), 210, 212–13
strike threatened by players (1991), xi–xiii
Stringer, Peter, 122, 219

Tabua, Ilie, 20, 21
Tainton, Mark, 219
Taking Irish Rugby Forward, 210
Talbot, Matt, 8
Taylor, Glenn, 62
Thames Valley v Ireland (1997), 73–4
Thomond Park, 121, 134, 135, 202
Thomas, Arwel, 88
Thomas, Clayton, 110
Thomas, Russ, 2
Thornley, Gerry, 80, 156, 174, 178
Tiatia, Ace, 64
Tierney, Tom, 106, 108, 111, 114, 122, 128,
  140
Toland, Liam, 176

Toulon, 131
Toulouse, 132
  v Munster (European Cup), 139–42
Tournaire, Franck, 139
training, 29, 32, 57, 104–5
Troncon, Alessandro, 31
Tucker, Colm, 131
Tuigamala, Inga, 80
Tweed, Davy, 30

Ulster
  All Ireland League and, 206–7
  1999 European Cup, 108, 127–8
Under 14s (national), 7–8

Waldron, Stan, 153
Wales v Ireland
  1993, 5
  1995, 30
  1995 World Cup, 39–40
  1997, 88–9
  2001, 159
Wallaby Players Marketing Ltd, 10
Wallace, David, 71, 74, 78, 133, 144
  career profile, 231
Wallace, Paul, 38, 60, 114, 115, 131, 136
Wallace, Richie, 5, 35, 36
Walsh, Brian, 15
Walsh, Gavin, 74, 75
  career profile, 229
Walshe, Nick, 130, 135
Waratahs, 11–14
Ward, Andy, 112, 113–14, 128
Ward, Tony, 172, 173, 174, 189
Warrington, Giles, 29, 32–3, 42
Wasps, 165, 220
Waters, Fraser, 51
Westin Excelsior, 178
Whangamata, 73
Whelan, Pa, 27–8, 33, 87, 212
  Ashton appointment, 84–5
  Ashton relationship deteriorates, 91–3,
    94–6
  assault on English, 98
  New Zealand/Samoa tour (1997), 59, 61,
    62, 75, 77, 80, 82, 83

proposes reducing All Ireland League, 93–4
resignation, 98–9
selection committee, 86, 89–90
White, Craig, 104–5, 165
White, Julian, 131
Wigglesworth, Eddie, 149, 151, 152, 161, 171, 173–4, 181
Wilkinson, Jonny, 181, 218–19
Williams, Bryan, 80
Williams, Matt, 160
Williams, Nigel, 136
Wilson, David, 110
Wilson, Jeff, 64, 65
Wilson, Roger, 11
Wood, David, 191
Wood, Gordon, 163–4, 191–2, 196
Wood, Keith, 191–6
  Australia tour (1994), 5–6, 8, 11, 15–16, 19
  captaincy of Ireland, 91, 96, 191–6
  contract stand-off, 103–4
  at Garryowen, 203
  Gatland sacking and, 163–4, 165
  at Munster, 122–3, 128, 129–31, 134, 135, 140–41, 145

O'Sullivan relationship, 191, 194, 195–6, 197, 201
  retirement, 201
  Six Nations, 159, 160
  World Cup (1995), 38, 40
  World Cup (1999), 110, 119
  World Cup (2003), 197, 198, 199–200
Woods, Niall, 6, 19, 62–3, 65, 70, 73–4, 80
  career profile, 225–6
Woodward, Clive, 48
World Cup, xi
  1991, xi–xiv, 4
  1995, 25–9, 32–44
    statistics, 238–9
  1999, 100–119
    statistics, 240–41
  2003, 184, 196–201
    statistics, 242–3
Wray, Nigel, 136
Wyllie, Alex, 107, 117, 118

Young Munster, 204

Zimbabwe v Ireland
  1991 World Cup, xiii
  1993 tour, 59–60